Hard Press

Contents

* * * * *

BOOK II.

* * * * *

BOOK III.

4

BOOK I.

CHAPTER I.

The festival.

The sufferings of the long war still continued; still stood Frederick the Great with his army in the field; the tremendous struggle between Prussia and Austria was yet undecided, and Silesia was still the apple of discord for which Maria Theresa and Frederick II. had been striving for years, and for which, in so many battles, the blood of German brothers had been spilt.

Everywhere joy seemed extinguished; the light jest was hushed; each one looked silently into the future, and none could tell in whose favor this great contest would finally be decided, whether Austria or Prussia would be victorious.

The year 1760, the fifth of the war, was particularly sad for Prussia; it was marked in the history of Germany with tears and blood. Even Berlin which, up to that time, had suffered but little from the unhappy calamities of war, assumed now an earnest, mournful aspect, and it seemed as if the bright humor and sarcastic wit which had always characterized the inhabitants of this good city had now entirely deserted them. Going through the wide and almost empty streets there were to be met only sad countenances, women clothed in black who mourned their husbands or sons fallen in one of the many battles of this war, or mothers who were looking with anxiety into the future and thinking of their distant sons who had gone to the army.

Here and there was seen some wounded soldier wearily dragging himself along the street, but hearty, healthy men were seldom to be met, and still more seldom was seen the fresh countenance of youth.

Berlin had been obliged to send not only her men and youths, but also her boys of fourteen years to the army, which, according to the confession of Frederick the Great, consisted, in the campaign of the year 1760, only of renegades, marauders, and beardless boys.

For these reasons it seemed the more strange to hear at this time issuing from one of the largest and handsomest houses on the Leipsic Street the unwonted sounds of merry dance-music, cheerful singing and shouting, which reached the street.

The passers-by stopped and looked with curiosity up to the windows, at which could be seen occasionally a flushed joyous man's face or pretty woman's head. But the men who were visible through the panes evidently did not belong to the genteeler classes of society; their faces were sunburnt, their hair hung down carelessly and unpowdered upon the coarse and unfashionable cloth coat, and the attire of the maidens had little in common with the elegance and fashion of the day.

"The rich Gotzkowsky gives a great feast to his workmen to-day," remarked the people in the street to one another; and as they passed on they envied with a sigh those who were able at the same time to enjoy a merry day in the rich and brilliant halls of the great manufacturer, and admire the splendor of the rich man's house.

The mansion of Gotzkowsky was indeed one of the handsomest and most magnificent in all Berlin, and its owner was one of the richest men of this city, then, despite the war, so wealthy and thriving. But it was not the splendor of the furniture, of the costly silver ware, of the Gobelin tapestry and Turkish carpets which distinguished this house from all others. In these respects others could equal the rich merchant, or even surpass him.

But Gotzkowsky possessed noble treasures of art, costly paintings, which princes and even kings might have envied. Several times had he travelled to Italy by commission from the king to purchase paintings, and the handsomest pieces in the Royal Gallery had been brought from the land of art by Gotzkowsky. But the last time he returned from Italy the war of 1756 had broken out, and the king could then spare no money for the purchase of paintings: he needed it all for his army. Therefore Gotzkowsky was obliged to keep for himself the splendid originals of Raphael, Rubens, and other great masters which he had purchased at enormous prices, and the wealthy manufacturer was just the one able to afford himself the luxury of a picture gallery.

The homely artisans and workmen who this day had dined in Gotzkowsky's halls felt somewhat constrained and uncomfortable, and their countenances did not wear a free, joyous expression until they had risen from table, and the announcement was made that the festival would continue in the large garden immediately adjacent to the house, to which they at once repaired to enjoy cheerful games and steaming coffee.

Bertram, Gotzkowsky's head book-keeper, had been commissioned by him to lead the company, consisting of more than two hundred persons, into the garden, where Gotzkowsky would follow them, having first gone in search of his daughter.

With lively conversation and hearty laugh the people retired, the halls were emptied, and now the deep silence of these state-apartments was only interrupted by the gentle ticking of the large clock which stood over the sofa on its handsomely ornamented stand.

When Gotzkowsky found himself at last alone, he breathed as if relieved. The quiet seemed to do him good. He sank down into one of the large chairs covered with gold-embroidered velvet, and gazed earnestly and thoughtfully before him. The expression of his countenance was anxious, and his large dark eyes were not as clear and brilliant as usual.

John Gotzkowsky was still a handsome man, despite his fifty years; his noble intellectual countenance, his tall proud figure, his full black hair, which, contrary to the custom of that period, he wore unpowdered, made an imposing and at the same time pleasing impression.

And certainly it was not because of his personal appearance that Gotzkowsky, notwithstanding the early death of his wife, had never contracted a second marriage, but had preferred to remain a solitary widower. Nor did this occur from indifference or coldness of heart, but solely from the love for that little, helpless, love-needing being, whose birth had cost his young wife her life, to whom he had vowed at the bedside of her dead mother to stand in stead of that mother, and never to make her bend under the harsh rule of a step-mother. Gotzkowsky had faithfully fulfilled his vow; he had concentrated all his love on his daughter, who under his careful supervision had increased in strength and beauty, so that with the pride and joy of a father he now styled her the handsomest jewel of his house.

Where then was this daughter whom he loved so dearly? Why was she not near him to smile away the wrinkles from his brow, to drive with light chat serious and gloomy thoughts from his mind? She it was, doubtless, whom his wandering glance sought in these vast, silent rooms; and finding her not, and yearning in vain for her sweet smiles, her rosy cheeks, he sighed.

Where was she then?

Like her father, Gotzkowsky's daughter sat alone in her room—her gaze, as his, fixed upon empty space. The sad, melancholy expression of her face, scarcely tinged with a delicate blush, contrasted strangely with her splendid dress, her mournful look with the full wreath of roses which adorned her hair.

Elise was the daughter of the wealthiest man in Berlin, the world proclaimed her the handsomest maiden, and yet there she sat solitary in her beautiful chamber, her eyes clouded with tears. Of a sudden she drew a golden case from her bosom and pressed it with deep feeling to her lips. Looking timidly at the door she seemed to listen; convinced that no one approached, she pressed a hidden spring of the medallion; the golden cover flew open and disclosed the portrait of a handsome man in Russian uniform.

The young girl contemplated this portrait with a strange mixture of delight and melancholy, and then, completely overpowered by its aspect, she approached it to her lips. "Feodor!" murmured she, so softly that it sounded almost like a sigh, and stretching out the hand which held the medallion, in order to be able better to contemplate the picture, she continued—

"Feodor, why did we meet, to be separated forever again? Why did not Fate allow me to be born as a poor serf upon one of thy estates, giving to thee the right to possess me, to me the sweet duty of loving thee? O Heaven, why art thou an enemy of my country, or why am I a German? Men call me happy; they envy me my father's wealth; they know not how wretched and forsaken I am."

She bowed her head upon her breast and wept bitterly. Suddenly steps were heard quite close to her door. She started, and concealed the medallion quickly in her breast. "My father," murmured she, and drying her tears she arose to open the door.

She was right, it was her father. He held out his hand to her. She took it and pressed it to her lips respectfully, but she did not see the look of almost passionate tenderness with which he regarded her, for she had cast down her eyes and did not dare to look at him.

"I have come, Elise, to lead you to our garden festival. You will go with me, my child?"

"I am ready," said she, taking her hat and shawl.

"But why in such a hurry, my child?" asked her father. "Let us leave these good people yet a little while to themselves. We will still be in time to witness their games. I would like to stay a quarter of an hour with you, Elise."

Without answering, she rolled an arm-chair to the window, and laid aside her hat and shawl.

"It is very seldom, father, that you make me such a present," said she.

"What present, my child?"

"A quarter of an hour of your life, father."

"You are right," said he, thoughtfully. "I have little time for pleasure, but I think so much the more of you."

She shook her head gently.

"No," said she, "you have no time to think of me. You are too busy. Hundreds of men claim your attention. How could you have time, father, to think of your daughter?"

Gotzkowsky drew a dark-red case from his breast pocket and handed it to her.

"Look, Elise! see if I have not thought of you. To-day is your birthday, and I have celebrated it as I have done every year by giving my workmen a festival, and endowing a poor bridal pair who on this day become betrothed. Their prayers and tears constitute the most beautiful thank-offering to you, and being happy they bless you, the authoress of their happiness. But how is this? You have not yet opened the case. Are you so little like other girls that diamonds cause you no pleasure?"

She opened the case, and contemplated the jewels with weary looks and scarcely concealed indifference.

"How wonderfully they shine and sparkle, and what tempting promises their brilliant colors hold forth! But this is a princely present, father; your poor Elise it not worthy to wear this diadem and collar."

"Oh, you are worthy to wear a crown!" cried her father with tender pride. "And let me tell you, my child, you have only to choose whether you will place on this beautiful hair an earl's coronet or a prince's diadem. And this, my child, is the reason of my visit to-day."

"On business," murmured she, almost inaudibly, with a bitter smile.

Gotzkowsky continued—

"Young Count Saldem applied to me yesterday for your hand."

"Count Saldem?" asked Elise. "I hardly know him. I have only spoken to him twice in the saloon of Countess Herzberg."

"That does not prevent him from loving you ardently," said Gotzkowsky, with scarcely perceptible irony. "Yes, Elise, he loves you so ardently that he would overcome all obstacles of rank and make you a genuine countess, if I will only promise to endow you with half a million."

The habitually pale countenance of Elise suddenly assumed life and color. She drew herself up and threw her head proudly back.

"Do you wish to sell me, father? Do you wish to give some value to this noble nonentity by the present of half a million, and will his lordship be kind enough in return to take the trifling burden of my person into the bargain?"

Her father gazed at her glowing countenance with eyes beaming with joy; but he quickly suppressed this emotion, and reassumed a serious air.

"Yes," he said, "the good count, in consideration of half a million, will consent to raise the manufacturer's daughter to the rank of a countess. But for a whole million we can obtain still more; we can rise yet higher in the scale. If I will advance his uncle, Prince Saldem, half a million to redeem his mortgaged estates, the prince promises to adopt the nephew, your suitor, as his son. You would then be a princess, Elise, and I would have the proud satisfaction of calling a prince my son."

"As if the king would consent to a nobleman thus demeaning himself!" cried Elise; "as if he would graciously allow the count so far to degrade himself!"

"Oh, the king will consent," continued her father in a light tone. "You know that he is fond of me. Only say whether you consent to become Countess Saldem."

10

"Never!" cried she proudly. "I am no chattel to be bartered, and this miserable title of princess has no charms for me. You can command me, father, to renounce the man I love, but you can never compel me to give my hand to a man I do not love, were he even a king!"

Her father clasped her vehemently in his arms.

"That is blood of my blood, and spirit of my spirit," cried he. "You are right, my child, to despise honors and titles; they are empty tinsel, and no one believes in them any longer. We stand at the portal of a new era, and this era will erect new palaces and create new princes; but you, my child, will be one of the first princesses of this new era. Manufactories will be the new palaces, and manufacturers the new princes. Instead of the sword, money will rule the world, and men will bow down before manufacturers and merchants as they are wont to do before generals. Therefore I say you are right in refusing Prince Saldem's offer, for I promise you, you shall be a princess, even without the title, and the great and noble shall bow as low before your riches as if they were a ducal diadem."

Elise shook her head with a melancholy smile: "I have no desire for such homage, and I despise the base metal with which you can buy everything."

"Despise it not!" cried her father, "prize it rather! Gold is a holy power; it is the magic wand of Moses which caused springs to gush forth from the sterile rock. See, my child—I, who despise all the rank and honors which the world can offer me, I tell you gold is the only thing for which I have any respect. But a man must perceive and understand the secret of this magic power. He who strives for wealth only to *possess* it is a heartless fool, and his fate will be that of Midas—he will starve in the midst of his treasures. But he who strives for wealth for the purpose of *giving*, he will discover that money is the fountain of happiness; and in his hands the dead metal is transformed into a living blessing. You may believe your father, who knows the world, and who has drunk the bitter cup of poverty."

"You were once poor?" asked Elise, looking at her father with astonishment.

Gotzkowsky smiled, and sank back in his chair, musing and silent. After a pause he resumed: "Yes, I was poor. I have endured all the horrors of poverty. I have hungered and thirsted, suffered misery and privation, even as a little boy. Thus lay I once, wretched and forsaken, in a ditch by the highway, and raised my hands to God on high, praying but for a drop of water, but for a morsel of bread. Ah! so strong was the belief of the goodness of God in my heart, that I was convinced He would open the heavens, and reach to me with His own hand the food for which I prayed. I waited and waited, in despairing anxiety, but the heavens were not opened, and not even a drop of rain came to cool my parched lips. But the cloud, which I had looked for in vain in the sky, was seen at last on the highway, and, as I saw this whirling cloud of dust, in the midst of which a splendid equipage came rolling on, I said to myself: 'Here comes God!' and then I found strength enough to raise myself from my knees, to hurry toward the rapidly passing vehicle, and to cry with a voice which was almost overpowered by the noise of the wheels, 'Pity! pity! give me a morsel of bread, a drop of water! Have pity on me!' A hand was stretched toward me out of the cloud of dust, and I saw a small, brightly shining object drop. The carriage rolled on, and disappeared in its cloud. But I sank on my knees and searched the dust for the piece of money, for in this coin lay for me life, health, and strength. I was obliged to hunt in the dust for a long time with hands tremulous with anxiety, and finally, when I found it, I rejoiced aloud and thanked God. Then I hurried with fleet steps toward the neighboring town, to the same baker's shop near the gate, where, shortly before, they had refused to my entreaties a bit of bread. Now, willingly and with smiles, they handed me a loaf, for I had money to pay for it. In that hour I said to myself: 'I must seek money, even if I have to grovel in the dust for it; for money is life, and poverty is death!' The hand which, from the cloud of dust threw me that piece of money, decided my whole future, for it taught me that even dust was not to be despised, as therein money might be found; but it taught me something more—it taught me compassion and charity. Then, as I crouched down with bleeding feet at the street-corner and devoured my loaf, I vowed to myself that I would become rich, and when I had grown rich, to be to each poor and needy one the helping hand stretched forth out of the cloud of dust."

Elise had listened to her father with deep emotion, and in the depth of her heart she at this moment absolved him from many a silent reproach, and many a suspicion, which her soul had harbored against him.

"You have kept your word, my father!" cried she. "How did you contrive to become a rich man from a beggar?"

Gotzkowsky laughed. "How did I contrive that?" said he. "I worked, that is the whole secret—worked from sunrise until late in the night, and by work alone have I become what I am. But no, I had one friend who often helped me with his sympathy and valuable counsel. This friend was the king. He protected me against my malicious enemies, who envied me every little piece of fortune. He cheered me on. Frederick's eye rested on me with pleasure, and he was delighted to see my manufactories thrive and increase. The king's satisfaction was for many years the only spur to my exertions, and when he looked on me with smiling benevolence, it seemed to me as if a sunbeam of fortune shone from his large blue eyes into my heart. I have learned to love the king as a man, and because I love mankind I love the king. It is said that he likes the French better than he does us, and prefers every thing that comes from them; but, indeed, he was the first to supply his wants from my manufactories, and in that way to encourage me to new undertakings.[1] Mankind, in general, do not like to see others favored by fortune in their enterprises and they hate him who succeeds where they have failed. I have experienced that often in life. I knew that men hated me because I was more fortunate than they were, and yet I saw how they cringed before me, and flattered me. Oh, my child, how many bitter and painful experiences do I not owe to my wealth! In wealth lies Wisdom, if one would only listen to her. It has humbled and subdued me, for I said to myself, 'How quickly would all these men who now surround me with attention and flattery, disappear if I became suddenly poor!' These princes and counts, who now invite me as a guest to their tables, would no longer know me if I appeared before them as a poor man. Wealth is rank and worth; and no prince's title, no star of honor, shines so brightly as golden coin. But we must learn how to use it, and not convert the means of fortune into the end. We must also learn to despise men, and yet to love mankind. My philosophy may be condensed into a few sentences. Strive for gold; not to take, but to give. Be kind and faithful to all men; most faithful, however, to thyself, thy honor, and thy country."

Elise looked at him with a strange expression: "You love all mankind! Do you then include our country's enemies?"

"The enemies of our country are the only men whom I hate," cried Gotzkowsky quickly.

"Even were they noble and good?" asked Elise with reproachful tone.

Gotzkowsky looked at her with astonishment and curiosity, and a cloud flitted across his brow. Then, as if shocked at his own thoughts, he shook his head, and murmured in a low tone, "No, that were too terrible!" He rose and paced the room in thoughtful mood. Suddenly a burst of lively music and gleeful shouts were heard from the garden. Gotzkowsky's brow brightened immediately, and he extended his hand with a tender look.

"Come, my child," exclaimed he, "come, and see how happy you have made men! Come, and see the power of wealth!"

[Footnote 1: "Gotzkowsky founded the first large velvet and silk manufactories in Berlin. He was also the first to attend the Leipsic fair with domestic goods, and thus open the commerce with Poland and Russia."—*History of a Patriotic Merchant of Berlin*, 1768, pages 10-12.]

* * * * *

CHAPTER II.

The Workman's holiday.

The garden, which stretched from behind Gotzkowsky's house to the limits of the city, was really of artistic beauty, and he had spent thousands in creating a park out of this dead level of sand. Now, his work was completed, and all Berlin spoke with praise and admiration of this garden, which ranked among the lions to be visited by every traveller. The most splendid groups of trees were seen here and there, interspersed among green plats of grass, ornamented by marble statues or graceful fountains; in other places, trimmed hedges stretched along, and from the conservatories exotic plants filled the air with perfume.

On this day, however, the garden presented a peculiarly lively spectacle. On the lawn, the young girls and lads were dancing to the music of a fiddle and bass-viol, while the older workmen and their wives had seated themselves around tables, on which all kinds of refreshments were spread.

At the largest of these tables, ornamented with flowers, was seated the betrothed couple, the workman Balthazar and Gretchen his young bride, who bashfully and affectionately clung to his side. They had loved each other long and faithfully in silence, but without hope, for they were both poor, and had to support themselves and their parents by the work of their hands. But Gotzkowsky had come to them as a helping benefactor; he had given Balthazar a considerable sum of money, and his daughter Elise had bestowed a dower upon the bride. On this day, Elise's eighteenth birthday, was to be celebrated the marriage of the happy couple. No wonder, then, that they regarded Gotzkowsky with feelings almost of adoration, and that this young girl appeared to them as a benevolent angel.

Elise had just come into the garden with her father, and had taken her seat at the table of the bridal pair. Next to her sat a young man, whose mild and noble countenance seemed to be lighted up with happiness and adoration whenever he looked upon her. He followed every one of her motions with watchful eyes, and the most trifling shade, the slightest change in the expression of her countenance, did not escape him. At times he sighed, reading perhaps in her features the secret thoughts of her soul, and these thoughts saddened him, and clouded his bright clear eye.

This young man, who sat at Elise's side, was Bertram, Gotzkowsky's head book-keeper. From his earliest youth he had been in the house of the rich manufacturer, who had adopted the poor orphan, and treated him as a tender father would have done, and Bertram loved him with all the affection of a son. And never by the lips of a true son was the name of father pronounced with more warmth and tenderness than by this son, adopted and won by deeds of generosity.

But Bertram, who called Gotzkowsky father, had never ventured to call Gotzkowsky's daughter sister. Brought up together, they had in their childhood shared their games, their childish joys and sorrows with one another; he had been a protecting brother to her, she an affectionate sister to him. But ever since Bertram had returned from a journey of three years, which Gotzkowsky had caused him to make, all this had changed. Elise, whom he had left almost a child, he found on his return a blooming young woman, and a feeling of joyous emotion flashed through him as he stood blushing before her; while she, perfectly collected, with a quiet look bade him welcome.

Under the charm of this look he had lived several weeks of rapture and yet of anxiety. He soon felt that he loved this young girl passionately, but he also felt that she returned his passion with the lukewarm affection of a friend or a sister, and that she had no suspicion of the tumult and pain, the joy and ecstasy which filled his breast. And yet he had a right to strive for the prize of her love; and if he raised his eyes to the daughter of his benefactor, it was not presumption, it was Gotzkowsky himself who emboldened him to do so. He had said to him, "Seek to win the love of my daughter, and I will cheerfully bid you welcome as my son, for I know that in your hands Elise's happiness is safe."

Thus he had the consent of her father, but Elise's love was wanting, and how could he ever deserve this love, how win this heart which shone as bright and clear, as hard and cold as rock crystal? Of what avail was it that he worked indefatigably in the service of his benefactor? how did it help him that the money, which Gotzkowsky had given to him as a boy, had borne rich interest and made him a man of means, and even, if he chose, of independence? What did it profit him that all men loved him, if this one being, by whom he so ardently longed to be loved, always remained the same, unchanged toward him, always affectionate and friendly, always open and candid, never abashed, never blushing, never casting her eyes down before him?

"It must at last be decided," thought Bertram, as he sat next Elise; "I must at last know whether she returns my love, or whether that be true which I have heard whispered since my return. I must at least have certainty, even if it annihilates all my wishes."

At this moment there sounded near him merry shouts and laughter. Gotzkowsky had accosted the bridal pair with a jest, and the grateful audience had taken up this jest with delight.

"Long life to the bridal pair!" cried he, raising his glass on high. "Health, wealth, and happiness to them!" A perfect uproar followed this appeal, and brought tears of delight into the eyes of the blushing little bride, who stood up with the bridegroom and bowed her thanks.

Balthazar laughed, and, as soon as every thing had become quiet, replied: "There, that will do! you have hurrahed enough. I don't wish for wealth; health, happiness, and content are enough for me with my little Gretchen; but for these blessings I have to thank, we have all to thank, our lord and master, our father Gotzkowsky.

Therefore, you boys up there, stop your clatter and dancing, and listen to what I have to say to you."

Balthazar's loud clear voice overpowered the music which now ceased, and the lads and maidens crowded around him.

"Balthazar is going to make a speech!" cried one with hearty laughter, in which the others joined lustily. "Silence, silence! Balthazar is going to make a speech. Come, Balthazar, out with it! It's a failing he has."

"Well, why shouldn't I?" said Balthazar, laughing; "many a great lord does nothing else all his life but make pretty speeches. Why shouldn't I play the great lord on this my wedding-day?" He drew himself up, cleared his throat, and continued: "I want to talk to you about our master, who turned us from good-for-nothing drones into industrious workmen, who gave us bread when nobody else had bread for us. Nobody, I say, not even our mayor, who is a very good mayor, but who cannot help the poor, feed the hungry, and give bread and work to hands willing to work. Who is able to do that, and who does it? Who in Berlin is the rich, the good man, who gives work to all, and in his large and celebrated mills procures us food and wages? Who is it?"

"Gotzkowsky, our father Gotzkowsky!" cried the crowd unanimously.

Balthazar waved his hat joyfully in the air. "Therefore, say I, long live Gotzkowsky our father!" cried he with stentorian voice. And loud shouts and cheers followed this appeal. Men and women surrounded Gotzkowsky and offered him their hand, and thanked him with those simple and plain words which never fail to reach the heart, because they come from the heart. All hailed him as friend and father, benefactor and master. Gotzkowsky stood in their midst, proud and erect. A deep emotion was evident in his noble features, and he raised his beaming, radiant face to heaven, thanking God in the humbleness of his heart for the proud joy of this hour.

"Long live Gotzkowsky, our father!" reiterated the happy multitude.

He lowered his eyes, and glanced with friendly looks at the cheerful assemblage.

"Thank you, my children," said he, "but I beg you not to overrate my merits. You are of as much service to me as I am to you. He who gives work is nothing without the worker; the one has need of the other, to increase and thrive. Of what avail would my looms and my money be if I had not your industrious hands and your good will to serve me? Money alone will not do it, but the good will and love of the workmen carry the day. I thank you all for your good will and your love; but above all," continued he, turning to Bertram, "above all things I must thank you, my friend. You have stood by me and helped me bravely, and it is full time that I should try to reward you. Children, one more surprise have I in reserve for you to-day. I

16

appoint Mr. Bertram my partner and sole director of the silk factory." "That's right, that's noble!" cried the workmen.

Bertram said nothing. He only turned his eyes, clouded with tears, toward Gotzkowsky, and the latter read in his looks his deep emotion and affectionate gratitude.

"My son," said he, opening his arms.

"My father, oh my dear, noble father," cried the young man, throwing himself, with streaming eyes, on Gotzkowsky's breast. The workmen stood round, deeply moved, and in silence; and in their hearts they sent up quiet prayers to God on high for their employer. At last Gotzkowsky raised himself from Bertram's arms and sought his daughter with his eyes. She was still sitting, silent and pensive, at the table, and did not appear to have observed what was going on around her. A light cloud crossed his brow as he took Bertram's hand and approached Elise.

"Well, Elise, have you no word of congratulation for him?"

She shuddered, as if awaking from a dream. "Oh," said she, "my good brother Bertram knows that I rejoice in his fortune."

"Brother! still brother?" murmured Gotzkowsky impatiently.

"And why should she not give me that sweet name?" asked Bertram, quickly. "Have you not often called me son, and allowed me to call you father?"

"Oh, I would like indeed to be your father, my son, without Elise's having to call you brother. But we will speak of this another time," said he, interrupting himself; and turning to his workmen, continued: "Come, let us be merry, and of good cheer. Who knows how long Heaven will grant us sunshine? Come, you young folks, I have caused a target to be set up in the court. Let us go there. He who makes the best shot shall get a new coat. Come, bride Greta, take my arm; I will be your groomsman to-day. Bertram, you and Elise follow us. Now, music, strike up a song for the bride."

Gotzkowsky offered his arm to the bride and led her out. Cheerfully the motley crowd followed him, and soon there was heard in the distance their happy laughter and the merry sound of the music.

* * * * *

17

CHAPTER III.

Brother and sister.

Elise did not follow the joyous multitude. She still sat musing, unaware that Bertram was standing opposite to her, considering her attentively. At last he ventured to pronounce her name softly. She looked up at him with perfect composure.

"You do not go with them, Elise?" asked he. "Do you not take any part in the general rejoicing?"

She tried to smile. "Oh yes," said she, "I am glad to see how much these good people love my father. And he deserves it too. The welfare of his workmen is his only thought, and the only fame for which he strives."

"You are too modest in your estimate of your father, Elise," cried Bertram. "Gotzkowsky's fame extends far beyond the walls of this town. All Germany, yes, even Holland and England, are familiar with his name, and the Prussian merchant is as much a hero on "'Change' as the Prussian king is on the battle-field."

"Only my father's victories are less bloody," said Elise, smiling.

A pause ensued. Both felt anxious and embarrassed, and neither dared to break the silence. It was the first time, since Bertram's return from his grand tour, that she had found herself in his presence without witnesses, for she had carefully avoided being alone with him. This had not escaped Bertram's notice, and he had therefore determined to take advantage of the present opportunity to have his fate decided. But yet he did not venture to speak, and the words died away on his lips as he remarked her silent, indifferent composure. As he contemplated her, memories of former days rose up before him. He saw her as, half child, half maiden, she clung trustingly and affectionately to his side, and with charming blushes listened to the teasing jokes of her father. Then her whole soul lay open and clear before him; then she disclosed to him the entire treasure of her pure, full heart, and all the fanciful and dreamy thoughts of her young virgin soul were perceptible; then he had participated in her joys, her little sorrows, every feeling which agitated her breast.

And now, why was it all so different?

A deep, painful melancholy took possession of him, and made him overcome his fear of her decision. He sat down resolutely at her side, and took her hand.

"Elise," said he, "do you still remember what you said to me three years ago, as I took leave of you?"

18

She shook her head and turned her eyes toward him. These eyes were full of tears, and her countenance was agitated with painful emotion.

Bertram continued: "You then said to me, 'Farewell, and however far you may travel my heart goes with you, and when you return I will be to you the same loving, faithful sister that I now am.' These were your words, Elise; you see that I have preserved them in my memory more faithfully than you, my sister."

Elise shuddered slightly. Then she said, with a painfully subdued voice, "You were so long absent, Bertram, and I was only a child when you left."

"The young woman wishes, then, to recall the words spoken by the child?"

"No, Bertram, I will always love you as a sister."

Bertram sighed. "I understand you," said he, sadly; "you wish to erect this sisterly love into an impassable barrier separating me from you, and to pour this cool and unsubstantial affection like a soothing balm upon my sufferings. How little do you know of love, Elise; of that passion which desires every thing, which is satisfied with nothing less than extreme happiness, or, failing that, extreme wretchedness, and will accept no pitiful compromise, no miserable substitute!"

Elise looked at him firmly, with beaming eyes. She too felt that the decisive hour had come, and that she owed the friend of her youth an open and unreserved explanation.

"You are mistaken, Bertram," said she. "I know this love of which you speak, and for that very reason, because I know it, I tell you I will always love you as a sister. As a true sister I bid you welcome."

She offered him her hand; but as she read in his pale face the agony which tormented his soul, she turned her eyes away and drew her hand back.

"You are angry with me, Bertram," said she, sobbing.

He pressed his hand convulsively to his heart, as if he would suppress a cry of agony, then held it firmly to his eyes, which were scalded by his hot tears. He wrestled with his sufferings, but he wrestled like a hero and a man who would not be subjugated, but is determined to conquer. As his hand glided from his face his eyes were tearless, and nothing was visible in his countenance but an expression of deep earnestness.

"Well, then," said he, recovering himself, "I accept this sisterly love as a sick man accepts the bitter medicine which he will not cast away lest he commit suicide. I accept you as my sister, but a sister must at least have confidence in her brother; she must not stand before him like a sealed book whose contents he is ignorant of. If I am to be your brother, I demand also the rights of a brother. I demand truth and trust."

"And who says that I will deny you either?" asked she, quickly.

"You, yourself, Elise; your whole conduct, your shyness and reserve, the manner in which you avoid me, the intentional coldness with which you meet me. Oh! even at this moment you would withdraw from me, but I will not let you, Elise; I will compel your heart to reveal itself to me. I will move you with my devotion, my tender anxiety, so that the cruel crust will fall from your gentle and pure heart, and you will become again my candid and confiding sister. Oh, Elise, have compassion on me! tell me what secret, mysterious charm has suddenly seized you; what wicked, hurtful demon has suddenly converted this bright ingenuous girl into a pale, sad, serious woman. Have courage and trust me, and let me read as in those happier days."

Elise looked at his noble countenance with a deep and painful emotion, and met his inquiring look with unabashed eye.

"Well, then," said she, "I will trust you, Bertram. I will tell you what I have confided to no human ear. Know, then, that my heart also has felt the pains which affect yours. Know that an ardent, hopeless love burnt my soul."

"A hopeless love?" asked Bertram.

"Yes, hopeless," said she, firmly; "for never can I hope for my father's blessing on this love, and never, without it, will I leave my father's house to follow the man I love."

"The man you love!" cried Bertram, painfully. "Does he also then love you, and does he know that you love him?"

She looked at him with astonishment. "Can one then love without being beloved?" asked she, with the unconscious pride of a young girl.

"You are right," said Bertram; "I was a fool to ask this question of you. But why do you doubt your father's consent? Why do you not go confidingly to him and confess your love? But how? Is this love such that it dare not face the light, and must conceal itself from the eyes of your father?"

"Yes, Bertram, it is such a love; but yet you must not doubt me, you must not think that this love which conceals itself from the eyes of my father need therefore fear the light of the world. My father would, perhaps, if he knew my secret, declare me unworthy of him; but never, be assured, never would I commit any act unworthy of myself, and for which I would have to blush. It is possible that not only my father but the whole world would pronounce me guilty if it knew my love; but, believe me,

20

that in the consciousness of my rectitude I would have the courage to brave the verdict of the whole world, provided that my own heart acquitted me, and that I am guilty of no other crime than this accidental one, which fate, and not my own will and trespass, imposes on me. Love allows itself neither to be given nor taken, and when it cannot command fortune, it can at least lighten misfortune. More I cannot tell you, my brother, and what is the use of words? Only depend on what I assure you, I will never be faithless to my honor nor my love. You may think," continued she, proudly and passionately, "that my love is a crime, but never that I could love unworthily, or that I could bow my head under the disgrace of a dishonorable love."

She looked beautiful in her proud, flashing maidenhood; and Bertram felt, as he looked on her handsome, glowing countenance, that he had never loved her so sincerely, and at the same time so painfully, as at this moment.

"Elise," said he, grasping her hand, "will you not have entire confidence in your brother? Will you not tell me the name of your lover?"

She shook her head earnestly. "Only God and my heart dare know it."

"Elise," continued he more urgently, "shall I tell you what has been whispered in my ear as I returned from a long absence? Shall I tell you what your enemies—for your youth and beauty and your father's wealth have made you enemies—shall I tell you what your enemies whisper to each other with malicious joy?"

"No, no!" said she anxiously, "how would it help me to know it?"

Bertram continued inexorably, "They say that the captive Russian, General Sievers, was welcomed by your father into his house as a friend, and that he overwhelmed the noble prisoner with kind attention."

Elise breathed more freely. "It was with the consent and by the wish of the king that my father was kind to the captive Russian general."

"And was it also by the wish of the king that Gotzkowsky's daughter accepted the homage of the Russian general's adjutant?"

A slight shudder ran through Elise's whole frame, and her cheeks became crimson.

"Ah," cried Bertram sadly, "I see you understand me. You will not tell me the name of your lover—let me tell it to you. It is Feodor von Brenda."

"No, no!" cried Elise, looking around in alarm, and fearful lest some treacherous ear had heard the dangerous secret.

"Yes," said Bertram, "his name is Feodor von Brenda; he serves as a colonel in the Russian army; he fights against our brothers and our king; he is the enemy of our country."

"You have no pity on me," cried Elise, wringing her hands, her eyes streaming with tears. "You wish to kill me with your cruel words."

"I wish to show to the daughter of the noblest and truest patriot, I wish to point out to the young, inexperienced, credulous maiden, to my sister, that she stands at the edge of an abyss. I wish to open her eyes that she may be aware of the danger which threatens her. I wish to draw her back from this abyss which threatens to engulf her."

"It is too late," said Elise, rising proudly and drying her tears. "I know it all, Bertram; I stand at the edge of this abyss with open eyes, conscious of the danger; but I will not, cannot draw back, for my heart holds me fast."

Elise took leave of him with a sad smile, and hurried rapidly down the dark walk which led to the retired and unfrequented parts of the garden.

Bertram looked after her until her pink dress disappeared behind the dark foliage of the hedge.

"She loves him," murmured he, letting his head drop upon his breast, "it is certain she loves him."

* * * * *

CHAPTER IV.

Feodor von Brenda.

Elise directed her hasty steps toward the now retired parts of the garden. She longed to be alone. Her soul, agitated by painful emotions, required silence and solitude, in order to settle down again gently to rest and peace. Slowly, and with bowed head, she traversed the dark, silent garden-walks. Her thoughts wandered afar off, and she sought some little comfort, some relief from the privations of the present, in the sweet and blissful recollections of bygone days.

"What can keep him?" asked she of herself; and as she thought of him, her countenance assumed a cheerful, almost happy expression. "He swore to brave every danger, every difficulty, in order to let me hear from him; and now, alas! ten weeks have passed, and no news, no token, from him. My God! is it possible that in all this long time he could have found no opportunity to write to me?—or perhaps his love has not survived the test of separation and silence."

At this thought she stopped, as if stunned, and pressed her hand to her breast. A sharp pain shot through her, and her heart seemed to cease to pulsate. But, in a moment, her countenance brightened up, and she murmured, with a gentle smile, "Oh, to doubt his love were a greater treason than to love my country's enemy. Oh, no! Feodor, my heart does not doubt you; and notwithstanding your silence, I know that your heart answers mine, and that we are forever and inseparably united."

With rapid step and cheerful mind she continued her wandering. She had now arrived at the darkest and most secluded part of the garden. Nothing stirred around her, and there was only heard the rustling of the dark fir-tree moved by the wind, or the melodious note of some bird hidden in the foliage.

The garden, elsewhere so carefully and artistically tended, stretching from the Leipsic Street to the Palisades, which surrounded the town in lieu of a wall at that time, was here overgrown with underwood, protecting the more beautiful parts like a quickset hedge. But this bush was, besides, surrounded by a high wall, running immediately next to the Palisades, and bounding the whole back part of the garden. It was seldom that any one wandered in this neighborhood, and Elise was certain, therefore, that no inquisitive eye could watch her, no treacherous ear listen to her half-whispered words.

She seated herself on a bench under a tree, not far from the wall, and looked up dreamingly and thoughtfully at the patches of blue sky visible through the tree-tops. Her whole soul was sunk in reminiscence. Ah, how often had she sat here, but not alone—not with this painful longing in her heart, but in the fullest contentment of happiness, listening with delighted ear to words spoken by him who sat next to her, holding her hand in his, and gazing on her with looks which made her heart tremble with happiness! Here, on this spot, he had taken leave of her, and since then it had become, as it were, the temple of her recollections, to which she daily made her pilgrimage to offer up her devout, sincere, and ardent prayer of love.

She sat and looked up to heaven, and her ear, dwelling on words which had died away long ago, did not hear sounds which were perceptible on the other side of the wall. It appeared as if some one were striving to climb it, and indeed there could be now seen a hand feeling about, and then a man's figure rising above the wall.

Cautiously spying around, large flashing eyes looked into the garden. One moment the figure rested upon the wall, as if exhausted by the exertion, or listening for some sound. It was a young man, in the garb of a peasant, who sat upon the wall; but the heavy, black mustache little suited this peaceful dress, and his bold air, verging on insolence, seemed to challenge the dangers which surrounded him.

He rested for a moment on the wall, and listened attentively. Then he drew a pistol from his breast, and examined carefully its lock and barrel. He then cocked it, and holding it in one hand, began carefully and noiselessly to descend. With one leap he sprang to the ground; the leaves rustled under his feet, and again he stood motionless in a listening attitude. His glance was as keen and bright as that of an eagle, and it seemed to penetrate the dark foliage. Suddenly a light flashed across his countenance, and a smile of delight played about his lips. He had seen the young girl, who was seated on the bench lost in deep thought, and that he had recognized her was betrayed by his animated expression. Quietly, carefully, he drew nearer, ever and again standing still and listening. Then he stood close behind her at the tree. Again he listens, but every thing is silent and hushed. Now he calls her softly by name, and whispers almost inaudibly, "Elise!"

She started and looked up, but saw no one, and as she recovered herself, she sighed gently, and said: "I was mistaken, it was only the wind."

But again he whispered: "Start not, Elise; do not utter a word or cry!"

"O God!" murmured she in a low tone, trembling in all her limbs. An ardent embrace, a glowing kiss upon her brow, and a well-beloved voice whispered her name.

"Feodor!" uttered she faintly. Overcome by the sudden violence of her feelings, her head dropped languidly on his breast. Then, drawing herself up, she gazed at him, and her eager, loving look encountered his flashing eye. She was, as it were, fascinated—happy as in a dream, and yet conscious of the most delicious waking.

"Do you know me, Elise? Do you recognize your Feodor in spite of his disguise?"

"Oh, speak again," said she as he ceased. "It is so long since I have heard your voice!"

24

"Ten weeks have passed," said he, pressing her still closer to his heart, "without my being able to see you or convey to you any information. I could endure it no longer. I said to myself, 'God is the friend of lovers,' and so I disguised myself as you see me, and ventured here."

Elise started up and gazed at him anxiously. Awaking from her ecstasy of delight, she just began to be conscious of the present.

"Good heavens!" she cried, "danger threatens you."

"Death, if I am found here!" said he, solemnly—"death, if it is known in the Russian camp why I came here!"

She uttered a cry, and clung anxiously to him. "You should not have come here," said she, trembling. "My God, if my father should find you here! It was cruel of you to come."

"It would have been more cruel," said he, smiling, "if being so near you, I had not come at all. I have watched and yearned so long for this meeting; I have longed so to read in your eyes that you have not forgotten me! Why do you cast them down, Elise?"

"Because, Feodor, you have already read too much in them, more than my father would ever forgive."

"Your father was always kind and friendly toward me but at that time I was his prisoner, now he regards me only as the enemy of his country; and yet, Elise, my object here is any thing but that of an enemy. It is not only the desire but also the anxiety of love which brings me here. Listen to me—my time is limited, and I am lost if I linger too long; but I had to see you to warn you, to avert the danger which threatens you, and all of you. Listen, therefore. Your father is the most powerful and influential man in Berlin. His influence will go far with the council and the citizens. Entreat him, Elise, to use all his influence to avert a terrible bloodshed from this city."

Elise shook her head seriously and sadly. Her sweet dream was dissipated; she was now no longer the dreaming, loving girl, but a conscious, reasoning, collected woman.

"How can my father do that?" said she, doubtingly.

"He must persuade the citizens to yield without fighting."

"That my father will never do," said she, warmly.

"Yes, he will do it," replied her lover, "when he learns that all fighting is useless. Let him have compassion on his native town, on himself. You are all lost if you fight. Already twelve thousand of our men, under General Tottleben, stand before the gates. At this moment, while I am speaking, Tschernitscheff, with twenty thousand regulars, is approaching from the other side. Count Lacy, too, with his Austrians, is drawing near. All this tell your father. Tell him, also, that General Tottleben has promised our Empress Elizabeth to take Berlin, if he has to lay it in ruins and ashes. Use all your influence, implore him to do all in his power to persuade the citizens to a peaceful surrender."

"I have no influence over my father," said she, sadly, "and if I had I would not abuse it. Such a surrender, without a fight, would be cowardice."

"But a fight, with the assured certainty of defeat, would be madness. Your father does not know the number of troops massed around Berlin. Do you tell him."

She looked at him mournfully. "And shall I tell him, too, from whom I received this information?"

After a little reflection, he replied: "Yes, if it cannot be otherwise, tell him. Your father will not betray me."

"No, but he will curse his daughter," cried Elise, painfully—"curse her for having had intercourse with our country's enemy, while the Russian cannon threaten our town. No, no, Feodor, it were no use to warn him. My father would not listen to me."

"So Berlin will run toward its ruin, and I cannot prevent it," said the colonel, sadly. "I have done all in my power. I wish to requite your father for all the kindness he has shown me, and for that reason I risked my life in order to warn him."

"Believe me, Feodor, I will never forget you for it," said she, offering him both her hands. "However angry my father may be, my heart still remains yours. Love does not recognize any national hatred. It yields itself without reserve to him who has won it."

She leaned her head upon his breast, and he imprinted a kiss upon her forehead.

"Thank you for these words," said he; "wherever I go they shall be my talisman."

"Are you going already?" asked she, anxiously.

"I must go, Elise," replied he.

26

"Oh, Feodor, I dare not bid you stay. I tremble at the thought of my father seeing you," sighed she; "but when, my beloved, when shall we see each other again?"

He looked at her a long time with a steady, piercing glance. He then exclaimed, almost rudely: "You have sworn me love and constancy till death. Do you remember it?"

"I remember it, and never will I be faithless to my vow," whispered she, smiling through her tears.

"You swore to me never to belong to any one but me. Have you forgotten that?"

"No, I have not."

"Well, then," said he, rising, "we shall soon see each other again."

"When, Feodor, when?"

"When Berlin is in our hands," said he, smiling proudly; "when we enter your gates as conquerors."

She shuddered painfully. He saw it, and a hateful, mocking expression passed across his features; but this lasted only a moment, and his changeable countenance appeared again bright and loving. He took Elise's hand and pressed it to his lips.

"Will you, even at such a time, allow me to see you? Will you, faithful to your vow, remember that my Elise has sworn by God and her love never to turn a deaf ear to my call? Will you expect me?" asked he, coaxingly.

"I will," answered she, in a low voice.

"And I will come," cried he, passionately, "if the way to you leads over mountains of dead bodies!"

She threw herself into his open arms, and nestled like a timid dove on his breast.

"Oh!" cried she, "when danger threatens you, then I think I would like to be a man to share it with you."

He covered her lips and eyes with kisses. "Farewell, farewell, Elise; and if it is God's will, we will meet again."

One last kiss, one last embrace, and he tore himself from her arms and hurried toward the wall. Now he climbs it, and throws his last greetings to her, then descends on the other side.

27

"He is gone, he is gone!" she shrieked, and, falling on her knees, raised her hands to heaven. "O God, have mercy on me, have pity on my love!"

It seemed as if God did grant her prayer, for a thick veil sank over her eyes, and a swoon robbed her of consciousness.

* * * * *

CHAPTER V.

Mr. Kretschmer, of the Vossian Gazette.

The editor of the *Vossian Gazette*, Mr. Kretschmer, sat at his desk, busily writing. That he was a learned man was seen by his earnest, care-worn forehead, his large, well-powdered wig, and above all by the disorder and confusion which reigned in the whole room. Besides which, Mr. Kretschmer wore a dressing-gown, thickly sprinkled with ink-spots, the official robe of his literary dignity. And whosoever beheld him in this robe, his long pipe in his mouth, filling the room with a thick blue smoke, seated on his high tripod before his desk, could not but believe that Mr. Kretschmer was a learned man.

But more than this, he was a great politician. Thereto testified the numerous journals which lay scattered about on the floor, but more especially the nineteen quarto volumes, which stood above on the book-shelf, lettered in gold on the back, "*Vossian Gazette*," and under that the number of the year, from 1740 to 1759. The *Vossian Gazette* was then a young, blooming rose, of scarcely nineteen summers. It could still pass for a vigorous, handsome, and perhaps even innocent young maiden; and Mr. Kretschmer was the editor of the *Vossian Gazette*. Had he not, then, a right to be regarded as a great politician?

Mr. Kretschmer was at this moment occupied in writing an article for the next morning's paper, and as he had just received news "by special courier" of another battle, subsequent to that of Liegnitz, which had resulted favorably for the Prussians, he was composing, with the courage of a lion, an extra, which fairly glowed with ardent hatred against the oppressors and cannibals, namely, the Russians and the Austrians; and declared that the salvation of all Germany depended on the supreme dominion of Prussia.

The bold editor of the *Vossian Gazette* in this article called upon the people to fly to arms against the "incendiary oppressors of Freedom and the people's rights," as he called the Russians; he exhorted even the women and girls to fight, and called upon them to grasp the sword in their tender hands instead of the needle. Finally, he entreated all Berlin, if ever the *incendiary enemy* should approach the gates, rather to let the whole city be destroyed by fire, and bury themselves in the ruins before they submitted to the foe.

Mr. Kretschmer then laid his pen down, and revised with a satisfied look what he had written.

"That will have an effect," said he, rubbing his hands together, delighted. "When his majesty, our heroic king, returns victorious to Berlin, I will send him this sheet of the *Vossian Gazette*, and I know that he will be satisfied with my heroism."

He looked again at the paper. "Beautiful, beautiful!" exclaimed he, with a self-satisfied smile. "My pen has shot nothing less than bomb-shells and grape, and my ink has turned into whole streams of the enemy's blood. And why should I not be bold, it being perfectly safe, since the king must certainly be victorious, and the enemy has no idea of visiting Berlin? Tschernitscheff and Tottleben are quietly encamped on the other side of the Oder; Soltikoff with his army is near Frankfort; and Count Lacy with his Austrians is waiting an opportunity to give battle to our king. Thus, as I said, I can safely exhort the good citizens of Berlin to defend themselves heroically against the infamous spoiler. How beautifully this peroration sounds: 'People of Berlin! rather let yourselves be buried under the ruins of your burning city than submit to an incendiary enemy!'—*Incendiary*," repeated he thoughtfully, "that is rather a strong expression, and if the Russians do come, they will revenge themselves for it; but, pshaw! the Russians are not coming, and I can safely send this article to the press. And, furthermore, did not the king himself stigmatize the Russians as such? Yes, I remember last year, after the unfortunate invasion of the Russians, he looked down from the steeple in Frankfort upon the devastation of the country, and cried out with angry indignation, 'Incendiaries! incendiaries!' The expression is at least official, and can therefore remain."

Mr. Kretschmer seized the bell-rope, and began to ring violently. Immediately the door opened, and a small boy entered with a portfolio under his arm.

"Devil," said Mr. Kretschmer, majestically, "here is my article; run as fast as you can to the printing-office with it, and impress upon the compositor the necessity of haste, and, above all things, not to make such mistakes as he did lately, when, in speaking of the Russians, he put 'friends' instead of 'fiends,' which was an unpardonable and most treasonable error of expression."

The little boy took the paper and laid it in his portfolio.

"The printer told me to ask you," said he, "if you had written nothing yet for the 'Miscellaneous.' *Spener's Journal* had yesterday such a beautiful 'Miscellaneous,' and told about a woman who had four children at a birth, and a stork which had arrived and built its nest, although it was the month of October."

Mr. Kretschmer frowned. "*Spener's Journal* always has some wonderful news, and amuses the Berlin people with all kinds of stupid gossip," grumbled he. "The rivalry of such a paper is unbearable."

"Well, how about the miscellaneous intelligence?" asked the printer's boy.

Mr. Kretschmer stamped his foot angrily. "Go to the devil!" said he.

At this moment there was heard a loud crying and shouting; and while the printer's boy pitched out of the door, Mr. Kretschmer hurried to the window to find out the cause of the uproar.

A heaving, noisy crowd filled the street below, and had halted right under the editor's window. In the midst thereof was seen the tall, lank figure of a man, whose extraordinary appearance enchained the attention of the multitude, and excited afresh their shouts and derisive laughter. And, in fact, nothing could be more striking or fantastic than this man. Notwithstanding the cool October weather, his gigantic figure was clothed from head to foot in gray linen, harmonizing strangely with the gray color of his skin and hair, which latter fell in long locks from his uncovered head down on his shoulders, and gave to the apparition the semblance of a pyramidical ash-heap, out of which his eyes shone like two burning coals. Around his shoulders hung a long cloak of gray linen, which, in addressing the multitude, he sometimes threw around him in picturesque folds, sometimes spread out wide, enveloping his long arms in it, so that he looked like an expanded bat.

"Ah! it is Pfannenstiel, our prophetic linen-weaver," said Mr. Kretschmer, smiling, as he opened his window, and exchanged a look of recognition with the man who was gazing up at him.

The linen-weaver and prophet had rapidly acquired some renown in Berlin by his prophecies and predictions. The people believed in his mystic words and soothsayings and mistaken fanaticism. He related to them his visions and apparitions; he told about the angels and the Lord Jesus, who often visited him; about the Virgin Mary, who appeared in his room every night, and inspired him with what he was to say to the people, and gave him pictures whose mystic signification he was to interpret to them. The prophet possessed more than a hundred of these pictures, given him by celestial apparitions. He had them carefully pasted together, and rolled up always with him. These pictorial sheets, roughly painted on coarse paper, served the linen-weaver in lieu of cards or coffee-grounds, for the purpose of prophesying to the people and announcing the future to them; and the good folks of Berlin believed in these prophecies with firm faith, and listened with devout confidence to the words of their prophet.

Pfannenstiel was in the act of unrolling his pictures, and the multitude, which, just before, had been shouting and screaming, became suddenly silent, and gazed up at the weaver with intense expectation. A breathless silence ensued, and, far down the street, sounded the prophet's loud and sonorous voice. He pointed to the last of his pictures, which, in coarse, clumsy drawing, represented a town, from the houses of which flames arose in the most variegated colors.

"Behold! behold!" cried the prophet, "and fall on your knees and pray! Yes, pray! for I tell you the Holy Ghost appeared to me, His wings dripping with blood, and in His burning and flaming beak He held this picture which I now show you."

"Well, then, how is it that the picture is not burnt too, if the Holy Ghost held it in His burning beak?" asked an impudent shoemaker's boy.

A low laugh ran through the crowd, but this was soon suppressed by angry, threatening voices, commanding silence and quiet.

The prophet turned with an air of majestic composure toward the questioner: "Why was not this picture burnt? Because God wished to perform a miracle, to manifest Himself to me in His glory, and to prove to me that this vision was from Him, and not from the devil. Yes, indeed, God gave me this picture that we might be warned—not to terrify us. Listen, therefore, to my voice, and learn what God announces to you from my mouth."

"I would like indeed to hear what the stupid rascal is going to announce to these poor foolish devils," muttered Mr. Kretschmer, leaning out of the window and listening attentively.

Pfannenstiel continued: "Behold these columns of fire rising from the houses of this town. This town is Berlin, and the fire will burst out of the roofs of your houses. Woe! woe! will sound in your streets, and weeping and lamentation will fill the air. I say unto you, watch and pray! Strew ashes on your heads, and fall down on your knees and pray to God for mercy, for the enemy is before your gates, and ere the sun sets the Russians will enter your town! I say unto you, verily I say unto you, God spoke to me in a voice of thunder, and said, 'The Russians are coming!' Fall down and pray, for the Russians are coming!"

"The Russians are coming!" cried the terrified multitude and some among them turned pale. The weeping women folded their hands in prayer; the men looked around timidly, and the frightened children clung to their mothers in dread of the Russians, whose name was synonymous with that of savages and cannibals. Even Kretschmer could not help feeling somewhat terrified. He drew back thoughtfully from the window, muttering with a shudder, "The Russians are coming!"

The people crowded around the prophet in still narrower circles, and in more piercing tones wept and cried out: "What shall we do? What shall we do to be saved? Have mercy, O God! Have mercy on Berlin, for the Russians are coming!"

"Yes, they are coming!" cried Pfannenstiel. "God told me so in the roll of His thunder and the lightning of His eyes; and he said to me: 'Go and say to the people of Berlin, "The Russians are coming!" and thou shalt see in the same hour how their hearts will shrink, and how cast down they will be; how their eyes will run tears, and their lips utter prayers, for the Russian is the sworn enemy of the Berlin people; and as often as the cry, "The Russians are coming," sounds through the streets of Berlin, there will be wailing and lamentation in every house and every heart; and they will bow down in timid contrition and abject obedience. Speak, therefore, to them, and say, "The Russians are coming!" that they may become humble and quiet; that the proud word may be silenced on their lips, and that they may submit in peace.'"

"What shall we do?" asked the people. "Help us, advise us, for thou art our prophet."

Pfannenstiel drew himself up to his utmost height, and an expression of triumphant cunning sparkled in his eyes. "Do you not understand the voice of God? God commands you to withdraw in silence and peace to your own dwellings, to weep and pray. Go, then! Let the word of your mouth and the rebelliousness of your hearts be silent. Go home to your huts, shut the doors and windows, and do not venture out, for without, death and the Russians await you!"

Obedient to the voice of their prophet, the crowd separated in different directions, and dispersed quietly.

Pfannenstiel looked after them with a smile of scorn; then silently rolled up his pictures, threw his gray cloak over his shoulders, and, casting a serious and significant look up at Mr. Kretschmer's window, strode down the street slowly and with an air of majestic dignity.

* * * * *

CHAPTER VI.

THE COWARDS' RACE.

The warning sounded loud and threatening in Mr. Kretschmer's ears—"The Russians are coming!" A cold chill ran through him, and he could not prevent an involuntary shudder. But he tried to rouse himself from this despondency, and laughed at himself for this credulous fear.

"This Pfannenstiel is a fool, and I would he a greater one if I believed his nonsense," said he. "No, no, my information is warranted and authentic. The king has had a sharp skirmish with the Russians near Reitwan, and driven them back, and then proceeded quietly to Meissen. Thus there is no ground for anxiety, and I can safely let off my bomb-shells against the Russians."

Mr. Kretschmer felt his courage return and his heart grow warm.

"Now I see the whole game," cried he, laughing. "Pfannenstiel wishes the *Vossian Gazette* to take notice of him. He wants to be talked about, and wishes the newspapers to spread his reputation. For that reason he stationed himself right under my window, for that reason he cast such significant looks at me, for that reason he addressed the crowd and poured forth his nonsense right here. Yes, that's it! He wishes to prove to me how great his power is over this people which believes in him, even when he utters the most incredible and unheard-of things. Well, we can help the man," continued he, laughing, as he stepped to his desk. "The desired article for the 'Miscellaneous' is found, and I think that the prophetic linen-weaver, Pfannenstiel, is well worth more than the four children at a birth and the miserable stork's nest of yesterday's *Spener's Journal*. Let's write it off quickly."

Kretschmer began to write most industriously, when he was suddenly interrupted by a violent knocking at the door. It opened, and a stately old gentleman entered, with well-powdered wig and long queue.

"Mr. Krause, my worthy colleague!" exclaimed Kretschmer, jumping up and hastening toward the old man. But Mr. Krause had no word of greeting. He sank sighing into a chair.

"Do you know the news?" asked he, in a whining tone, folding his trembling hands, and looking at Kretschmer timidly, as he stood before him.

"Know what?" demanded the latter in reply, feeling his heart sink.

"The Russians are coming!" sighed Mr. Krause.

"That is a silly tale," cried Kretschmer peevishly, with an impatient gesture.

34

"Would to God it were!" groaned Krause; "but the news is, alas, but too true, and it can no longer be doubted!"

"Man of misfortune," cried Mr. Kretschmer, "who told you so?"

"Pfannenstiel."

"Pfannenstiel?" repeated Kretschmer, laughing heartily; "oh, yes! Pfannenstiel prophesied it just now in the streets, under my window. Now don't distress yourself, dearest friend and colleague. That was only a clumsy trick of the scoundrel to get me to write an article about him in the *Vossian Gazette*. I have already gratified his wish."

"You are mistaken," said Krause, mournfully. "I sent Pfannenstiel into the streets, to quiet the people, and to admonish them to behave peaceably and soberly, even if the Russians should come."

"Oh! you believe in all these dreams of Pfannenstiel?"

"I believe in the truth, and in what I know!" exclaimed Krause emphatically. "Pfannenstiel has for a long time been my agent, and for a considerable stipend, paid every month, informs me of all that happens, is talked and thought of in the town. He is a very useful man, peculiarly suited to this service."

"The approach of the Russians is then town-talk, and nothing more?" asked Kretschmer, who was still anxious to throw doubt on the bad news.

"No, it is a fact," said Krause seriously. "Pfannenstiel is, as you know, not only a prophet, but also a quack doctor, and his herbs and decoctions are certainly often of astonishing efficacy. He always gathers the plants for his mixtures himself, and roams about in search of them in the neighborhood of Berlin for days together. Last evening he was outside the town, on one of these tramps, intending to pass the night sleeping under a tree. He was awoke by the sound of troops marching, and as he looked carefully around, he could plainly distinguish in the bright moonlight the uniforms of the Russian army. It was a long column of many thousand men. They halted not far from the place where Pfannenstiel lay, and he crept carefully nearer. He then ascertained from their conversation that this was only a small division of the army, which had advanced by forced marches from Frankfort, and was commanded by General Tottleben."

"By Tottleben!" cried Kretschmer in dismay.

"Yes, by Tottleben," whimpered Krause, and they both looked in silence on the ground. "Yes, his vengeance will be terrible," said Krause, after a long and anxious pause. "Have you not heard," continued he in whisper—"have you not heard the sad story of what occurred last year in Erlangen? The editor of the *Erlangen Gazette* admitted into his columns an article abusive of our great king. A Prussian officer came in person to Erlangen to call the editor to account. And what do you think he did? He caused the unfortunate and pitiable journalist to be beaten with cudgels, and then gave him a receipt for the bastinado he had gotten."

"Horrible!" cried Mr. Kretschmer, wringing his hands.

Mr. Krause continued: "When a refined Prussian, officer can behave in this way, what have we to expect from these rough, uncivilized enemies, the Russians? Oh! they will murder us, for we, too, have ventured to write boldly and energetically against them."

"Yes, you particularly," said Mr. Kretschmer quickly. "Do you recollect the famous article in your paper, in which you called General Tottleben a notorious adventurer, who had deserted to the enemy after having enjoyed the unmerited favor of our king? This was, certainly, rather strong; it might even be called indiscreet."

"Not as indiscreet as your 'Earnest and Confidential Country Talk,'" cried Krause sharply.

"I never avowed myself the author of that pamphlet," said Kretschmer quickly.

"But every one knows that you are, and you never denied it," replied Krause maliciously. "This 'Country Talk' is more than indiscreet, it is foolhardy. In it you nicknamed Maria Theresa, Aunt Tilla; the Elector of Saxony, Brother Osten; the Empress of Russia, Cousin Lizzy; and our king, Neighbor Flink. And don't you remember what words you put into Cousin Lizzie's mouth, and how you made neighbor Flink ridicule her? Ah, I am afraid you will pay dearly for this" piece of boldness."

"It is not quite so bad as your calling Tottleben a notorious adventurer; for the princes are not here, but Tottleben is before the gates of Berlin, and will revenge himself."

"I am afraid our prospects are equally bad, and for that reason I have come to you, that we might consult together as to what we had best do, to avert this threatening blow from our heads."

"You are right," said Kretschmer, drawing nearer to his brother editor. "Let us consider. Above all things, no exciting calls, no appeals to the people to perform deeds of heroic valor. Berlin is too weak for defence; why, then, should we irritate the enemy by useless opposition?"

"You, too, are right," said Krause thoughtfully; "let us rather advise the citizens of Berlin to be quiet; let us wheel boldly round, and speak in our journals with respect and deference of our worthy enemy."

"Besides which, it would be well to consult with some of the principal men who have an influence on the people. For example, let us go to Gotzkowsky," said Kretschmer.

"Gotzkowsky gives a great holiday to his workmen to-day."

"So much the better, for then he can immediately use his influence on his workmen. Come, let us go at once to Gotzkowsky, this Croesus of Berlin, who bought for our king three hundred thousand dollars' worth of pictures in Italy, without having been paid for them up to this day, and yet is able to take a contract for commissary stores to the amount of eight millions. Let us go to him; and, hark ye! it would be as well to take Pfannenstiel with us to back us."

"Yes," said Krause, raising himself quickly by the arm of his younger friend, "let us go to Gotzkowsky with Pfannenstiel, and preach mildness and submission to him and his workmen."

They both prepared to go. Suddenly Kretschmer stopped as if struck by lightning, and sank down on a chair stunned. "My article, my article!" moaned he. "I am a lost man!"

"What article do you mean, my dearest friend?"

"The leading article in tomorrow's paper," whimpered Kretschmer. "Oh, it was a beautiful article, full of inspiration, but it is not suitable to the times or the circumstances. I wrote it under the erroneous impression that our armies had gained a victory, and in it I spoke with great contempt of the incendiary enemy."

"My God, what rashness!" exclaimed Krause, clasping his hands in despair.

Kretschmer flew from his stool, and grasped his hat. "My article! I must have my article back. The printer must give it up to me. Wait for me in the street. I come either with my article or not at all."

Bidding Krause a hasty farewell, he hurried out.

* * * * *

CHAPTER VII.

THE INTERRUPTED FESTIVAL.

Gotzkowsky had as yet received no intelligence of the danger which threatened the town, and was enjoying the festival in his garden in the midst of his people.

They were all collected on a grass-plat for target-shooting. In the midst of the plat rose a pole with a target. The women and girls were standing around, attentively and curiously watching the men, who, collected under a tent, were shooting with crossbows at the target. Every lucky shot was greeted with a cheer, every unlucky one with derisive laughter; and the prizes which were assigned to the fortunate marksmen only served to increase the joy and merriment of the happy crowd.

Suddenly loud cries of weeping and lamentation were heard from a distance. The people looked at each other with anxiety and alarm. The dismal noise came nearer and still nearer, and then appeared at the entrance gate near by the strange and wild figure of the linen-weaver, accompanied by the two editors, Krause and Kretschmer.

"Pfannenstiel! it is Pfannenstiel, our prophet!" shouted the crowd, while they hastened with joyous laughter and words of greeting toward their beloved seer.

The linen-weaver strode forward with a serious and majestic air, answering the greetings of the workmen with patronizing nods, and from time to time stretching out his hand as if to bless them. The multitude crowded around him, and seemed to look upon the advent of the prophet as part of the programme of the entertainment. But Gotzkowsky hastened toward the two editors with a cheerful smile, bidding them a courteous welcome. They responded to his friendly greeting with a solemn earnestness, and requested a conference with a mysterious and important air. Gotzkowsky looked at them with astonishment; but as he read in their countenances an expression of deep and anxious concern, he motioned to them and preceded them to a summer-house on the other side of the lawn.

"Here we can talk without being observed," said he, casting a look across at his workmen. "You see my guests are still busy with the scarecrow which you brought here; and what business has this man, indeed, among merry people?"

"He maintains that God ordered him to come to you, to warn you in His name, and call upon you to protect Berlin," said Krause.

"Yes," continued Kretschmer, "and he entreated us to accompany him, trusting to our influence with our dear friend."

Gotzkowsky looked at both of the men with astonishment. "Tell me, my worthy friends, which of us is crazy?" asked he, smiling, partly in derision, partly in pity. "I am called on to protect Berlin, and from what?"

"Because the Russians are coming," said Mr. Krause, solemnly.

Gotzkowsky shrugged his shoulders. "That is an idle rumor," said he; "two days ago they were still in Frankfort. You see, therefore, that some wag has amused himself by teasing you and frightening you a little for the thunderbolts which you two, and particularly the *Vossian Gazette*, have launched against the Russians."

Mr. Kretschmer shuddered and turned pale. "I beg you," cried he, "do not speak of it! Good Heavens! the *Vossian Gazette* is the organ of the popular mind, and it is its duty to take each day the exact tone of public opinion. I abused the Russians, therefore, because—"

"Because they were still a hundred miles from Berlin. Oh, yes! we know you, gentlemen of the press. You are full of courage as long as no enemy is in the field, but as soon as you scent him and see the points of his lances, you become quite humble and mild; and when he comes threateningly down upon you, assure him of your respect and swear to him that you love him," interrupted Gotzkowsky.

"You are pleased to jest," said Mr. Krause, casting a rapid glance of hatred at Gotzkowsky; "it is well, indeed, that the rich and powerful Gotzkowsky is so cheerful. I will notice it in my journal. It is news for 'Change, and the funds will rise when people hear that Gotzkowsky has laughed."

Gotzkowsky's countenance became sad and serious. "You may tell the world," said he, "that my lips laugh; but how my heart feels, that you gossips and newspapers know nothing about."

"God be praised," said Kretschmer, ironically, "you are now talking earnestly, and I can request you to listen to our serious representations. It is no idle rumor that I have told you. The Russians are already at the gates of Berlin. They have hurried thither by forced marches. This news is no longer a secret. All Berlin knows it, and it is only accidentally that you have not learned it earlier."

"Oh, Heavens!" sobbed Krause, wringing his hands, "what a terrible fate awaits our unfortunate town!"

Gotzkowsky looked at him with a gloomy frown. "You are, it is true, an old man," said he, "but even old men should, at such a time, possess some manhood. But you, Mr. Kretschmer, are young and hearty; what do you say to this approach of the Russians?"

"I say," replied Kretschmer, sharply, "I say that it would be madness to excite the wrath of the enemy by resistance. I say, that those citizens who call on the people to fight are rash fools."

"Oh!" cried Gotzkowsky, joyfully, "if there be any such *rash fools*, then all is not lost!"

"Can you comprehend such madness?" whispered Krause, "to wish to oppose an overwhelming force while all our capable men and youths are with the army in Silesia, and we have no troops but the sick and maimed; no artillery save two old rusty cannon?"

"A people willing to fight for liberty," cried Gotzkowsky, "such a people have the strength of a giant even without cannon and bayonets. God has given them hands and paving-stones. If we cannot shoot down the enemy who threatens our liberty, we can beat him down."

"What do you say?" stammered Krause, looking with amazement at Gotzkowsky's glowing countenance.

"I say," said Gotzkowsky, "that you have mistaken your man. I will not advise the brave Berlin people to yield without having at least fought for their freedom."

"But only reflect!" exclaimed Kretschmer, while Krause paced up and down, wringing his hands and moaning in a low tone; "have you forgotten that the Russian generals have proclaimed that the empress has commanded them to leave nothing but air and earth to the inhabitants of every conquered town and province of Prussia?"

"Oh, pshaw!" cried Gotzkowsky, laughing, "they will have to conclude to leave us something more."

"And did you hear London's terrible threat? He has said his soldiers should massacre every one, and not spare even the child in its mother's womb."

"And did you not hear the brave Schwerin's answer to this Austrian bravado?" asked Gotzkowsky. "He said, 'My soldiers are not with child, neither am I.' Well, our men of Berlin are not with child, and therefore they need not be afraid."

"But you must be afraid!" whined Krause. "It is disgraceful madness not to be afraid. How! You can be so unreasonable as to advise war? But war is the most bitter enemy of prosperity, and threatens property above all things."

"Then shame on the proprietors," cried Gotzkowsky, "if their property is to make cowardly poltroons of them! Liberty is our greatest possession, and all else must yield to it."

At this moment loud cries and sounds of wailing were heard in the garden from the collected workmen, who surrounded the prophet in a dense group, and listened to his prophecies with anxious wonder as he uttered them from a high bench.

Gotzkowsky frowned. "Ah, I understand!" said he, "this good linen-weaver is your accomplice, my brave gentlemen, and as you wish to convert me, so does he wish to convert my honest workmen into old women. Let us see first in what sort of gibberish he preaches his wisdom to these good people."

Without taking any further notice of the two editors, Gotzkowsky left the summer-house rapidly and approached the listening multitude.

* * * * *

CHAPTER VIII.

THE LEADER OF THE PEOPLE.

The inspired prophet stood on a bench, and, as he unrolled his pictures, he endeavored to explain these mystical paintings to his devout gazers and listeners in equally mystical language. Gotzkowsky hastened toward this group, and pressed in silent observation close up to Pfannenstiel's side.

The linen-weaver, wholly possessed by his prophetic god, had in the mean while unrolled another picture, and holding it up high with solemn countenance, exclaimed with a screaming voice: "The day of judgment is at hand, and destiny is at your door! In my dream I saw a face like unto no other face, and I heard a voice, and the voice was like unto no other voice!"

"And yet you heard it! What ears you must have!" said Gotzkowsky, laughing.

The prophet answered calmly, "Yes! for then were seen invisible things, and then were heard inaudible sounds!" And showing a fresh picture to the crowd, he continued: "Look at this picture, which I found this morning on my sheet. It contains the history of your future, and God announced it to me as I sat at my loom weaving. I heard a voice crying, 'Pfannenstiel, my beloved son, dost thou hear me?' And I fell on my knees and answered, 'Yes, I hear.' 'Dost thou know what thou art weaving?' asked the voice. 'Yes,' said I, 'it is linen shirting for the almshouse.' 'No,' said the voice, 'it is a cloth of weeping for the town of Berlin, for the daughters of your fathers will shed tears, and there will be moaning and weeping.'"

These last words he accompanied with a sobbing and plaintive howl, in which his trembling hearers joined. They assured each other in uncomfortable whispers that Pfannenstiel's prophecies usually came true, and that, even before the war, he had predicted the coming of this day of terror.

But soon Pfannenstiel raised his voice, and its hoarse croaking sounded above the loud conversation and anxious cries of the multitude. "Woe unto Berlin!" cried he, with shrieking pathos. "Blood will flow within her walls! The voice said unto me, 'I will look upon red, but it will not be a scarlet cloak, and when the red banner waves thrones will tremble, and there will be no end to the lamentation. And the cock will crow, and the heavens will shine blood-red, and everywhere and in all places men will cry, "Blood! blood is the drink of new life; blood makes young what is old; blood wipes out sworn debts; blood makes the proud humble. Let us drink blood!"'"

Here the prophet was interrupted by the loud cries and wailing of the multitude. The women broke out in tears, sank on their knees and prayed, or clung trembling and weeping to their moody-looking husbands.

Pfannenstiel looked with an air of proud triumph on this evident effect of his speech, and then continued in a more subdued tone: "But the voice said to me, 'Hope, and every thing will turn out well, and the blood which flows will transform itself into a purple robe, and men will call it freedom. Out of death will arise life.' Therefore fall down on your knees, for the hour of judgment has come, and prayer alone, but not the sword, can save you."

The multitude, carried away by the deception, were in the act of obeying this order, when Gotzkowsky, who could no longer restrain himself, stepped rapidly forward, his countenance radiant, and his eyes sparkling with anger.

"Listen not to this hypocritical set, this lying prophet, my people!" cried he, with a voice of thunder. "He will make cowards of you all, cowards who will submit to the yoke, howling and whining. You would not have this ignominy put upon you. You will be men, who will defend their liberty with noble courage to the last drop of their blood, against the invading hordes of barbarians. For the barbarians are coming, and their fierce wrath threatens your wives and children. Will you submit to the Russians with a humble whine?"

"No, no!" cried the men, and many a clinched fist was raised, and many a wild but muttered oath was heard.

At this moment there arose in the street a confused sound of screams and yells, then the hollow roll of the drum, and the deep clang of the alarm-bell, which summoned the citizens to the town-hall.

The garden gates were now violently thrown open, and a band of stout workmen was seen hastening in wild disorder toward Gotzkowsky.

These were the workmen from Gotzkowsky's factories, industrious men, who had preferred working in the factory, and not losing their time, to the enjoyment of the day's festival, and to whom Gotzkowsky had ordered double wages to be paid, that they might not lose their share in the celebration of his daughter's birthday.

"The Russians are at the gates!" cried they. "All the citizens are arming themselves. We have no arms. Give us arms, master!"

The cry was taken up by those who had just been listening to Pfannenstiel's words. "Yes, give us arms, give us arms. We are no cowards, we will fight!" Gotzkowsky's flashing eye flew across the multitude, and he saw in the earnest countenances of the men that they were serious in their demand, and in their desire to fight. "Well, then, if you will fight, you shall not want for weapons," cried he, joyfully. "I have, as you know, in my house, a collection of costly arms. Follow me, my children; we will go to the armory, and each one shall take what he likes best. On such a day as this, arms do not belong to any one in particular, but are the property of him who can find and make use of them. That is the sacred right of manhood. The country is in danger! Come to my armory and arm yourselves!"

The men shouted for joy at Gotzkowsky's words, and pushed after him with wild impetuosity into the house, and the large hall, in which the costly weapons were tastefully grouped and ornamentally arranged against the walls. With eager haste the men possessed themselves of these arms, and Gotzkowsky saw with glad pride his rare Damascus blades, his delicately carved silver-mounted pistols, his daggers inlaid with gold, his costly ornamented sabres and guns in the hands of his warlike workmen. He then armed himself, and his men, always accustomed to look upon him cheerfully and willingly as their leader, fell into line behind him in a long military procession.

"Now, then, my children," cried he, "let us go to the town-hall and offer our services to the magistrates."

And at the head of his workmen he left the house. Soon deep silence reigned in these rooms, so lately filled with noise and tumult. The garden, too, had become deserted and empty. Pfannenstiel alone remained in his elevated position, gazing pensively, as in a dream, on his collection of pictures.

After this silence had lasted some time, Krause and Kretschmer crept, cautiously looking around them, out of the summer-house in which they had secreted themselves up to this moment. Their countenances were pale and angry.

"Gotzkowsky is a puffed-up fool," exclaimed Krause, with a dark frown. "With his swaggering phrases he has seduced these workmen away from us, to rush into the fight like wounded wild boars, and to bring the Russians down upon us."

"We must not give up all hope," said Kretschmer; "the people are timid and fickle, and whoever will give them the sweetest words wins them over to his side. Come, let us try our luck elsewhere. Every thing depends upon our being beforehand with this braggart Gotzkowsky, and getting first the ear of the people. You, Pfannenstiel, come with us, and get up your words strong and spirited, so that the stupid people may believe you."

Pfannenstiel clapped up his picture-book, and threw his cloak with majestic dignity over his lean shoulders. "The people are like a flock of sheep," said he; "they want a leader, never mind who. Only the leader must be there at the right hour; and if God has bestowed upon him the gift of eloquence, he can lead them either into the church to contrite prayer, or to the slaughterfield to bloody combat. The people are a flock of sheep, nothing more!"

"Come, then," cried Kretschmer pathetically; "come and be their bellwether, and lead the people into the church."

* * * * *

CHAPTER IX.

THE RUSSIAN IS AT THE GATES.

In a few minutes quiet, peaceful, industrious Berlin was transformed into an open encampment. From all the streets there poured throngs of armed men toward the town-hall, where the wise magistrates were consulting on the possibility of resistance, or toward the commander of Berlin, General Rochow, who had the streets patrolled, and called upon the citizens, by beat of drum, to assemble with arms, and assist in the defence of the town.

"The Russian is at the gates!" This cry of terror seemed to cure the sick and feeble, and give courage and strength to the wavering. The old national hatred of the German toward the Russian broke out in its entire vigor; and vehemence made even the faint-hearted fly to arms, and caused words of imprecation to rise to the lips of those who were in the habit of uttering prayers and timid complaints.

The council of war was assembled at the commander's office, and, strange to say, it consisted of only old men and invalids. There were present the infirm veteran general and commander, Rochow, and the eighty-year-old Field-Marshal Lehwald, the severely-wounded General Seidlitz, and General Knoblauch, also wounded. These four composed the whole council, and fully aware of the danger and of the smallness of their forces, were debating whether they should yield to the demand of the Russian troops, and give up the town without any defence, or, with twelve hundred garrison troops, two rusty cannon, a few thousand wounded soldiers, and an inefficient body of citizens, give battle to the twelve thousand irregular troops of General Tottleben, who would soon he reenforced by the army of General Tschernitscheff, twenty thousand strong, and fourteen thousand Austrians under Count Lacy, who, as they well knew, were coming on by forced marches. But so great was the heroic exasperation and eagerness for the fight of these noble and war-worn veterans, that not one of them advised submission; but, on the contrary, they unanimously determined to defend Berlin as long as a drop of blood flowed in their veins. As these brave generals had no army to lead into the fight, they would defend the town, not as commanders of high rank, but as fighting soldiers, and waiving their military rank and dignity to their noble love of country, like other soldiers, they would each one defend his intrenchment or redoubt.

But while the military commanders were adopting these heroic resolutions, the Town Council was engaged in secret session at the town-hall. The wise fathers were staring at each other with terror in their countenances, and considering, in pusillanimous faint-heartedness, whether they would really assume the heavy responsibility of engaging the peaceful citizens in a fight, which, after all, would be, in all probability, useless and without result.

"I vote for submission," stammered out the chief burgomaster, Herr von Kircheisen, with heavy tongue, as he wiped off the big drops of sweat which stood upon his brow with his silk handkerchief. "I vote for submission. The honorable citizens of this

46

town are not called on to spill their blood in useless fighting, nor to irritate the wrath of the enemy by resistance. And besides, the enemy will doubtless lay a war tax on us, and this will certainly be lighter if we submit at once than if we resist. Further, it is the sacred duty of a prudent magistrate to protect and preserve, to the best of his ability, the property of the citizens. It is therefore my opinion that, in order to save the hard-earned possessions of the poor citizens of Berlin, already sufficiently oppressed, we submit at once to an overwhelming force."

By the brightening countenances of the worthy councilmen it could be plainly perceived that the eloquence of the chief burgomaster had told powerfully upon them, and that the question of money which he had raised would prove a powerful and decisive argument in favor of submission at this momentous period.

The assistant burgomaster had already expressed his entire concurrence in the views of Herr von Kircheisen, and the first alderman was in the act of opening his mouth to do the same, when the patriotic deliberations of the worthy gentlemen were interrupted by shouts and cries from the street below, which drove them in terror from their seats. They hastened to the windows, and, carefully concealed behind the curtains, ventured to peep down into the street.

Down there they beheld a much more lively sight—men and youths, old men and boys streamed toward the town-hall, and, raising their eyes and arms to the windows, demanded from the city fathers, with genuine enthusiasm, weapons and ammunition. Perhaps, indeed, it was only fear which had suddenly made these peaceful citizens of Berlin so bold and lion-hearted: one thing is certain, that is, that at this moment they were all animated by one sentiment, one impulse, and that their deadly hatred against Russian and Austrian tendered peaceable submission impossible. The tailor threw away his needle and grasped the sword, the shoemaker exchanged his awl for a dagger, and all these quiet, humble citizens had been transformed by hatred and fear, anger and terror, into most belligerent heroes.

"Give us arms!" was the reiterated cry.

An heroic tailor climbed up on the shoulders of a hunchback shoemaker, and sawing the air violently with his arms, cried out: "The people of Berlin demand their rights; they will fight for their liberty. Give the people of Berlin their due. Give them arms—arms!"

"Arms!" roared the crowd. "We will have arms!"

"And what do you want with arms?" cried suddenly a shrill, piercing voice. All eyes were turned toward the spot whence the voice proceeded, and there was seen the meagre figure of the linen-weaver, who had leaped upon a bench, and from his elevated position was looking down upon the people with the confident air of a conqueror. But Pfannenstiel observed, to his dismay, that this time his appearance did not produce the desired effect; on the contrary, angry looks were cast upon him, and occasionally a threatening fist was raised against the divinely-inspired prophet.

"What do you want with arms?" cried he once more. "Prayer is the only weapon becoming peaceful citizens."

A burst of scornful laughter was the answer. "Down with the linen-weaver! Tear him to pieces!" roared the crowd, becoming infuriated.

"We mean to fight, and not to pray," cried the valorous tailor.

"We want none of your poltroonery, you blackguard of a linen-weaver!"

"The tailor is right! Pfannenstiel is a false prophet!" cried another voice.

"Hang him!"

"He wants to make cowards of us!"

The crowd raged still more furiously, and pressed toward the spot where Pfannenstiel stood. Threatening hands were raised against him, and the situation of the prophet of peace began to be uncomfortable enough, when suddenly two new figures rose near him, and, by their unexpected appearance, restrained for a moment the wrath of the people.

* * * * *

48

CHAPTER X.

BE PRUDENT.

These two men, who so unexpectedly appeared at the side of the prophetic weaver, were none else than the two editors, Kretschmer and Krause, who came to support him in his exhortations in favor of peace, and to use their eloquence on the multitude assembled in front of the town-hall.

Mr. Krause opened: "Listen to me, good citizens of Berlin; look at my gray hairs. Age has the advantage, if not of wisdom, at least of experience. Listen to my advice. You who wish to fight for liberty, be at least prudent and moderate."

"None of your moderation!" cried the tailor. "We won't be moderate!"

"But you will be reasonable and prudent, won't you?" cried Mr. Kretschmer, with his clear, penetrating voice, raising himself on tiptoe, and casting his large, light-blue eyes over the crowd. "You will be reasonable, certainly, and in reason you can tell me what you wish, and we can deliberate, and decide whether that which you wish, is reasonable."

"We want arms."

"But why do you want arms?"

"To fight the enemy," cried the shoemaker, whom the crowd seemed tacitly to recognize as their mouthpiece.

"You really wish, then, to fight?" asked Mr. Kretschmer. "You wish to precipitate yourselves into a fight, with the certainty of being defeated. You wish to put yourselves in opposition to an enemy who out-numbers you ten times; who, with sneering pride, will drive your little band of warriors, with his cannon, to destruction! Consider what you are about to do! Twelve thousand Russians are now before your gates; their cannon pointed against your walls, your houses, your churches, and they are awaiting only an opportunity of springing upon you like a tiger on his prey. And what have we to oppose them? Our little garrison consists of invalids and wounded men; for our young men, able to fight, are all with the king on the bloody fields of Silesia, and only a small band of worthy citizens remains here. Can they fight against an overwhelming enemy, ten times their number? Can they wish to do it?"

No one answered this question. The countenances became thoughtful, and the redness of anger grew paler on their cheeks.

"Yes," cried one of the people, "we are very weak."

"We cannot think of gaining a victory," grumbled out another.

Mr. Kretschmer perceived, by the darkening faces and downcast look of his audience, that the prudence he was preaching had already commenced to press the courage of the poor people into the background, and raising his voice still higher he continued:

"Your fighting will be a species of suicide. Your wives and children will curse you for having killed their husbands and fathers. Worthy citizens! be prudent, and remember that work and not war is your calling. Go home, then, and mind your business; take care of your wives and children, and bow your heads in humbleness, for necessity will teach you prudence."

Mr. Kretschmer stopped, and the silent assembly seemed to be considering whether they should listen to his prudent advice. Even the heroic tailor had climbed down from the hump of the shoemaker, and remained thoughtful and silent.

"The man is right," cried the shoemaker, in his grumbling, bass voice.

"Yes, indeed," said his gossip, the glover; "why should we sacrifice our legs and arms? We can't beat them anyhow."

"Now, my friends," whispered Kretschmer to his associates, "now is your turn to speak. My breath is exhausted. You speak now and finish the good work I commenced. Admonish the people to be moderate."

"I will make them perfectly enthusiastic in the cause of peace and quiet," said Mr. Krause, in a low voice. "You shall see how irresistible the stream of my eloquence will be," and striding forward with pathetic mien, and raising both arms as if to implore the people, he exclaimed in a loud voice: "You say so, and it is so! We cannot be victorious. Now, my opinion is, that as we cannot beat the enemy, we ought not to fight him, and in that way we can cheat him out of his victory. For where there is no fight, there can be no victory. Resist the armed bands with the quiet obstacle of mental fortitude. Do not act, but submit. Submit with a defiant air. Do not use your weapons, but do not yield them up to the enemy. Keep your hands on the hilts of your swords, and be quiet. When they mock and abuse you, be silent; but let them read your defiance in your countenances; when they press upon you with sword and cannon, retire with a proud smile, and do not defend yourselves, and we will see whether they are brutal enough to attack peaceful non-combatants. Act in this way, and the moral victory is yours, and you then will have conquered the enemy by your moral greatness, even if you are physically subdued. Against cannon and bayonets a people cannot defend themselves except by passive resistance, by submission, with secret and silent hatred in their hearts. Use no other weapons than this passive resistance, and posterity will praise you, and say of you, with admiration, that you were no heroes of fight, but heroes of passive resistance. Your country will be proud of you!"

Mr. Krause paused, and leaned, worn out, on the shoulder of the prophetic linen-weaver.

"You may be in the right," said the tailor, still rebellious at heart; "all that sounds right and reasonable, but still it don't suit me, and I don't see how the country can be proud of us, if we behave like cowards, and let ourselves be bamboozled this way."

"Do you hush, tailor!" cried the hunchbacked shoemaker. "The chap thinks because he can manage a sharp needle, he must be able to yield a broadsword; but let me tell you, my brave boy, that a stick with a sword hurts worse than a prick with a needle. It is not only written, 'Shoemaker, stick to your last,' but also, 'Tailor, stick to your needle.' Are we soldiers, that we must fight? No, we are respectable citizens, tailors and shoemakers, and the whole concern is no business of ours. And who is going to pay us for our legs and arms when they have been cut off?"

"Nobody, nobody is going to do it!" cried a voice from the crowd.

"And who is going to take care of our wives and children when we are crippled, and can't earn bread for them? Perhaps they are going to put us in the new almshouse, which has just been built outside of the King's Gate, and which they call the Oxen-head."

"No, no, we won't go into the Oxen-head!" screamed the people. "We won't fight! let us go home."

"Yes, go home, go home!" cried Krause and Kretschmer, delighted, and Pfannenstiel repeated after them—

"Let us go home!"

And indeed the groups began to separate and thin out; and the two editors, who had descended from their bench, mixed with the crowd, and enforced their peaceful arguments with zealous eloquence.

But it seemed as if Fortune did not favor them, for now down the neighboring street came Gotzkowsky with his band of armed workmen. He drew them up in front of the town-hall. The sight of this bold company of daring men, with determined countenances and flashing eyes, exercised a magical influence on the people; and when Gotzkowsky addressed them, and with overpowering eloquence and burning words implored them to resist, when with noble enthusiasm he summoned them to do their duty, and to remember their honors as men, the versatile crowd began again to cry out—"Arms, arms! give us arms!"

But the humpbacked shoemaker still remained cowed and timid, and the threatenings of the preachers of peace still sounded in his ears. He threw up his arms and cried out: "Children, remember what the gentlemen told us. Have nothing to do with fighting. Be wise and prudent!"

"The devil take your prudence!" cried Gotzkowsky. In an hour like this we have no need of prudence; we want courage! Won't you fight?"

"No, we won't!" cried the shoemaker, resolutely. "We want to keep our arms and legs."

"We don't want to go to the Oxen-head!" exclaimed another.

Gotzkowsky broke out impetuously: "Are you men, who dare to talk in this way? You are afraid of losing your limbs, and you are not afraid of losing, by your cowardice, your most valuable possessions, your liberty and your honor. Even if you do crawl through our streets as cripples, your wives and children will point to you with pride, and men will whisper to each other, 'He too was one of the heroes who fought for liberty, one of the brave men who, when Berlin was besieged, met the enemy, and fought bravely for our rights.'"

"That's fine," cried the tailor, carried away by Gotzkowsky's fiery words. "Yes, let us be heroes, let us fight!"

At the windows of the town-hall above, hid behind the curtains, the wise members of the city Council still stood and listened with anxious hearts to what was going on below. The countenance of the chief burgomaster became ashy pale, and drops of cold sweat stood on his brow. "This Gotzkowsky will ruin us all," sighed he heavily. "He does not think what he is doing. His foolhardiness will compel us all to be brave. But we will have to pay for our liberty, not only with our blood, but with our fortunes. And this man, who calculates so badly, pretends to be a merchant! But we must yield to this rash mob, for to oppose an excited people might bring even the honorable Council into danger. Good Heavens!" cried he, interrupting himself, "what is this again?"

To the sound of martial music, there was seen coming down the street a band of scar-covered veterans, the invalids of the first years of the war. Some limped, others carried their arms in slings, others again had their heads bound up; but one could perceive, by their serious, determined faces, that they were animated by a high and cheerful courage, which placed them above physical suffering. In their midst, on a litter, was borne the brave General von Seidlitz, whose wounds, received in the battle of Kunersdorf, had not yet healed; but the danger which threatened Berlin had roused him from a bed of suffering, and, as he could not walk, he had himself carried to the battery at the Kottbuss Gate, the defence of which he had undertaken.

As the hero turned to the people with a friendly greeting, and exhorted them to courage, with short and appropriate words, there sounded from a thousand voices an enthusiastic "Hurrah!" The people waved their hats, and cried loudly and tumultuously up at the windows of the Council, "Give us arms—arms!"

At the window above stood the chief burgomaster, with trembling limbs and livid face. "It is decided," said he, softly; "the people of Berlin are determined to die as heroes, or purchase their liberty with all the wealth of the town," and, with a weak cry of grief, he sank fainting into the arms of the head alderman.

The assistant burgomaster opened the window and cried out: "You shall have arms. We will defend Berlin with our last breath, and to the last drop of our blood!"

* * * * *

CHAPTER XI.

THE NIGHT OF HORRORS.

Thus, once more, had the impetuous boldness of the patriots carried the day against braggart cowardice. The Council, yielding to necessity, had resolved to be brave. The chief burgomaster, who had revived, donned his robe of office, adorned himself with his golden chain, and followed by the councillors, proceeded to Commander Rochow, to ask for arms for the citizens of Berlin. This petition was readily granted; the armory was thrown open, and there were seen, not only men and youths, old men and boys, but even women and girls, arming themselves for the sacred fight for fatherland and freedom. As if on a pilgrimage, the people proceeded to the armory in a long, solemn procession, silent and devout, a noble determination, a brave and cheerful but subdued expression observable in every face. No loud cries, not a rude word, nor boisterous laughter was heard from this crowd. Each one spoke in low and earnest tones to his neighbor; every one was conscious of the deep significance of the hour, and feared to interrupt the religious service of the country by a word spoken too loud. In silent devotion they crossed the threshold of the armory, with light and measured steps the crowd circulated through the rooms, and with solemn calmness and a silent prayer in their hearts, the people received from the hands of the veteran soldiers the weapons for the defence of their country. And the flags which hung around on the walls as shining mementoes of former victories, seemed to greet the people as patriots who were arming themselves for the holy fight against the enemy of their country, the destroyer of liberty.

For it was no longer a fight for Silesia, a strip of territory, which was to be fought, but a struggle between intellect and brute power, between civilization and barbarism, the inevitable companion of the Russian hordes. Prussia represented Germany, and on her waving banner she bore the civilization, refinement, science, and poetry of Germany. Her opponent was no longer the German brother, sprung from the same stock; it was the Austrian, who had called in the assistance of foreign barbarians, and who was fighting the Germans, the Prussians, with the help of the Russians. For that reason, the hatred against the Austrian was among the Prussian troops much more bitter and bloody than the hatred and abhorrence of the Russians, the sworn enemy of the German; and when, therefore, the Berlin citizens learned that the Austrians, too, were approaching under Count Lacy, this news was considered by these soldier-citizens as a consecration of their arms.

"Better be buried under the walls of Berlin than yield to the Austrian!" was the war-cry of the people, who flocked in constantly renewed streams to the armory for weapons, the watchword of the brave militia who hastened to all the gates to defend them against the enemy.

But all the streets did not offer so lively or proud an appearance. Whilst the citizens and the warriors scarcely recovered from their wounds, whilst the people were arming themselves to defend wife and child, and the sacred liberty of fatherland; whilst these brave troops were hurrying toward the Dresden and Kottbuss Gates to meet the Russians, others were seen hastening down the Linden and Frederick Streets. But these crowds were unarmed, though not empty-handed; their faces were pale, and their eyes were gloomy and dull. These were the faint-hearted and irresolute, who, in fear and trembling, were turning their backs on a town in which was to be fought the fight for the noblest possessions of mankind. This was the crowd of boasting, versatile flatterers and parasites, who worshipped no other God but fortune, and possessed no other faith than that of property and personal safety. Berlin might be reduced to ashes, barbarism and slavery might conquer, a foreign ruler might erect his throne in the midst of the down-fallen city, what did they care, provided their own lives and money were safe?

At this time they were hurrying along, pale with fright, death and terror in their distracted countenances. Women of the highest nobility, whose silken-shod feet had never before trod the rough pavement, fled with hasty steps down the street; shoulders which had never borne the least burden of life or sorrow, were now laden with treasures, and gold was the parent whom these modern Aeneases sought to save from the ruins of the threatened town. All ranks and conditions were confounded; no longer servant and master, fear had made brothers of them all. Countesses were seen smiling on their valets, in order to obtain the assistance of their arm to a more rapid flight; high-born gentlemen were seen laden down, like the meanest of their servants, with gold and silver ware, which they were seeking to save from the beleaguered city.

What did these people care whether Berlin fell, and was taken or not? What did they care if the throne of the house of Hohenzollern was overthrown? They had but one thought, one object—safety in flight. So they hurried down the street, moaning and wailing, breathless and trembling in every limb, toward the town gates. They reached the goal; they stood before the gates beyond which were escape and safety. But these gates were closed, and the soldiers who guarded them declared that none should pass them, that the men must stay to defend the town, the women to nurse the wounded and dying. All begging and pleading were in vain; in vain did the Jew Ephraim, who had become a millionnaire by the farming of the mint, offer the sentinel thousands to open the gates; in vain did the gentlemen, once so proud, entreat; in vain did the beautiful countesses wring their white hands before the poor despised workman who now stood as sentinel at the gates. In this moment this poor man was richer than the Hebrew mint-farmer Ephriam, for he was rich in courage; mightier than the proudest countess, for to his hands were intrusted the keys of a town; and the town gates were not opened to these bands of cowards. They were condemned to remain, condemned to the torture of trembling fear, cowardly, inactive supplication.

Howling and whining, they fled back again into the town, in order at least to bury their treasures, and hold themselves in readiness to meet the victor, whoever he might be, with flags of peace and hymns of welcome.

But before they had reached their houses, bombs had commenced to fly into the town, and here and there mortar-shells were heard whizzing through the air; with the cries of the flying and the wounded, and the screams of the dying, was now heard the moaning toll of the alarm-bell, telling that to the terrors of the siege were added those of the elements. Like gigantic torches of a funeral procession shone the flames of the burning houses, and covered the heavens with crimson as deep as the blood of those wounded unto death. At last night set in, but brought no rest for the sick, no refreshment for the weary. The fire-balls and bomb-shells still flew into the town, the alarm-bells still continued their mournful toll, the burning houses still flamed up to the sky; but yet the courage of the besieged did not sink. They still held their ground intrepidly, and they still bade an heroic defiance to the attacks of the enemy. In vain did the Russians attempt to storm the gates, the brave defenders drove them back again and again. Suddenly the cannon ceased firing, and the enemy drew back.

"What is the meaning of this?" asked the combatants at the gates.

"The meaning is," said Gotzkowsky, who had just arrived from another part of the town with a squad of his workmen—"the meaning is that help is approaching. It means that God is on our side, and succors our noble and righteous cause. The Prince of Wurtemberg has just arrived from Pasewalk with his division, and General Huelsen is hastening hither as rapidly as possible from Koswig."

The brave warriors received this news with a loud hurrah, and embraced each other with tears in their eyes and thanksgiving in their hearts.

"We are saved!" cried they to each other; "Berlin will not be surrendered, Berlin will be victorious, for help has arrived." And then they sank down on the pavement, to rest for an hour on this hard bed, after the fatigue of the fierce combat.

But Gotzkowsky could not rest. For him there was no leisure, no sleep; neither was there any fear or danger for him. As he had left his house, his daughter, and his riches unguarded, with the same unconcern did he move among the rain of balls and the bursting of shells. He did not think of death nor of danger! He only thought of his country, and one great, lofty idea—the idea of liberty—burned in his heart and animated his whole being. The Council, knowing his influence over the citizens, had, therefore, as soon as the Prince of Wurtemberg had arrived with his regiment in Berlin, communicated this intelligence to the brave patriot, and commissioned him to acquaint his men with the fact. With glistening eye and beaming countenance did he announce this significant intelligence to his brave warriors, reviving their courage, and redoubling their strength as they drove the enemy back from the gates and silenced his cannon.

But yet in his soul Gotzkowsky was sad and full of care. He had seen the regiments of the Prince of Wurtemberg as they marched in, and he had read in the dull countenances of the soldiers, staggering and sinking from fatigue, that they were not able, nor even in a condition, to hold a sword. But yet his heart did not fail him. The elasticity of his courage seemed only to increase with the danger. Perhaps a short rest, strengthening food, refreshing wine, might restore to these men their lost strength.

56

And now for the first time since the attack of the enemy did Gotzkowsky turn toward his home; but not to visit his daughter, not to inquire after his property, but to open his wine-cellars, and to let his cashier fill his pockets with gold.

He then returned rapidly down the street directly to the town-hall, where the Council were in session, and had invited the most venerable citizens to consult with them.

Appearing before this august body, Gotzkowsky painted, with glowing eloquence and impressive words, the destitute condition of the regiments which had entered the town. He demanded for them nourishment and support; he entreated the Council to give these weary troops shelter and rest.

"First let them eat and sleep," said he, "and then they will fight for us and conquer. We cannot expect courage from a tired and starved man."

From the Council he hastened to the rich merchants and factory lords. The rich man went begging for his hungry brethren, and his pride did not feel itself lowered by the petition. No one could resist his impetuous eagerness; every one was carried away by his unselfish and impulsive magnanimity. For the moment, even earthly treasures lost their value, for more valuable possessions were at stake, namely, liberty and honor. Every one gave cheerfully and most liberally.

And now it was a glorious sight to see how, in a few hours, the whole city changed its appearance. As the night before had been full of horrors and dread events, the next morning and day were like a festival, the preparation to a great and solemn feast. Forty of the largest and fattest oxen were slaughtered, to afford a strengthening meal to those so much in need of nourishment. About mid-day, a strange procession moved down the Koenig's Street and across the Palace Square. And what was the meaning of it? It was not a funeral, for there were no mourning-wreaths and no hearse; it was not a bridal procession, for the bridal paraphernalia and joyous music were wanting. Nor did it wend its way toward the church nor the churchyard, but toward the new and handsome opera-house, recently erected by the king, whose gates were opened wide to receive it. It looked like a feast of Bacchus at one time, from the enormous tuns driven along; at another time like a festival of Ceres, as in solemn ranks came the bakers bringing thousands of loaves in large wagons. Then followed the white-capped cooks, bringing the smoking beef in large caldrons. The rear was finally brought up by the butlers, with large baskets of wine.

And the beautiful and resplendent temple of art was thrown open to the reception of all these things, although they only served for material nourishment, and in the magnificent hall in which formerly Frederick the Great, with his generals and chosen friends, listened to the magic strains of Gluck, there sounded now a wild confusion of discordant cries. The butlers stood by the wine-casks, filling the bottles which were carried out by the nimble and active *vivandieres*, and on the same stage on which once Galiari and Barbarini, Ostroa and Sambeni enchanted the public with their marvellous singing, were seen now large caldrons of beef; and, instead of the singers, the performance was conducted by cooks, who drew the meat out of the pots, and arranged it neatly on enormous dishes. Gotzkowsky had attained his object, and Berlin fed this day the exhausted and hungry troops of the Prince of Wurtemberg. The merchant of Berlin had given his choicest and best wines to the banquet of patriotism.

* * * * *

CHAPTER XII.

RUSSIANS AND AUSTRIANS.

After so many horrors and so many hours of anxiety, at last, on the evening of the second day of the siege, a momentary suspension of hostilities occurred. Berlin rested after the excitement and turmoil, and even the besiegers seemed to be reposing. Shells and fire-balls no longer hissed through the groaning air, and the thunder of the cannon had died away. Peace—the peace arising from disabling exhaustion on the part of the combatants, reigned for a short while, and the belligerents rested for a few hours to invigorate themselves for a renewal of the fight. The streets of Berlin, lit by the dull lamplight, were forsaken and empty, and only occasionally from the dark houses was heard wailing and moaning, either the death-struggle of a wounded man or the lamentations of his mourning friends. This death-like silence prevailed for several hours, when it was broken by a peculiar noise, sounding like the dull, muffled beat of drums, followed by the measured tread of marching troops. The sound approached nearer and nearer, and by the dim light of the street lamps one could distinctly recognize a column of men marching in close order from the opera-house down the Linden Street.

It consisted of more than six thousand men, moving down the "Linden" in deep silence, unbroken even by a word of command. To see this dark and silent column passing along the gloomy and deserted street, was calculated to produce a feeling of awe in the spectator. Any one inclined to be superstitious might have imagined this warlike force, marching through the streets at the hour of midnight, noiseless and silent as the grave, to be, not living soldiers, but the large and daily increasing cohort of spirits of those fallen in battle, taking its way through the dying town, as birds of prey fly with prophetic wing in circles round the fields of death.

And now the head of the column reaches the Brandenburg Gate. The sentinel stands to arms and challenges. The leader steps up to the officer of the guard and whispers a few words in his ear. This officer bows deeply and respectfully, and gives his sentinel a short order in an under-tone. He then steps back to his command and presents arms. The leaves of the gate then turned creaking on their hinges, and in solemn silence the column marched out. This long, dark procession, lasted nearly an hour; the gate then closed, and the same quiet resumed its sway in the streets.

Berlin was dreaming or sleeping, praying or weeping, but knew not that in this hour fresh misfortune had fallen upon it; knew not that the Prince of Wurtemberg had just left the town, and retired upon Spandau with his regiments, feeling himself too weak to resist an enemy three times his number. And furthermore, it was not aware that the Austrian Count Lacy, who had already occupied Potsdam and Charlottenburg, with his division of ten thousand men, would in a few hours be at the gates of Berlin.

In serious consultation, in anxious and wavering expectation, the city fathers were assembled in the town-hall, which they had not quitted for two days. But, at this moment, a pause seemed to have occurred in their deliberations, for both the chief burgomaster, Von Kircheisen, and the aldermen were leaning back in their high, carved chairs, in sleepy repose, contemplating the wax-lights in their silver candelabras, which shed a dim and uncertain light into the more distant parts of the hall. One or the other occasionally threw an inquiring glance toward the door, and leaned forward as if to listen. After a while, steps were heard in the antechamber, and the countenances of the honorable members of the Council lighted up.

"At last he comes," said the chief burgomaster, raising himself with an effort in his chair, and arranging the chain on his breast, which had got a little out of order.

The door now opened, and the merchant Gotzkowsky entered.

He approached the assembly with a firm and hurried step. The light of the candles shone upon his countenance, and in his pale, worn features you could read the traces of the hardships, the efforts and dangers he had undergone during the last two unfortunate days; only his eye still shone with its mild and yet fiery glance, and in his breast there beat still a brave and cheerful heart.

"Ye have called me, honorable gentlemen, and, as ye see, I have not delayed in answering your call."

"Yes, we have summoned you," answered the chief burgomaster. "The Council desire your advice."

A slight, mocking smile played about Gotzkowsky's lips. "It is not the first time," he said, "that the Council have done me this honor."

Herr von Kircheisen plucked uneasily at his golden chain, and frowned. Gotzkowsky's answer had wounded his pride. "Yes, you gave us your advice yesterday, and it was only by your urgent appeal that we were induced to feed and lodge the Prince of Wurtemberg's troops. We might have spared ourselves the trouble, and our forty oxen remained unslaughtered."

"The Prince of Wurtemberg has left us, I know," said Gotzkowsky, sorrowfully, "and we are thrown again on our own resources. Oh, I could weep over it! Two days and nights have the citizens of Berlin fought with the courage of a lioness defending her young, and all in vain. So much noble blood shed in vain!"

"We must surrender, then?" said Kircheisen, turning pale.

"Unless the honorable Council can sow dragons' teeth and reap armed men, unless we can mould cannon and create gunners to serve them, we must, indeed, surrender!" said Gotzkowsky, in a sad tone. "Yes, if we had a dozen cannon like the two at the Kottbuss Gate served by the brave artillerist, Fritz, there might be some hope for us. Those were beautiful shots. Like the sickle of death did they mow down the ranks of the enemy, and whole rows fell at once. Fritz is a hero, and has built himself a monument with the dead bodies of the Russians—and all this for nothing!"

"For nothing! do you say?" sighed the chief burgomaster. "On the contrary, I rather think it will cost us a mint of money. The Austrians have sent Prince Lowenstein in with a flag of truce, to demand the surrender of the town. The Russians have also sent in a flag of truce with the same demand. Now comes the important question, To which of these two powers shall we surrender? Which will give us the best bargain?" and as the burgomaster stammered out this question, he seized a large goblet of wine which stood before him and emptied it at a draught. He then ordered the servant, who stood at the door, to replenish it with Johannisberger.

The aldermen and senators looked significantly at each other, and the second burgomaster ventured timidly to suggest that the heavy wine might possibly be injurious to the health of his honor the chief burgomaster.

"Wine makes a man brave," he drawled out, "and as long as the city fathers have good wine in their cellars, the citizens of Berlin may sleep in peace, for so long will the Council have the courage to brave the enemy! Let me have wine, then, and be brave!" and again he emptied the replenished goblet. He then stared complacently at the ceiling, and seemed lost in contemplation of the laurel-wreath painted above.

The second burgomaster then rose gently from his seat, and taking Gotzkowsky's arm, led him with the two principal councillors to one of the more remote window-seats. With a slight motion of the hand and a compassionate shrug of the shoulders, he pointed across to Herr von Kircheisen.

"Our poor oppressed chief wishes to acquire pot-valor," said he, "and to stimulate himself into a delirium of firmness; but I am afraid that the *delirium tremens* of fear is the only kind that he will experience. The poor man is very much to be pitied. It is just at such a time, when presence of mind is most requisite, that the good burgomaster regularly loses his head, and his brain rushes off with him like a mad horse to death and destruction."

"And such a man is the chief magistrate of the town of Berlin," said Gotzkowsky, mournfully.

"The citizens chose him, and the king confirmed their choice," said the burgomaster; "so we ought to be satisfied. But now let us come to the subject which induced us to disturb your slumbers, my friend. We need your counsel. The Russians and Austrians both summon us to surrender, and the Council of Berlin wish your advice, Gotzkowsky, as to which of these two enemies they shall yield."

"That is, by Heavens! a choice that the devil himself must envy us," cried Gotzkowsky, with a sad smile. "To which party shall we surrender? To the Austrian, who wears the imperial German crown, and yet is the enemy of Germany!

or to the Russian, the northern barbarian, whose delight it is to trample every human right in the dust! Let me consider a little while, for it is a sad and painful choice." And Gotzkowsky strode up and down, absorbed in the deepest reflection. Then turning to the gentlemen, after a long pause, he asked, "To whom shall we yield? If my brother were among my enemies, I would fear him above all others; for a brother's hatred is most unnatural, and, for that very reason, the most violent. The Austrian is the German brother of the Prussian, and yet they are striving for the right of the first-born, instead of confederating for the general good in unity, in equal authority, equal power, and equal determination. On the contrary, Austria allies herself to Russia, the sworn enemy of Germany, and with the assistance of this enemy fights against her German brothers. Therefore, my opinion is that, if we really must surrender, and if the Prussian really must yield, let it not be to Austria. Subjection to an equal is doubly humiliating. It is less painful to suffer death at the hand of a barbarian than to be butchered by a brother. I would, then, in this instance, give the preference to Russia."

"That is also my opinion," said the burgomaster, and the councillors agreed with him. They returned to the table, at which the chief burgomaster still sat, gazing stupidly at the wine-cup.

"Gotzkowsky is of our opinion," said the second burgomaster, turning toward him; it would be best to yield to the Russian."

"The Russian is a capital fellow!" stammered the chief burgomaster. "The Russian has a great deal of money, and spends it freely. I esteem the Russian astonishingly; and my decided opinion is, that we surrender to the Russian."

* * * * *

CHAPTER XIII.

A MAIDEN'S HEART.

Elise had passed the last two days and nights in her room; nevertheless she had felt no fear; the thunder of the cannon and the wail of the wounded had inspired her with mournful resignation rather than with fear. As, at one time, she stood at the window, a shell burst near the house, and shattered the window-panes of the ground floor.

"Oh, if this hall had only struck me," cried she, while her cheeks burned, "then all this suffering would have been at an end, this doubt would have been cleared up: and if my father ever again gave himself the trouble to visit his house, and ask after his daughter, my death would be the proper rebuke to his question." Her father's long absence and apparent indifference tormented her and converted her grief into anger.

During these days of danger and mortal peril he had never once entered his house to visit his daughter. With the unmitigated egotism of her sex, she could not comprehend the greatness, the noble self-denial, the manly firmness which dictated his conduct; she could see in it nothing but indifference and cold-heartedness.

"The most insignificant and unpolished workman is dearer to him than his own child," said she, proudly, drying her tears. "He is now, perhaps, watching in the cabins of his laborers, and does not care if his own house is burned to the ground; but even if he were told that it was so, if he heard that his daughter had perished in the flames, he would calmly say, 'My country demands this sacrifice of me, and I submit.' No tear would dim his eye; his country would not leave him time to mourn for his daughter. Oh, this country! what is it? My country is where I am happy, and where I am beloved!" She sighed deeply, and her thoughts wandered to her lover, her Feodor, the enemy of her country, in whose heart she thought she would find her real country, her true home.

The spoiled child of fortune, always accustomed to see every wish fulfilled, Elise had not learned the power of self-control, nor to bend her will to any higher power. Fortune seemed anxious to spare yet awhile this warm, loving heart, and to allow her a little longer the freedom of happy ignorance, before it initiated her into the painful and tearful mysteries of actual life. Besides this, Elise had inherited from her father a strong will and dauntless courage, and behind her bright, dreamy eyes dwelt a proud and spirited soul. Like her father, her whole soul yearned for freedom and independence; but the difference between them was, that while she only understood freedom as applying to herself personally, Gotzkowsky's more capacious mind comprehended it in its larger and more general sense. She wished for freedom only for herself; he desired it for his country, and he would willingly have allowed his own person to be cast into bonds and fetters, if he could thereby have secured the liberties of the people. Out of this similarity, as well as from this difference of character, arose all the discord which occasionally threatened to disturb the harmony of these two hearts.

Gotzkowsky could not understand the heart of the young maiden, nor Elise that of the noble patriot. To these two strong and independent natures there had been wanting the gentle, soothing influence of a mother's love, acting conciliatingly on both. Elise's mother had died while she was young, and the child was left to the care of strangers. Her father could seldom find time to be with his daughter; but, though seldom personally present, yet his whole soul was faithfully, unalterably devoted to her. Elise did not suspect this, and in consequence of seldom seeing or meeting him, and the want of mutual intercourse, the heart of his daughter became estranged from him, and in the soul of this young girl, just budding into life, brought up without companions, in the midst of wealth and plenty, arose at first the doubt, and later the conviction, of the indifference of her father toward his only child. But proud as she was, and full of a feeling of independence, she never met him with a reproach or complaint, but withdrew into herself, and as she believed herself repelled, strove also, on her part, to emancipate herself.

"Love cannot be forced, nor can it be had for the asking," said she, as, yielding sometimes to a natural childish feeling, she felt an irresistible longing to go to her father, whom she had not seen the livelong day; to hunt him up in the midst of his work, to lay herself gently on his breast, and say to him: "Love me, father, for without love we are both so lonely!" Once she had yielded to the impulse of her heart, and had gone down to his work-room, to take refuge with all her love and all her desire in her father's heart. It was on the very day that Gotzkowsky had returned from a most important journey. He had been absent for weeks from his daughter, and yet his first visit had not been to her, but to the work-room, which he had not left since his arrival. But Elise did not know that he had travelled with relays of horses, and that, in spite of the intensely bitter weather, he had driven day and night, allowing himself no rest nor refreshment, in order to reach home as rapidly as possible, solely from desire to see his daughter, whose fair and lovely countenance was the star which lighted his dreary, lonesome hours of toil, and inspired him with courage and cheerfulness. Nor could she know that he had only undertaken this journey because, by the failure of one of the largest mercantile firms in the Netherlands, his own house had been put in danger, and he had been threatened with the loss of his hard-earned wealth.

With palpitating heart, and tears of love in her eyes, she entered his room. Her whole bearing was sublime, full of tenderness and warmth, full of the humble love of a child. But Gotzkowsky scarcely raised his eyes from his books and papers, did not advance to meet her, did not leave the circle of his officials and servants, did not even break off the conversation he was engaged in with the directors of his silk-factory. And yet Elise drew nearer to him, her heart yearned so to bid him welcome. She laid her hand on his shoulder, and whispered an affectionate greeting in his ear. Gotzkowsky only looked at her hastily, and replied almost impatiently, "I pray you, my child, do not disturb me; we are busy with very important matters."

It certainly was business of great importance, which monopolized Gotzkowsky's attention immediately on his return. It was a question of nearly half a million, which he would probably lose in consequence of a royal decree just issued. This decree ordained that the new *Frederick d'ors* coined by the Jewish farmer of the mint, and which were much too light, should be received at par all over the whole kingdom, and even at the treasury offices. It was, therefore, but natural that all debtors would hasten to pay their creditors in this coin which had imparted to it so sudden and unexpected a value. Gotzkowsky had received from his debtors upward of eight hundred thousand dollars in this light coin, while his foreign creditors absolutely refused to take them, and demanded the payment of their debts in good money. Gotzkowsky, who, in consequence of his large and extensive connections abroad, had about three hundred thousand dollars in exchange against him, paid his creditors in gold of full weight, and lost by these transactions three hundred thousand dollars in one day.

Just at the moment when this heavy loss befell him, Elise appeared, to welcome him. His heart sank as he beheld her, for as he looked at her this loss appeared in its full magnitude; it seemed as if not he, but his child, had lost a portion of her wealth.

Elise knew and suspected nothing. She only felt that she had been repulsed, and she withdrew, deeply wounded and mortified, with the vow never to run the risk again of such another rebuff, such another humiliation.

Gotzkowsky lost in this hour, not only the three hundred thousand dollars, but, what he valued above all earthly treasures, the affection of his daughter, and both without any fault of his own. Elise forced herself to close her heart against her father, or at least to conquer her grief at the supposed indifference, or quiet, lukewarm inclination. And yet this ardent heart longed for love, as the plant longs for the sunshine which is to penetrate it, and ripen it into wonderful bloom. Had the friend and companion of her youth, Bertram, been near her, she would have confided all her sorrows to him, and found consolation on his breast. But he had been absent for about a year on his long journey; and Elise's heart, which had always clung to him with a sisterly affection, became more and more alienated from the friend of her youth.

But fate or perhaps her evil destiny ordained that, about this time, she should make the acquaintance of a young man who quickly won the love of her vacant heart, and filled its void.

This young man was Colonel Feodor von Brenda, whom the fortune of war had thrown into Berlin.

Elise loved him. With joy and delight, with the unbounded confidence of innocence, she gave her whole heart up to this new sensation.

And, indeed, this young colonel was a very brilliant and imposing personage. He was one of those Russian aristocrats who, on the Continent, in their intercourse with the noblest and most exclusive society of Germany and France, acquire that external adroitness and social refinement, that brilliant graceful polish, which so well conceals the innate barbarism and cunning of the natural character of the Russian.

He was a bright companion, sufficiently conversant with arts and sciences to talk on every subject, without committing himself. He knew how to converse on all topics fluently enough, without betraying the superficial character of his knowledge and his studies. Educated at the court of the Empress Elizabeth, life had appeared to him in all its voluptuousness and fullness, but at the same time had soon been stripped of all its fancies and illusions. For him there existed no ideals and no innocence, no faith, not even a doubt which in itself implies a glimmer of faith; for him there was nothing but the plain, naked, undeceivable disenchantment, and pleasure was the only thing in which he still believed.

This pleasure he pursued with all the energy of his originally noble and powerful character; and as all his divinities had been destroyed, all holy ideals had dissolved into myths and hollow phantoms, he wished to secure one divinity, at least, to whom he could raise an altar, whom he could worship: this divinity was Pleasure.

Pleasure he sought everywhere, in all countries; and the more ardently and eagerly he sought it, the less was he able to find it. Pleasure was the first modest, coy woman who cruelly shunned him, and the more he pursued her, the more coldly did she seem to fly him.

And now he converted his whole life into an adventure, a kind of quixotic pursuit of the lost loved one, Pleasure. In the mean time, his heart was dead to all the better and nobler feelings. But, at one time, it seemed as if a higher and more serious inclination promised permanently to enchain this dreaded rival of all husbands and lovers.

Feodor von Brenda, the most *blase*, witty, insolent cavalier at the court of his empress, became suddenly serious and silent. On his proud countenance was seen, for the first time, the light of a soft and gentle feeling, and when he approached his beautiful bride, the Countess Lodoiska von Sandomir, there beamed from his dark eyes a glow holier and purer than the fire of sensuality. Could he have fled with her into some desert, could he have withdrawn into the stillness of his mountain castle, he would have been saved; but life held him with its thousand minute, invisible threads, and the experiences of his past years appeared to mock him for his credulity and confidence.

Besides this woman, whom he adored as an angel, arose the demon of skepticism and mistrust, and regarded him with mocking smiles and looks of contempt; but still Feodor von Brenda was a name of honor, a cavalier to whom his pledged word was sacred, and who was ready to pay the debt of honor which he had incurred toward his betrothed; and this love for the Countess Lodoiska, although cankered by doubt and gnawed by the experiences of his own life, still had sufficient power over him to cause the future to appear not gloomy but full of promise, and to allow him to hope, if not for happiness, at least for rest and enjoyment.

The war-cry roused him from these dreams and doubts of love. Elizabeth had united with Maria Theresa against Frederick of Prussia, and the Empress of Russia was about to send an army to the support of her ally. Feodor awoke from the sweet rest into which his heart had sunk, and, like Rinaldo, had torn asunder the rosy chains by which his Armida had sought to fetter him. He followed the Russian colors, and accompanied General Sievers as his adjutant to Germany.

As to him all life was only an adventure, he wished also to enjoy the exciting pastime of war. This, at least, was something new, a species of pleasure and amusement he had not yet tried, and therefore the young colonel gave himself up to it with his whole soul, and an ardent desire to achieve deeds of valor.

But it was his fate to be carried early from the theatre of war as a prisoner, and in this character he arrived with General Sievers at Berlin. But his durance was light, his prison the large and pleasant city of Berlin, in which he could wander about perfectly free with the sole restriction of not going beyond the gates.

General Sievers became accidentally acquainted with Gotzkowsky, and this acquaintance soon ripened into a more intimate friendship. He passed the greater part of his days in Gotzkowsky's house. As a lover of art, he could remain for hours contemplating the splendid pictures which Gotzkowsky had bought for the king in Italy, and which had not yet been delivered at Sans Souci; or, by the side of the manufacturer he traversed the large halls of the factory in which an entirely new life, a world of which he had no idea, was laid open to him. And then again Gotzkowsky would impart to him the wide and gigantic plans which occupied his mind; and this disclosed to him a view into a new era which arose beyond the present time, an era when industry would command and raise the now despised workman into the important and respected citizen.

While Gotzkowsky and his friend the general were discussing these extensive plans, and speculating about the future of industry, the young people, Elise and the adjutant, were dreaming about the future of their love.

The colonel had only commenced this love-affair with the daughter of the rich manufacturer as a new adventure. It was so piquant to go through all the stages of a romantic, dreamy German love, with a pure, innocent German girl, and to let himself be led by her through the sacred mazes of innocent romance, holy transports, and chaste affection—it was so pleasant a diversion of his captivity, why should he not enjoy it?

This attachment to Elise was for him at first only a temporary amusement, and he toyed with his vows and wooing, until, imperceptibly, he found his heart entangled in his own net. The ardent yet innocent love of the young girl touched his feelings. It was something new to be the object of so chaste and devoted an affection. He was ashamed of himself in his inmost soul to perceive with what childish trust, what sacred security and humble resignation this young, rich, and beautiful maiden gave herself up to him.

For the first time, he experienced an ardent desire to be worthy of so noble an affection, and to resemble, at least in some slight degree, the ideal picture which Elise had formed of him—to be something of the hero, the knight, the noble being whom Elise worshipped in him.

At the same time it was so surprising and strange to meet a girl, who, all submission and devoted love, yet remained firm and immovable in her purity and chastity, so bright and proud that even he felt respect for this innocence which surrounded the beloved one like a halo, and his lips refused to utter words at which her pure soul might tremble.

With his fiery and mercurial temperament, he had, with a kind of passionate curiosity, adopted the *rôle* of a Platonic lover, and the libertine in his character had been subdued by the love of the eccentric. He had converted this love into a kind of adoration. He placed Elise upon the altar, and worshipped her as a saint to whom he had turned from the turmoil and wild lust of life, and in the contemplation and worship of whom he could obtain forgiveness of all his sins and errors. It affected him to think that Elise was praying for him while he, perhaps, forgot her in the whirlpool of pleasure; that she believed in him so devotedly and truly, that she looked up to him so lovingly and humbly—to him who was so far her inferior. And in the midst of his wild life of pleasure he felt the need of some saint to intercede for forgiveness for him. All these new and unaccustomed feelings only enchained him the more closely, and made him consider the possession of her as the most desirable and only worthy object of his life.

She must be his; he was determined to wear this brilliant diamond, the only one he had ever found genuine and without flaw, as his most costly possession; to become, in spite of all difficulties and impossibilities, unmindful of his betrothed bride and his solemn vows, the husband of this beautiful German maiden, who had given herself to him heart and soul.

In proportion to the difficulties that opposed such a union, increased his fierce determination to overcome them. He was betrothed, and the Empress Elizabeth herself had blessed the betrothal. He could not, therefore, retract his vows without exciting the anger of his mistress, and history had more than one example to show how violent and annihilating this anger could be. In like wise, Elise dared not hope ever to obtain the consent of her father to her union with a man who was the enemy of her country. She was obliged to conceal this love with anxious care from his eyes, if she did not wish to expose herself to the danger of being separated from her lover forever. She knew that her father, in every thing else uniformly kind and yielding toward her, was on this one subject implacable, and that no tears, no pleading, were capable of moving the firm and energetic will of the ardent patriot.

Both were obliged, therefore, to preserve their love a secret, and in this concealment lay for Feodor a new charm which bound him to her, while it estranged Elise's heart still more from her father, and chained it in unbounded devotion to her lover.

In the mean while the time arrived for Feodor to leave Berlin with General Sievers. He swore eternal love and fidelity to Elise, and she vowed to him cheerfully never to become the wife of another, but in patience and trust to await his return, and to hope for the end of the war and the coming of peace, which would solve all difficulties, and remove the opposition of her father.

That besides her father there could be any obstacle, she did not suspect; Feodor had so often sworn that she was his first and only love, and she, young and inexperienced as she was, believed him.

* * * * *

CHAPTER XIV.

A FAITHFUL FRIEND.

Elise's father had not yet returned. She was still alone, but in her soul there was neither fear nor trembling, but only a defiant grief at this apparent indifference to the danger which had threatened her, in common with the rest of Berlin, for the last two days.

She had shut herself up in her room, not that she anticipated any danger, but because she wished to be alone, because she wished to avoid Bertram, the faithful friend, who had watched over her during this time with the most attentive devotion. Truthfully had he remained in the house, deserted by her father, as a careful watchman; had never left its door; but, armed with dagger and pistol, he had stationed himself as a sentinel in the antechamber, ready to hasten at the slightest call of Elise, to defend her with his life against any attack or any danger, and Elise felt herself bound to him in gratitude, and yet this duty of gratitude was a burden to her. It was distressing and painful to her to see Bertram's quiet and mournful countenance, to read in his dimmed eyes the presence of a grief so courageously subdued. But yet she had endeavored to overcome this feeling, and she had often come to him lately to chat with him about past times and to reward him with her society for his protection and faithful presence. And yet Bertram's tender conscience was well aware of the constraint Elise had put herself under, and the harmless and cheerful chat was to him all the more painful as it reminded him of past times and blasted hopes.

He had, therefore, with a melancholy smile of resignation, requested Elise not to come any more into the hall, as it would be better, by the anticipated occupation of the enemy, to remain in her room, in the upper story of the house, and to lock the door in order to secure her from any possible surprise.

Elise had completely understood the delicacy and nobleness of this request, and since then had remained quiet and undisturbed in her room.

Thus the second night had commenced. She passed it like the one preceding, wandering up and down, not needing sleep, but kept awake by her thoughts and cares. In the middle of the night she was interrupted in her anxious reveries by Bertram, who came to her door, and in a low and timid voice requested permission to enter.

Elise knew very well that she could trust Bertram like a brother, as an unselfish, disinterested friend. Therefore, fearlessly she opened the door, and bade him come in. Bertram entered timidly and confused, almost overpowered by happiness, for this room into which he came was Elise's bedroom, the sanctuary of maidenhood and beauty, and he felt disposed to kneel down and pray, so evidently did this room seem to him a temple of innocence.

It appeared to him as if his unholy foot was not worthy to tread this ground, nor to approach the bed which, with its white curtains, seemed to wave before his dazzled eyes like a white swan.

In soft and gentle words he brought to Elise greeting from her father. He related to her how Gotzkowsky had visited his house, not to take rest, but to see Elise; how, scarcely arrived there, a messenger from the Council had called him back to the town-hall. There he had commissioned Bertram to request his daughter to withdraw from the front rooms of the house, and to retire into those next to the garden, where she would be safer and have less to fear from the enemy as he marched in.

"At last, then, my father has consented to think of me," said Elise, with a bitter smile. "His patriotism has allowed him leisure to remember his only daughter, who would have remained solitary and forsaken in the midst of servants and hirelings if my noble and faithful brother had not assumed the duties of my father, and watched over and protected me." She reached out both her hands to Bertram with a look full of gratitude, but he scarcely touched them; he held them for a moment lightly and coldly in his, and then let them go. This slight and transient touch had shot through him like an electric shot, and reawakened all the sorrows of his soul.

"You will then leave this room?" asked Bertram, approaching the door.

"I will go into the hall immediately next to it."

"All alone?" asked Bertram; and then fearing that she might suspect him of wishing to force his company upon her, he added, quickly, "You ought to keep one of your maids near you, Elise."

Smilingly she shook her head. "For what purpose?" asked she. "Bertram is my protector, and I am quite safe. I have sent my maids to their rooms. They were tired from long watching and weeping; let them sleep. Bertram will watch for all of us. I have no fear, and I would not even leave this room, if it were not that I wished to comply with the rarely expressed and somewhat tardy desire of my father."

Saying which, she took the silver candelabras from the table and quietly traversed the room in order to proceed to the adjoining hall. At the door she stopped and turned round. The full light of the candles shone on her handsome, expressive face, and Bertram gazed on her with a mixture of delight and anguish.

"Bertram," said she gently and timidly, "Bertram, my brother, let me thank you for all your love and constancy. Would that I could reward you more worthily! In that case all would be different, and we would not all be so sad and despondent as we now are. But always remember, my brother, that I will never cease to love you as a sister, and that if I cannot compel my heart to love you otherwise, yet no other power, no other feeling can ever lessen or destroy my sisterly affection. Remember this, Bertram, and be not angry with me." She nodded to him with a sweet smile, and retreated through the door.

Bertram stood rooted to the floor like one enchanted, and gazed at the door through which this vision of light had departed. He then raised his eyes to heaven, and his countenance shone with excitement. "God grant that she may be happy!" prayed he, softly. "May she never be tormented by the agonies of error or repentance; may he whom she loves prove worthy of her!"

Overpowered by bitter and painful thoughts, his head sank upon his breast, and tears coursed down his cheeks. But he did not abandon himself long to his sad and anxious thoughts, nor did he allow sorrow long to take possession of his heart. After a short pause he raised himself and shook his head, as if to roll off the whole burden of care and grief with all the power of his will.

"At least I will always be at her side," said he, his countenance beaming from the noble decision. "I will follow her like a faithful, watchful dog, and ward off from her every danger and every misfortune which comes from man and not from God. She has called me her brother! Well, a brother has both rights and duties, and I will perform them!"

* * * * *

CHAPTER XV.

AN UNEXPECTED MEETING.

The hall to which Elise had retired, next to her bedroom, was on the garden side of the house, and its glass doors opened on a porch from which handsomely ornamented bronze steps led winding down into the garden. Notwithstanding the advanced season of the year, the night was mild, and the moon shone brightly. Elise opened the glass doors and stepped out on the porch to cool her burning forehead in the fresh night air; and, leaning on the balustrade, she looked up smiling and dreamily at the moon. Sweet and precious fancies filled the soul of the young maiden, and brought the color to her cheeks.

She thought of her lover, who so lately had appeared to her as in a dream; she repeated to herself each one of his words. With a sweet but trembling emotion she remembered that he had bidden her to await him; that he had sworn to her to come, even if his way should be over dead bodies and through rivers of blood.

With all the pride of a loving girl she recalled his bold and passionate words, and she rejoiced in her heart that she could call herself the bride of a hero. Even if this hero was the enemy of her country, what did she care? She loved him, and what to her were nationalities or the quarrels of princes? She was his—his in love and faith, in purity and innocence; what cared she for aught else?

Elise started suddenly from her dreams. She had heard a noise down in the garden, and leaned listening over the balustrade. What was the meaning of this noise? Was it perhaps some thief, who, under cover of the general confusion, had stolen into the garden? Elise remained motionless, and listened. She had not deceived herself, for she distinctly heard footsteps. A feeling of fear took possession of her, and yet she did not dare to move from the spot, nor to cry for help. Might it not be her lover, for whom she had promised to wait?

With strained attention she gazed down into the garden; her eye seemed to penetrate the darkness with its sharp, searching look. But she could distinguish nothing; not an object moved through these silent paths, where the yellow sand was sufficiently lighted up by the moon to betray any one sufficiently bold to tread them. Every thing was again quiet; but Elise shuddered at these long, black shadows cast on both sides of the alleys; she was afraid to remain any longer on the porch. She retired into the hall, the door to which she had left open on purpose to perceive any noise coming from that quarter.

Now again she became aware of steps approaching nearer and nearer. She wished to rise, but her feet refused their office. She sank back powerless into her chair and closed her eyes. She could not determine whether it was fear or happy expectation which pervaded her whole being.

And now the footsteps ascended into the porch, and came quite near to the window. Would a thief dare to approach these lighted windows? She raised her eyes. He stood before her!—he, her beloved, the friend of her heart, her thoughts, her hopes! Feodor von Brenda stood in the doorway of the hall, and uttered softly her name. She could not rise, her feet trembled so; and in her heart she experienced an uneasy sensation of fear and terror. And yet she stretched her arms out to him, and welcomed him with her looks and her smile.

And now she lay in his arms, now he pressed her firmly to his heart, and whispered tender, flattering words in her ear.

She pushed him gently back, and gazed at him with a smile of delight. But suddenly her look clouded, and she sighed deeply. Feodor's brilliant Russian uniform pained her, and reminded her of the danger he might be incurring. He read her fear and anxiety in her countenance.

"Do not be afraid, my sweet one," whispered he gently, drawing her into his arms. "No danger threatens us. My people are now masters of the town. Berlin has surrendered to the Russians. *The enemy* is now conqueror and master, and no one would dare to touch this uniform. Even your father must now learn to yield, and to forget his hatred."

"He will never do it," sighed Elise sadly. "You do not know him, Feodor. His will never bends, and the most ardent prayers would not induce him to grant that to his heart which his judgment does not approve of. He is not accustomed to yield. His riches make him almost despotic. Every one yields to him."

"He is the king of merchants," said Feodor, as he passed his fingers playfully through the dark tresses of the young girl, whose head rested on his shoulder. "His money makes him as powerful as a prince."

"That is exactly my misfortune," sighed Elise.

The colonel laughed, and pressed a kiss upon her forehead. "Dreamer," said he, "do you call yourself miserable because you are the daughter of a millionnaire?"

"Millions alone do not make one happy," said she sadly. "The heart grows cold over the dead money, and my father's heart is cold toward his daughter. He has so many thousand other things to do and think of besides his daughter! The whole world has claims upon him; every one requires his advice, submits to and obeys him. From all parts of the world come letters to be answered, and, when at last, late in the evening, he remembers he is something besides the king on 'Change, the man of speculation, he is so tired and exhausted, that he has only a few dull words for his child, who lives solitary in the midst of all this wealth, and curses the millions which make her poor."

She had spoken with increasing excitement and bitterness. Even her love had for a moment been eclipsed by the feeling of an injured daughter, whose grief she now for the first time disclosed to her lover.

As she finished speaking, she laid her arm on Feodor's shoulder, and clung still more closely to him, as if to find in his heart protection and shelter against all pain and every grief. Like a poor, broken flower she laid herself on his breast, and Feodor gazed at her with pride and pity. At this moment he wished to try her heart, and discover whether he alone was master of it. For that purpose had he come; for this had he risked this meeting. In this very hour should she follow him and yield herself to him in love and submission. His long separation from her, his wild soldier's life had crushed out the last blossoms of tender and chaste affection in his heart, and he ridiculed himself for his pure, adoring, timid love. Distrust had resumed power over him, and doubt, like a mildew, had spread itself over his last ideal. Elise was to him only a woman like the rest. She was his property, and as such he wished to do with her as he chose.

But yet there was something in her pure, loving being which mastered him against his will, and, as it were, changed his determination. In her presence, looking into her clear pure eye, he forgot his dark designs and his dreary doubts, and Elise became again the angel of innocence and purity, the saint to whom he prayed, and whose tender looks shed forgiveness on him.

This young girl, resting so calmly and confidingly on his breast, and looking at him so innocently and purely, moved him, and made him blush for himself and his wild, bold desires. Silent and reflecting he sat at her side, but she could read in his looks, in his smile, that he loved her. What further need had she of words?

She raised her head from his breast, and looked at him for a long time, and her countenance assumed a bright, happy expression.

"Oh," said she, "do I call myself poor when I have you? I am no longer poor since I have known you, but I have been so; and this, my friend, must be the excuse for my love. I stood in the midst of the cold glitter of gold as in an enchanted castle, and all around me was lifeless, stiffened into torpidity by enchantment, and I knew no talisman to break the charm. You came, and brought with you love. The talisman was found; a warm life awoke in me, and all the splendor of gold crumbled into dust. I was rich then, for I loved; now I am rich, for you love me!"

"Yes, I love you," cried he; "let your father keep his treasures. You, and only you, do I desire."

She sprang up startled from his arms. In the overpowering happiness of the hour she had entirely forgotten the danger which threatened her lover. She suddenly remembered, and her cheek paled.

"My father!" cried she, "if he should come at this moment! His look alone would be enough to kill me." And anxiously and tremblingly she clung to Feodor.

"Fear not, dear one," he whispered, "he is not coming. God protects and watches over those who love each other. Do not think of danger. Banish all care, all fear. This hour belongs to us, and as I now fold you in my arms with delight, so let it be always and forever. For you know, precious child, that you are mine, that you can never belong to another; that you have pledged yourself, and at some future time must follow me as your husband."

"I know it, I know it," she murmured; and, in blissful self-forgetfulness, she leaned her head on his shoulder, and listened with beating heart to the burning, passionate words which he poured into her ear.

Of a sudden, with the rapidity of lightning, she sprang up, as if an electric shock had pervaded her body, and listened eagerly.

As Feodor was about to speak, to inquire the cause of her sudden terror, she quickly pressed her hand to his mouth. "Silence," whispered she softly. "I heard it distinctly. My father is coming hither through the garden!"

They both listened in silence. In the quiet of the night Gotzkowsky's voice was now heard. He ordered his servants to shut the garden gates carefully, and watch them well, as the Russians entering the town would pass by this wall.

"You are right," said Feodor; "it is your father. Truly this is an unlucky accident."

"He will kill me if he finds you here," murmured Elise, clinging, half fainting, to her lover's arm.

"I will protect you with my life," said he, pressing her more firmly to him.

"No, no!" cried she breathlessly; "he must not find you here. No one must see you. Oh, Feodor, listen to me. He is not alone; Bertram and his servants are with him. Oh, my God, they will kill you! Save yourself; leave me, Feodor, and conceal yourself!" And drawing him with irresistible strength to the door, she whispered, "In there, in my bedroom conceal yourself."

"Never," said he firmly and decidedly. "Never will I hide myself, or sneak away like a coward!"

"You must do it," entreated she; and as she saw that he hesitated and drew back unwillingly, she continued: "Not for your sake—for the sake of my honor, Feodor. Remember it is night, and I am alone with you."

76

"Yes, you are right," said Feodor sadly. "Hide me; no spot must tarnish your honor."

With convulsive haste, Elise drew him to the door of her chamber. Gotzkowsky's voice was heard just outside the window.

"Quick! hasten, they are coming!" said she, pulling the door open, and pushing him hurriedly on.

"He is saved," cried her heart joyfully, as she closed the door after him, and, sinking down, half fainting in a chair, her lips murmured, "Have mercy, gracious God; have mercy on him and me!"

At this moment her father, accompanied by Bertram and the factory workman, Balthazar, entered the room through the door of the balcony.

* * * * *

CHAPTER XVI.

THE FUGITIVE.

Gotzkowsky at length returned to his home. Sad and sorrowful was his soul, and his brow, at other times so smooth and clear, was now dark and clouded. He mourned for his country, for the fruitless battles, the blood shed in vain, and, in the bitter grief of his heart, he asked himself what crime he had committed, that to him should be assigned the painful duty of deciding to which of the enemies they should surrender. And yet the decision was imperative, and Berlin had to be surrendered to the Russians.

In gloomy sadness, hardly casting a passing glance at his daughter, whose anxiety and death-like paleness he did not even perceive, Gotzkowsky entered the hall, Bertram carefully bolting the doors behind him, and then in an undertone gave Balthazar and the servants directions for the protection of the house.

"What a dreadful night!" said Gotzkowsky, sinking down on a sofa exhausted; "my heart aches as much as my limbs."

For a moment he closed his eyes, and lay silent and motionless. Elise was still leaning trembling and breathless on the chair near the door. Gotzkowsky raised his head, and his eyes sought his daughter. As he perceived her, a gentle and pleased expression passed over his face, and his brow grew clearer. He hastened to her and raised her in his arms.

"Bless you, Elise, my child! for two days have I been nothing but citizen and soldier; now at last I am permitted to remember that I am a father. I had almost forgotten it during these wild sad days. Good-evening, my darling child!"

Elise kissed his hand respectfully, and muttered a low welcome.

Gotzkowsky said in a gentle tone, "This is a comfort which makes me forget all my sufferings. Come, my children, let us for one bright hour put aside all care and trouble, and be happy and cheerful together. Let us have breakfast. This poor, weak body needs refreshment, for it reminds me that, for two days, I have been living on prison fare, bread and water. Come, then, let us breakfast. Bertram, sit by my side, and our sweet little housekeeper will help us to coffee."

Elise rose with difficulty and gave the necessary orders to the servants; and while the latter were hurrying to and fro, serving up breakfast, Gotzkowsky reclined on the sofa, half asleep from exhaustion; and Bertram and Elise sat opposite to each other in silence. Suddenly there were heard in the distance wild yells, and loud noises and cries. Then hasty steps flew up the staircase; the hall door was pulled open, and a soldier rushed in. With breathless haste he bolted the door behind him, threw off the white cloak which concealed his figure, and the broad-brimmed hat which covered his head, and sank with a loud sigh into a chair. Gotzkowsky hurried up to him and looked at him attentively. Elise, with an instinctive feeling of the danger which threatened Feodor, turned to the door behind which he was hidden.

"The artilleryman, Fritz!" cried Gotzkowsky, with visible astonishment.

"Yes, it is me," groaned the soldier. "Save me, Gotzkowsky; do not deliver me up to these barbarians!"

Gotzkowsky laid his hand on his shoulder with a friendly smile. "I would not betray the enemy himself, if he sought refuge in my house; and you ask me not to betray the most valiant and renowned defender of Berlin. Bertram, this man here, this simple cannoneer, has performed miracles of valor, and earned for himself an enviable name in these last unfortunate days. It was he who had charge of the only two cannon Berlin possessed, and who, never tiring, without rest or relaxation, gent death into the ranks of the enemy. Be assured, my son, you have fought these two days like a hero, and it cannot be God's wish that, as a reward for your bravery, you should fall into the hands of the enemy."

"They pursue me everywhere," said the artilleryman. "Hunted by De Lacy's chasseurs like a wild beast, I fled down the street hither. You told me yesterday that if ever I wanted a friend in need, you would be one to me. Therefore have I come to you. The Austrians have sworn vengeance on the cannoneer, whose balls swept their ranks so murderously, and have set a large price on my head."

"Ah!" cried Gotzkowsky, laughing, "the Austrians advertise rewards before they have got the money to pay them. Let them set a thousand ducats on your head, my son. They will have to do without the ducats, and your head too, for Berlin will give them neither. If we must pay the money, the Russian shall have it; and as for your head, well, I will pay for that with my life. You have fought like a lion, and like lions we will defend you."

"What have I gained by fighting?" said Fritz, with a mournful shrug of the shoulders. "The enemy have succeeded in getting into the town, and their rage is tearful. They have sworn to kill me. But you will not give me up! and should they come here and find me, then have pity on me and kill me, but do not give me up to the enemy!"

"To kill you, they must kill both of us first!" cried Bertram, taking the brave cannoneer by the hand. "We will hide him in your house; won't we, Father Gotzkowsky?"

"Yes, and so safely that no one will be able to find him!" cried Gotzkowsky, cheerfully, raising the soldier up by the hand. "Follow me, my son. In my daughter's chamber is a safe hiding-place. The mirror on the wall covers a secret door, behind which is a space just large enough to conceal a person. Come."

He led the artilleryman toward the door of Elise's room. But before this door Elise had stationed herself, her cheeks burning and her eyes flashing. The danger of her lover lent her courage and determination, and enabled her to meet the anger of her father unflinchingly.

"Not in there, father!" said she, in a tone almost commanding; "not into my room!"

Gotzkowsky stepped back in astonishment, and gazed at his daughter. "How," asked he, "do you forbid me the entrance?"

"Behind the picture of the Virgin in the large hall is a similar hiding-place," said Elise, hurriedly; "carry him thither."

Gotzkowsky did not answer immediately. He only gazed firmly and inquiringly into Elise's countenance. Dark and dismal misgivings, which he had often with much difficulty suppressed, now arose again, and filled his soul with angry, desperate thoughts. Like Virginius of old, he would have preferred to kill his daughter to delivering her into the hands of the enemy.

"And why should he go there, and not remain here?" asked he at last with an effort.

"Remember, father," stammered she, blushing, "I—"

She stopped as she met the look of her father, which rested on her with penetrating power—as she read the rising anger of his soul in the tense swollen veins of his brow, and his pale, trembling lips.

Bertram had witnessed this short but impressive scene with increasing terror. Elise's anxiety, her paleness and trembling, the watch which she kept over that door, had not escaped him, even on his entrance, and filled him with painful uneasiness. But as he now recognized in Gotzkowsky's features the signs of an anger which was the more violent for the very reason that he so seldom gave way to it, he felt the necessity of coming to the assistance of his distressed sister. He approached her father, and laid his hand lightly on his shoulder.

"Elise is right," said he, entreatingly. "Respect her maiden hesitation."

Gotzkowsky turned round upon him with an impatient toss of the head, and stared him full in the face. He then broke into a fit of wild, derisive laughter.

"Yes," said he, "we will respect her maiden hesitation. You have spoken wisely, Bertram. Listen: you know the partition behind the picture of the Madonna in the picture-gallery. Carry our brave friend thither, and take heed that the spring is carefully closed."

Bertram looked at him sadly and anxiously. He had never before seen this man, usually so calm, so passionately excited.

"You will not go with us, father?" asked he.

"No," said Gotzkowsky, harshly; "I remain here to await the enemy."

He cast on Elise, still leaning against the door, a threatening look, which made her heart tremble. Bertram sighed, and had not the courage to go and forsake Elise in this anxious and critical moment.

"Hasten, friend," said Gotzkowsky, sternly. "The life of a brave man is at stake. Hasten!"

The young man dared not gainsay him, but he approached Gotzkowsky, and whispered softly: "Be lenient, father. See how she trembles! Poor sister!"

And with a painful glance at Elise, he took the hand of the artilleryman, and led him out of the room.

* * * * *

CHAPTER XVII.

THE EAVESDROPPER.

Elise was now alone with her father. She had sunk down near the fatal door, and her colorless lips murmured faint prayers.

Gotzkowsky stood there, still relentless; but his agitated countenance, his lowering brow, his flashing eyes, betrayed the deep and passionate emotion of his soul. Struck and wounded fatally in his most sacred feelings, he felt no pity, no compassion for this poor trembling girl, who followed his every motion with a timid, anxious eye. His whole being was filled with burning rage against his daughter, who, his misgiving heart told him, had trampled his honor in the dust.

A long and dreadful pause occurred. Nothing was heard but Gotzkowsky's loud, heavy breathing, and Elise's low-muttered prayers. Suddenly Gotzkowsky drew himself up, and threw his head proudly back. He then walked to the door leading into the balcony, and to the opposite one, and ascertained that they were both closed. No one could intrude, no one interrupt this fearful dialogue.

Elise was terribly conscious of this, and could only whisper, "Pity, pity, merciful God! I shall die with terror!"

Gotzkowsky approached her, and, seizing her hand, raised her rapidly from the floor. "We are alone now," said he with a hoarse, harsh voice. "Answer me, now. Who is concealed there in your room?"

"No one, my father."

"No one!" repeated he, sternly. "Why, then, do you tremble?"

"I tremble because you look at me so angrily," said she, terrified.

Her father cast her hand passionately from him. "Liar!" cried he. "Do you wish me to kill him?"

He took his sword from the table, and approached the door.

"What are you going to do, my father?" cried she, throwing herself in his way.

"I am going to kill the thief who stole my daughter's honor," cried Gotzkowsky, his eyes flashing with rage.

"Father, father, by the God in heaven I am innocent!" cried she, convulsively, striving to hold him back.

"Then let me have the proof of this innocence," said he, pushing her back.

But she sprang forward with the agility of a gazelle, rushed again to the door, and clung with both hands to the lock.

"No, no, father, I remain here. You shall not insult yourself and me so much as to believe what is dishonorable and unworthy of me, and to require a proof of my innocence."

This bold opposition of Elise only excited Gotzkowsky's anger the more, and was to him a fresh proof of her guilt. His rage overpowered him; with raised arm and flashing eye he strode up to Elise, and cried out: "Away from the door, or by Heaven I will forget that I am your father!"

"Oh," cried she breathlessly, "you have often forgotten that, but think now; remember that I am the daughter of the wife whom you loved! Trust me, father. By the memory of my mother, I swear to you that my honor is pure from any spot; and, however much appearances may be against me, I am nevertheless innocent. I have never done any thing of which my father would have to be ashamed. Believe me, father; give me your hand and say to me—'I believe your innocence; I trust you even without proof!'"

She sank down on her knees, raising her arms imploringly to him, while burning tears streamed down her cheeks. Gotzkowsky gazed at her long and silently, and his child's tears touched the father's heart.

"Perhaps I do her injustice," said he to himself, looking thoughtfully into her weeping face. "She may be really innocent. Let us try," said he, after a pause, pressing his hands to his burning temples. As he let them drop, his countenance was again calm and clear, and there was no longer visible any trace of his former anger. "I will believe you," said he. "Here, Elise, is my hand."

Elise uttered a cry of joy, sprang up from her knees, rushed toward her father, and pressed her burning lips on his extended hand. "My father, I thank you. I will ever be grateful to you," cried she, fondly.

Gotzkowsky held her hand firmly in his own, and while speaking to her approached, apparently by accident, the door so bravely defended by Elise. "You are right, my child; I was a fool to doubt you, but I am jealous of my honor, the most precious property of an honest man. Much can be bought with gold, but not honor. True honor is bright and clear as a mirror, and the slightest breath dims it. Oh, how would this envious, grudging, malignant world rejoice if it could only find a spot on my honor! But woe to him who dims it, even if it were my own child!"

Elise turned pale and cast down her eyes. Gotzkowsky perceived it. He still held her hand in his, and approached the door with her, but he compelled his voice to be gentle and mild.

"I repeat," said he, "I wronged you, but it was a terrible suspicion which tortured me, and I will confess it to you, my child. The Russian flag of truce which came into town to negotiate with the authorities was accompanied by ten soldiers and two officers. While the commissioner was transacting business in the Council-chamber above, they remained below in the lower story of the building. I accompanied the commissioner, as he left the Council, down-stairs, and we found his military escort in a state of anxiety and excitement, for one of the officers had left them two hours before, and had not yet returned, and they had called and hunted for him everywhere. The Russians were furious, and cried out that we had murdered one of their officers. I succeeded in quieting them, but my own heart I could not quiet; it felt convulsively cramped when I heard the name of this missing officer. Need I name him?"

Elise did not answer. She looked at her father, with tears in her eyes, and shook her head languidly.

Gotzkowsky continued: "It is the name of a man to whom I formerly showed much friendship; toward whom I exercised hospitality, and whom I made free of my house, and who now shows his gratitude by stealing the heart of my daughter, like a pitiful thief. Oh, do not attempt to deny this. I know it, Elise; and if I have hitherto avoided speaking to you about this matter, it was because I had confidence in your sound sense, and in the purity of heart of a German girl to sustain you in resisting a feeling which would lead you astray from the path of duty and honor. I do not say that you loved him, but that he wished to seduce you into loving him clandestinely, behind your father's back. That is his gratitude for my hospitality."

Speaking thus, Gotzkowsky pressed his daughter's hand more firmly in his own, and continued approaching more closely to the door. "Only think," continued he, "the mad thought crossed my mind—'How if this man should be rash and foolhardy enough to have gone to my daughter?' But I forgot to tell you his name. Feodor von Brenda was the name of the treacherous guest, and Feodor von Brenda was also the name of the officer who left the commissioner, perhaps in search of some love adventure. But why do you tremble?" asked he in a loud tone, as her hand quivered in his.

"I do not tremble, father," replied she, striving for composure.

Gotzkowsky raised his voice still higher till it sounded again. "Forgive me this suspicion, my daughter. I should have known that, even if this insolent Russian dared to renew a former acquaintance, my daughter would never be so mean, never stoop so low as to welcome him, for a German girl would never throw away her honor on a Russian boor."

84

"Father," cried Elise, terrified and forgetting all her prudence, "oh, father! do not speak so loud."

"Not so loud? Why, then, some one can hear us?" asked Gotzkowsky, pressing the arm of his daughter. "I will speak loud, I will declare it aloud. He is a scoundrel who conceals himself in a dastardly and dishonorable manner, instead of defending himself! a coward who would put the honor of a maiden in the scale against his own miserable life. No German would do that. Only a Russian would be base enough to hide himself, instead of defending his life like a man!"

At this moment the door of the bedroom was violently torn open, and the Russian colonel appeared on the threshold, his cheeks burning and his eyes flashing with anger.

* * * * *

CHAPTER XVIII.

THE TWO CANNONEERS.

Elise uttered a cry of terror, and stared at her lover with wide-opened eyes. But Gotzkowsky's countenance was illuminated with a dark and savage joy. "Ah, at last, then!" said he, letting go the arm of his daughter, and grasping his sword.

But the colonel advanced proudly and collectedly toward him. "Here am I, sir," said he; "here am I, to defend myself and avenge an insult."

"I have driven you out of your hiding-place, as the fox draws the badger out of his kennel," cried Gotzkowsky, with derisive laughter, purposely calculated to irritate the anger of the young officer to the highest pitch.

The two men stood opposite to each other, and gazed at one another with faces full of hatred and rage. Elise threw herself between them, and falling on her knees before her father, exclaimed, "Kill me, father; save your honor—kill me!"

But Gotzkowsky slung her pitilessly aside. "Away!" cried he, roughly. "What do you here? Make room for us! Here is a man with whom I can fight for my honor."

Feodor stepped quickly toward Elise, who was still kneeling on the floor, wringing her hands, and sobbing from intense pain. He raised her up, and whispering a few words in her ear, led her to the sofa. He then turned to Gotzkowsky, and said, "Your honor is pure and unspotted, sir! Whatever you may think of me, you must respect the virtue of your daughter. She is innocent."

"Innocent," cried Gotzkowsky derisively, "innocent! why, your very presence has polluted the innocence of my daughter."

"Father, kill me, but do not insult me!" cried she, a dark glow suffusing her cheeks.

"Pour out your anger on me," said Feodor ardently. "It is a piece of barbarism to attack a defenceless girl."

Gotzkowsky laughed out loud and scornfully: "You speak of barbarism, and you a Russian!"

An exclamation of rage escaped the colonel; he seized his sword and drawing it quickly advanced toward Gotzkowsky.

"At last!" cried Gotzkowsky, triumphantly, raising his blade. But Elise, beside herself, and heedless of the flashing steel, threw herself between them. With burning words she entreated Feodor to spare her father, and not to raise his sword against him. But Gotzkowsky's voice overpowered hers. Such wild words of contempt and insulting rage issued from his lips, that the young officer, hurt in his military honor, did not dare to listen to the voice of his beloved. It was he now who pressed Elise back, and with raised arm placed himself opposite to her father.

"You must kill me, sir, or wash out this insult with your blood," cried he, preparing himself for the combat.

Both were then silent. It was a terrible, unearthly silence, only broken by the clash of their swords or the occasional outcries of anger or savage joy, as one or the other received or gave a blow. Elise raised her head to heaven and prayed; every thing became confused before her eyes, her head swam, and she felt as if she would go crazy. She prayed God that He would release her by madness or death from the suffering of this hour, or that He would point out to her some way of deliverance or escape. But in the violence of their dispute and combat, the two men had not heard that there arose suddenly in the house a loud tumult and uproar; they had not perceived that a guard of soldiers was drawn up in the street, and that the commanding officer with a loud voice was demanding the delivery of the cannoneer who had taken refuge in this house.

As no attention was paid to the demand, the officer had ordered his soldiers to break open the doors of the house and enter by force. But Bertram had anticipated this proceeding by having the door opened, and requesting the Austrian officer to search the house with his men, and convince himself that no one was concealed in it. With most industrious energy, and mindful of the price which had been set on the head of the cannoneer, the soldiers searched every room in the house, and had finally arrived at the closed door of the hall.

Just as the combat between the two had reached its greatest violence, it was interrupted by fierce blows at the door from butts of muskets, and they were compelled to refrain from their imbittered struggle. They stopped and listened, but Elise sprang from her knees, rushed with a cry of delight to the door and threw it open. An officer of De Lacy's chasseurs entered with some of his soldiers, while the rest of the men filled the entrance hall and passages of the house with noise and confusion.

With a commanding tone the Austrian officer demanded the delivery of the cannoneer, who, he asserted, had been seen by all to take refuge in this house, whence it was impossible that he could have escaped, as it had been immediately surrounded. And as no one answered his threats, but only a sullen silence was opposed to his violently repeated demand, he swore that he would burn down the house and let no one escape if the refugee was not given up at once.

Gotzkowsky had at first stood like one stunned, and scarcely heard what the officer demanded of him. Gradually he began to recover from his stupefaction and regain strength to turn his attention to things around him. He raised his head from his breast, and, as if awaking from a dream, he looked around with bewildered amazement. The Austrian officer repeated his demand still more haughtily and threateningly. Gotzkowsky had now recovered presence of mind and composure, and declared with a determined voice, that no one was concealed in his house.

"He is here!" cried the Austrian. "Our men have followed his track thus far, and marked this house well. Deliver him up to us, to avoid bloodshed," and, turning to his soldiers, he continued, "Search all the rooms-search carefully. The man is hidden here, and we—"

Suddenly he interrupted his order, and gazed earnestly at the door through which his soldiers were pressing in.

"Had not this cannoneer, as he fled thither, a white cloak around him, and did he not wear a broad-brimmed hat?" asked he.

As the soldiers answered affirmatively, the officer stepped toward the door, and drew from under the feet of his men the cloak and hat of the cannoneer. A wild yell of joy broke from the soldiers.

"Do you still persist in denying that this man is concealed here?" asked the officer, raising the cloak.

Gotzkowsky did not answer, but gazed on the ground absorbed in deep thought.

As the soldiers thronged into the room, the young Russian colonel had withdrawn himself to a remote part of the room, and taken the most lively interest in the scene acted before him. A word from him would have brought the whole affair to an end, for, as an involuntary listener, he had heard all that had transpired concerning the cannoneer. Consequently he knew exactly the hiding-place in which the latter had been concealed. But it had never come into his mind to play the informer and traitor. He was only intensely interested in the issue of the scene, and firmly determined, if the danger should grow more urgent, to hasten with his weapon to Gotzkowsky's assistance, and to defend him against the fury of the Austrians.

Gotzkowsky still stood silent. He was trying to devise some plan by which he might save the brave defender of Berlin, whose presence, after such positive proof, he could no longer deny.

As suddenly as lightning an idea seemed to penetrate his mind, his countenance cleared, and he turned with a singular expression in his eye to Colonel von Brenda.

"Well!" asked the officer, "do you still deny it?"

"No, I cannot deny it any longer," said he, in a determined tone. "You are right, sir; the cannoneer who shattered your ranks is here in my house!"

The soldiers broke out again in a triumphant roar. But Elise looked at her father with anxious terror, and sought, trembling, to read in his countenance the meaning of these words. "Can he possibly be capable of betraying this man whom he has sworn to protect?" thought Feodor, and yielding to his curiosity he approached the group in the middle of the hall. Suddenly he felt Gotzkowsky's hand laid on his shoulder, and met his dark eye, full of hatred.

"Well," said Gotzkowsky, with a loud, defiant voice, "you are looking for the artilleryman, Fritz. Here he is!"

A scream and a burst of laughter were heard. It was Elise who uttered the scream, and the colonel who greeted this unexpected turn with a merry laugh. But Gotzkowsky did not allow himself to be confused by one or the other.

He laid his arm on Feodor's neck, and forced his countenance to assume a friendly expression. "Dear friend," said he, "you see it is vain any longer to deny it. Our stratagem has unfortunately failed."

"What stratagem?" asked the Austrian and Feodor, simultaneously.

Gotzkowsky replied in a sorrowful tone to Feodor: "Do not disguise yourself any longer, my son! you see it is useless." Then turning to the officer, he continued: "We had hoped that he might escape detection in this Russian uniform, left here by the adjutant of General Sievers, who was formerly a prisoner of war in my house, but unfortunately the hat and cloak have betrayed him."

Feodor von Brenda looked at Gotzkowsky with admiring wonder, and this rapidly invented *ruse de guerre* pleased him astonishingly.

It was a piquant adventure offered him by Gotzkowsky's hate and cunning, and he did not feel inclined to throw away such an original and interesting chance of excitement. He, the Russian colonel, and Count von Brenda, the favorite of the empress, degraded to a Prussian cannoneer, whose life was in danger! His wilful and foolhardy imagination was pleased with the idea of playing the part of a criminal condemned to death.

"Well," asked the Austrian officer, "do you acknowledge the truth of this statement, or do you deny being the cannoneer, Fritz?"

"Why should I deny it?" answered Feodor, shrugging his shoulders. "This gentleman, who ought to have saved me, has already betrayed me. I am the man whom you seek!"

With a scream of surprise, Elise threw herself toward her lover.

"No!" cried she, loudly, "no, he is—"

Her father's hand pressed heavily on her lips. "Another word, and you are a murderess!" whispered he.

The officer looked suspiciously at them. "You do not deny," asked he of Feodor, "that you are he who directed such a murderous fire on our lines? You do not deny that you are the artilleryman, Fritz, and that this cloak and hat belong to you?"

"I deny nothing!" replied Feodor, defiantly.

The officer called to some of his men and ordered them to shoulder arms, and take the prisoner in their midst; enjoining them to keep a sharp watch on him, and at the first attempt to escape, to shoot him down. But when he demanded his sword of the colonel, the latter recoiled, shocked, and resisted.

He now became aware of his foolhardiness and rashness, and that he had not considered or foreseen the dangerous and perhaps dishonorable consequences. However, as he had gone so far, he considered that it would be disgraceful and cowardly to retreat now. He was also desirous of pursuing to the end this adventure which he had begun with so much boldness and daring. He drew his sword, and with considerable strength breaking it in pieces, he threw them at the feet of the Austrian officer.

That officer shrugged his shoulders. "Your insolence will only make your situation worse. Remember, you are our prisoner."

"He must and shall die!" shouted the soldiers, thronging around Feodor, angrily.

The officer ordered silence. "He must die," said he, "that is true; but we must first carry him to the general, to obtain the price offered for him."

The soldiers surrounded him and shoved him toward the door. But Elise broke through the crowd. With flashing eyes, and cheeks burning with a feverish excitement, she rushed toward Feodor. "No!" cried she, with all the ardor of love, "no, I will not leave you. You are going to your death!"

Feodor kissed her lightly on the forehead, and replied with a smile, "I fear nothing. Fortune does not forsake a brave soldier."

He then took her by the hand and led her to her father. Gazing on him with a long and speaking look, he continued: "Here, Father Gotzkowsky, I bring your daughter to you: be a better father to her than you have been a friend to me. These are my farewell words."

He leaned forward as if to give Gotzkowsky a parting embrace, and whispered to him: "I hope we are now quit! I have atoned for my fault. You will no longer wish to punish your daughter for my transgression."

90

He then threw the white cloak around him, and bidding Elise, who leaned half fainting against her father, a tender farewell, he stepped back into the ranks of the guard.

"Attention! shoulder arms!" commanded the officer; and the Austrians left the hall with closed ranks, the prisoner in their midst.

* * * * *

CHAPTER XIX.

FATHER GOTZKOWSKY.

The door had closed behind the soldiers and their prisoner. Gotzkowsky and Elise remained behind, silent and immersed in the deep sorrows of their souls. Neither spoke a word; both stood motionless and listened.

They heard the soldiers hurry down the steps; they heard the house door violently thrown open, and the officer announce in a loud voice to those of his soldiers who were waiting in the street, the lucky capture of the artilleryman.

A cry of triumph from the Austrians was the answer; then was heard the loud word of command from the officer, and the roll of the drum gradually receding in the distance until it was no longer audible. Every thing was silent.

"Have mercy, Father in heaven have mercy! They are leading him to death!" cried Elise in a heart-rending tone, and she sank on her knees in prayer.

"The brave cannoneer is saved!" murmured Gotzkowsky in a low voice to himself, and he too folded his hands in prayer. Was it a prayer of gratitude, or did it proceed from the despairing heart of a father?

His countenance had a bright and elevated expression; but as he turned his eyes down on his daughter, still on her knees, they darkened, and his features twitched convulsively and painfully. His anger had evaporated, and his heart was filled with boundless pity and love. He felt nothing but painful, sorrowful compassion for this young girl who lay deathly pale and trembling with suffering on the floor. His daughter was weeping, and his heart yearned toward her to forgive her every thing, to raise her up and comfort her.

Suddenly Elise started up from her knees and strode toward her father. There was something solemn and imposing in her proud bearing, her extraordinary composure, which only imperfectly veiled her raging grief and passionate excitement.

"Father," said she solemnly, and her voice sounded hoarse and cold, "may God forgive you for what you have done! At this moment, when perhaps he is suffering death, I repeat it, I am innocent."

This proud composure fell freezingly on Gotzkowsky's heart, and drove back all the milder forgiving impulses. He remembered only the shame and the injured honor of his daughter.

"You assert your innocence, and yet you had a man concealed in the night in your bedchamber!"

"And yet I am innocent, father!" cried Elise vehemently. "Read it on my forehead, see it in my eyes, which do not fear to meet yours. I am innocent!"

And completely overpowered by the bitter and desperate anguish of her soul, she continued, still more excited, "But how does all this concern you? It was not my honor that you were interested in; you did not seek to avenge that. You only wished to punish me for daring to assert my freedom and independence, for daring to love without having asked your leave. The rich man to whom all bend, whom all worship as the priest of the powerful idol which rules the world, the rich man sees with dismay that there is one being not dazzled by his treasures who owns an independent life, a will of her own, and a heart that he cannot command. And because this being does not of her own accord how down before him he treads it in the dust, whether it be his own child or not."

"Elise," cried Gotzkowsky, shocked, "Elise, are you mad? Do you know that you are speaking to your father?"

But her tortured heart did not notice this appeal; and only remembering that perhaps at this moment her lover was suffering death through her father's fault, she allowed herself to be carried away by the overpowering force of her grief. She met the flashing eye of her father with a smile of contempt, and said, coldly: "Oh yes, you may look at me. I do not fear your angry glances. I am free; you yourself have absolved me from any fear of you. You took from me my lover, and at the same time deprived yourself of your child."

"O God!" cried Gotzkowsky in an undertone, "have I deserved this, Father in heaven?" and he regarded his daughter with a touching expression.

But she was inexorable; sorrow had unseated her judgment, and "Oh!" cried she in a tone of triumph, "now I will confess every thing to you, how I have suffered and what I have undergone."

"Elise!" cried he painfully, "have I not given you every thing your heart could desire?"

"Yes!" cried she, with a cruel laugh, "you fulfilled all my wishes, and thereby made me poor in wishes, poor in enjoyment. You deprived me of the power of wishing, for every thing was mine even before I could desire it. It was only necessary for me to stretch out my hand, and it belonged to me. Cheerless and solitary I stood amidst your wealth, and all that I touched was turned into hard gold. The rich man's daughter envied the beggar woman in the street, for she still had wishes, hopes, and privations."

Gotzkowsky listened to her, without interrupting her by a word or even a sigh. Only now and then he raised his hand to his forehead, or cast a wandering, doubtful look at his daughter, as if to convince himself that all that was passing was not a mad, bewildering dream, but painful, cruel reality.

But when Elise, breathless and trembling with excitement, stopped for a moment, and he no longer heard her cutting accents of reproach, he pressed both hands upon his breast, as if to suppress a wail over the annihilation of his whole life. "O God!" muttered he in a low voice, "this is unparalleled agony! This cuts into a father's heart!"

After a pause, Elise continued: "I too was a beggar, and I hungered for the bread of your love."

"Elise, oh, my child, do you not know then that I love you infinitely?"

But she did not perceive the loving, almost imploring looks which her father cast upon her. She could see and think only of herself and her own tormented heart.

"Yes," said she, "you love me as one loves a jewel, and has it set in gold in order to make it more brilliant. You loved me as a costly ornament of your rooms, as something which gave you an opportunity of exercising the splendor of your liberality, and to be produced as an evidence of your renowned wealth. But you did not love me as a father; you did not perceive that I wept in secret, or if you did see it, you consoled me with diamonds, with rich dresses, to make me smile. But you did not give me your father's heart. At last the rich man's child discovers a happiness not to be bought with gold or treasures, a happiness that the millions of her father could not purchase for her. This happiness is—love. The only possession that I have owned, father, contrary to your will, you have deprived me of, because it was mine against your will. Now, poor rich man, take all your gold, and seek and buy yourself a child with it. Me you have lost!" and staggering back with a sob, she sank fainting on the carpet.

A dread silence now reigned in the room. Gotzkowsky stood motionless, with his eyes directed toward heaven. The cruel, mocking words of his daughter sounded over and over again in his ears, and seemed to petrify the power of his will and chain him fast, as if rooted to the floor. Gradually he recovered from this apathy of grief. The stagnant blood revived in his veins, and shot like burning streams of fire to his heart. He bent over his daughter, and gazing for a long time at her, his features assumed a gentler and softer expression. Tenderly with his hand he smoothed the tresses from her clear, high forehead; and as he did so, he almost smiled again, so beautiful and charming did she seem to him in her death-like repose.

"She has fainted," whispered he, low, as if fearful of awakening her. "So much the better for her; and when she recovers, may she have forgotten all the cruel words that she has uttered!"

94

He laid his hand on her head as if to bless her, and love and forgiveness were expressed in his looks. A perfect peace seemed to pervade his whole frame. In this moment he forgave her all the pain, all the suffering she had caused him. He pardoned her those unjust reproaches and accusations, and with lofty emotion, raising his eyes toward heaven, he exclaimed, "O God! thou seest my heart. Thou knowest that love alone has possession of its very depths, love to my child! and my child has no faith in me. I have worked—I am rich—I have amassed wealth—only for her. I thought of my child as I sat at my desk during the long, weary nights, busied with difficult calculations. I remembered my daughter when I was wearied out and overcome by this laborious work. She should be happy; she should be rich and great as any princess; for this I worked. I had no time to toy or laugh with her, for I was working for her like a slave. And this," continued he with a sad smile, "this is what she reproaches me with. There is nothing in which I believe, nothing but my child, and my child does not believe in me! The world bows down before me, and I am the poorest and most miserable beggar."

Overpowered by these bitter thoughts, which crowded tumultuously upon his brain, he leaned his head upon his hand and wept bitterly. Then, after a long pause, he drew himself up erect, and, with a determined gesture, shook the tears from his eyes.

"Enough!" said he, loudly and firmly, "enough; my duty shall cure me of all this suffering. That I must not neglect."

He rang the bell, and ordered the servant-maids, who appeared, to raise up the insensible girl and bear her to her room.

But when the maidens called the waiting-man to their assistance to raise their mistress, Gotzkowsky pushed them all aside, and carried her softly and gently, as carefully and tenderly as a mother, to a couch, on which he placed her. He then pressed a fervent kiss upon her brow. Elise began to move, a faint blush overspread her cheeks, she opened her eyes. Gotzkowsky immediately stepped back, and signed to her maids to carry her into her room.

He looked after her until she had disappeared, his eyes dimmed with tears. "My child," said he, in a low voice, "she is lost to me. Oh, I am a poor, pitiable father!" With a deep groan he pressed his hands to his face, and nothing was heard but the painful sobs wrung from the heart of this father wrestling with his grief.

Suddenly there arose from without loud lamentations and cries for help. They came nearer and nearer, and at last reached Gotzkowsky's house, and filled its halls and passages. It was not the outcry of a single person. From many voices came the sounds of lamenting and weeping, screams and shrieks:

"Help! help! have pity on us, save us! The Austrians are hewing us down—they are burning our houses—save us!"

Gotzkowsky dropped his hands from his face and listened. "What was that? who cries for help?" asked he, dreamingly, still occupied with his own sorrows, scarcely conscious of the reality. But suddenly he started, and from his eyes beamed life and courage. "Ah!" cried he aloud, "mankind is suffering, and I am thinking of my own griefs. I know these voices. The wives and children of my workmen, the poor and oppressed of the city are calling me. The people need me. Up, Gotzkowsky! give them your heart, your life. Endeavor to be a father to the unfortunate, and you will not be poor in children!"

Without the wailing and cries for help continued to resound, and the voices of weeping and trembling women and plaintive children cried aloud, "Gotzkowsky, help us! have pity on us, Father Gotzkowsky!"

"Father!" cried he, raising his head, his countenance beaming with delight. "They call me father, and yet I complain. Up! to my children who love me, and who need my help!"

* * * * *

BOOK II.

CHAPTER I.

THE TWO EDITORS.

On the morning succeeding the night of horrors and confusion in which Berlin had surrendered to the conqueror, the vanguard of the Russians marched into the town through the Koenig's Gate. But the commanding general, Tottleben, wished to make his triumphal entry with his staff and the main body of his army through the Kottbuss Gate, and had ordered the magistracy of the town to meet him there, and to bring with them a deputation of the merchants, to determine what contribution should be laid upon them. But before the Russian general could make his entry, the vanguard of De Lacy's army corps had penetrated into the Frederick Street suburb, and were committing the most atrocious acts of cruelty in the New Street. With wild yells they entered the houses to rob and plunder, ill-treating those who refused to give up their valuables, and by violent threats of incendiarism, raising forced levies from the frightened inhabitants.

But it was not alone this lust of plunder in the soldiers which spread terror and dismay in each house and in every family. Count De Lacy possessed a list of those persons who, by word, deed, or writing, had declared against Austria or Russia, and he gave it to his officers, with the order that they should not hesitate at any measures, any threats or acts of violence, to obtain possession of these people. Besides which, he promised a considerable reward for each "traitor" brought to him; and it was therefore no wonder that these officers, with brutal and avaricious zeal, had scarcely arrived in the city before they commenced the pursuit of these outlaws. With fearful yells they rushed into the houses, shouting out the names of those on the pursuit of whom they were bent, and whose seizure would secure them a golden reward.

Naturally enough, the writers and journalists were the first on whom the vengeful wrath of the conqueror was poured, for it has ever been the lot of authors to suffer for the misfortunes of the people, to be made responsible for the being and thinking, the will and action of the nation to which they belong. But it is only in days of misfortune that the responsibility of authors and poets commences. They must answer for the ill luck, but are never rewarded for the happiness of the nation.

Three names, especially, did De Lacy's chasseurs cry out with a raging howl for vengeance, through the Frederick-Stadt and down the Linden Street, and they searched for their owners in every house.

"De Justi! De Justi!"—with this cry one of the Austrian officers rushed through the street, knocked with his sword violently against the closed house doors, and demanded with savage threats the delivery of this criminal for whose arrest a high premium had been offered.

M. De Justi was indeed a notorious criminal. Not that he had written much or badly, but principally because he had dared to use his sharp pen against the Austrian empress, and her allies the Russians and Saxons. It was especially three pamphlets which excited the wrath of the victorious enemy. These pamphlets were called: "Proof that the Empress should be deposed;" "Why and wherefore Certain Nations in Europe are disposed to become Anthropophagous," and lastly, "Account of the life of Count Bruehl." He had offended not only the Austrians, but also the Russians and Saxons. It was therefore natural that these three powers reigning in Berlin should wish to take their revenge on the writer of these insulting pamphlets.

But De Justi had been prudent enough to escape from the pursuit of his revengeful enemies. During the siege he had betaken himself to the house of a friend in a more secure street, and had hidden in the cellar, where it was impossible to find him. As they could not get possession of the writer, they were obliged to cool their wrath on his treasonable writings. They were dragged in his stead, as prisoners of state and dangerous criminals, to headquarters at the New Market.

The two other writers, whom the Austrians pursued with furious zeal, were the two newspaper editors, Kretschmer and Krause. These two had no idea of such pursuit; indeed, they did not even know that the Austrians had penetrated into the city. In the safe hiding-place in which both of them had passed the night they had only learned that Berlin had surrendered to the Russians, and that General Tottleben had ordered the magistrates to receive him the next morning at the Kottbuss Gate at eight o'clock.

It was intended that the reception should be a brilliant and solemn one, and that the general should be mollified and conciliated by humble subjection; it was also determined to endeavor, by an offering of money made to him individually, to induce him to make the contribution laid on the town moderate and light.

The news was like a thunder-clap to the two editors, for it compelled them to leave their safe hiding-place, and to venture out into the dangerous world. For these gentlemen, editors of such renowned journals, who prided themselves on giving their readers the most recent and important intelligence, would not dare to be absent at the reception of the Russian general. For the love of their country they had to forget their own fears, and, for the honor of their journals, face danger like true heroes.

Day had scarcely dawned, and deep silence and death-like stillness reigned at the Kottbuss Gate. The wings of the gate were closed, and the watchman had withdrawn into his little box, and was resting from the events of the past days. Dawn still lay like a veil over poor, anxious Berlin, and concealed her tears and bloody wounds.

The silence was suddenly interrupted by the sound of approaching footsteps, and around the nearest corner glided the cowering figure of a man. He remained still for a minute and listened; then, convinced that all around him was quiet and silent, he crept along, keeping anxiously close to the houses, and reached unperceived the pillar on the right side of the gate, in the dark shadow of which he concealed himself. This man was no other than Mr. Kretschmer, the editor of the *Vossian Gazette,* who made himself comfortable in his hiding-place.

"This is quite nice and right," said he, shoving a stone behind the pillar, in order to raise himself to a higher point of view. "From here I can hear and observe every thing."

So, settling himself on the stone, he leaned back in the corner of the door-pillar, as if it were the leathern arm-chair in his *sanctum*. A comfortable smile stole over his features.

"This time," said he, "at least, I have forestalled my rival, good Mr. Krause. To-morrow the *Vossian Gazette* will be the only one which will be able to report, from actual observation, on the formal entry of the Russian general. Oh, how vexed *Spener's* will be! There is seven o'clock striking. In an hour the ceremony will begin. *Spener's Journal* still sleeps, while the *Vossian Gazette* wakes and works, and is alert to satisfy the curiosity of Berlin."

Poor, benighted editor of the *Vossian*! You, indeed, could not see him, but the veil of the dawning day, which spread over Berlin, concealed your rival, as well as yourself, in its folds. His drawn-up figure was not visible to your dimmed sight, as he sneaked along the houses, and hid himself behind the pillar on the left of the gate. While you were rejoicing over the long sleep of *Spener's Journal*, its editor, Mr. Krause, was standing opposite to you, behind the pillar, whither he had come, notwithstanding his sixty-eight years, like you, to witness the entrance of the Russians. And happy was he in spirit at this victory obtained over his rival, the editor of the *Vossian Gazette*, and it made him very proud indeed to think that this once he had forestalled Mr. Kretschmer, and consequently would have the monopoly of describing in the morning's paper, to the people of Berlin, the magnificent and pompous entrance of the Russians!

The editor of the *Vossian Gazette* had no idea of the vicinity of his rival. He continued to congratulate himself on the advantage he had obtained, and proceeded cheerfully in his soliloquy. "It makes me laugh to think of *Spener's Journal*. I, myself, advised Mr. Krause to conceal himself, and the good man faithfully followed my advice. Perhaps the little old gentleman dreams that I am at this moment sitting by my fireside, while there is so much matter for my newspaper here. Good matter, too, that can be moulded into an interesting article, is not so common that it can be carelessly squandered. Sleep, therefore, sleep, good *Spener*—the *Vossian* wakes."

But *Spener* did not sleep. He was at the opposite pillar, smirking and saying to himself, "How lucky it is that I have anticipated the *Vossian*!" He then was silent, but his thoughts were active, and in the bottom of his heart he instituted some very serious reflections upon the superfluousness of a second newspaper, how perfectly unnecessary it was in fact.

"This *Vossian Gazette* is perfectly intolerable," thought he. "There ought to be a law prohibiting the publishing of more than one newspaper in each town. Then the public would always get reliable news, and draw its political opinions from one source, which would be undoubted, and it would accept as true what we gave forth for truth. If the government would follow this plan, and allow only one newspaper to each town, and conciliate this one with money or patronage, mankind would be much happier and more contented, and less liable to be distracted by the most opposite political views and information. What profits the existence of this *Vossian Gazette*? What does it do but rob me of my subscribers? By Heavens! I wish the Russian would exterminate it thoroughly."

While Mr. Krause was thus speaking to himself, Mr. Kretschmer had followed the same course of thought, and, very naturally, arrived at a similar conclusion. He, too, had to confess that *Spener's Journal* was very inconvenient, and hated its editor from the bottom of his heart. In the vehemence of his vexation, he overlooked the necessary precaution, and cried out, "Cursed be this rival, this man who has the presumption to imagine he can compete with me!"

Mr. Krause shuddered at the sound of this voice, which seemed to him as it were the echo of his own unspoken thoughts, but he mastered his alarm, and cried aloud, "Did any one speak?" "Did any one speak?" sounded back again, and two heads were seen protruding from the pillars on each side of the gate, the eyes in them inquiringly peering at each other. The morning in the mean while had become lighter, and, with an inward shudder, the two gentlemen recognized each other.

"It is *Spener's*! May the devil take him!" thought Mr. Kretschmer.

"It is the *Vossian*! Damn the fellow!" thought Mr. Krause.

But while they thought this to themselves, they rushed forward and embraced each other, with greetings and assurances of friendship, to all appearances warm and sincere.

"I am not mistaken! It is my dear friend Krause."

"Oh, what happiness! my dear Kretschmer!"

And they shook each other's hands and repeated their asseverations of friendship and esteem, but, at the same time, breathed in their hearts their curses and execrations. But the two editors were not the only persons who had sought the Kottbuss Gate at this early hour. An Austrian officer with a guard of soldiers, in his search after the two editors, had also reached the spot, and was marching with his men from the corner near the gate, looking eagerly right and left and up at all the windows. His eye fell upon these two men who were shrinking from his sight, uttering pious ejaculations to Heaven. The officer approached them and demanded their names. Neither answered. The officer repeated his question, and accompanied it with such threats as convinced Mr. Krause of the imperative necessity of answering it. He bowed, therefore, respectfully to the officer, and pointing to his friend, said, "This is Mr. Kretschmer, the editor of the *Vossian Gazette*."

Kretschmer cast upon him a look full of hatred and revenge. "And this," said he, with a wicked smile, "is Mr. Krause, editor of *Spener's Journal.*"

An expression of joyous triumph shone in the countenance of the officer: "You are my prisoners, gentlemen," said he, as he beckoned to his soldiers to arrest them.

Pale did Mr. Krause grow as he drew back a step. "Sir, this must be a mistake. We are quiet, peaceable citizens, who have nothing to do with the war, but only busy ourselves with our pens."

"Our arrest is contrary to all national law," cried Mr. Kretschmer, at the same time endeavoring to defend himself from the weapons which were pointed at him.

The officer laughed. "In war we know no national law. You are my prisoners." And disregarding their struggles and cries for help, they dragged the two editors as prisoners to the guard-house at the New Market.

* * * * *

CHAPTER II.

THE CHIEF MAGISTRATE OF BERLIN.

After a short interval of quiet and lonesomeness at the Kottbuss Gate, there appeared, first far down the street, then approaching nearer and nearer, a solemn procession. Foremost staggered the chief burgomaster, Von Kircheisen, in full uniform, adorned with his golden chain, which rustled as it rose and sank with his hurried, feverish respiration. He was followed by the second burgomaster, with the Town Council, and deputation of merchants, headed by Gotzkowsky. With solemn, serious air, these gentlemen took up their position at the gate.

The chief burgomaster then beckoned Gotzkowsky to his side. "Stand by me, my friend," said he, with a groan, and offering his hand to Gotzkowsky with a dismal air. "I am suffering terribly, and even the two bottles of Johannisberger are not sufficient to inspire me with courage. Is it not terrible that the honorable Council should be obliged to attend in person? It is an unheard-of indignity!"

"Not only for you, but for the Berlin citizen is the insult equally great," said Gotzkowsky.

Herr von Kircheisen shook his head in a most melancholy manner. "Yes," said he, "but the Berlin citizen does not feel it so deeply. It does not affect his honor as it does that of the magistracy."

Gotzkowsky smiled scornfully. "Do you think," asked he, "that the magistrates possess a different kind of honor from that of any citizen of the town? The sense of honor is keener among the people than it is among the noblest lords."

The chief burgomaster frowned. "These are very proud words," replied he, with a shrug of his shoulders.

"Pride belongs to the citizen!" cried Gotzkowsky. "But believe me, noble sir, my heart to-day is not as proud as my words. It is sore with pain and grief over our deep, unmerited degradation."

"Silence, silence!" whispered the chief magistrate, leaning tremblingly on Gotzkowsky's arm. He heard a noise behind the closed gates, and his mind misgave him that the dreaded enemy was at hand.

Suddenly there sounded on the other side of the walls the loud notes of a trumpet, and the warder hastened to throw open the gate. A rare and motley mixture of Russian uniforms now came in sight. There were seen Cossacks, with their small horses and sharp lances; body-guards, with their gold-adorned uniforms; hussars, in their jackets trimmed with costly furs, all crowding in in confused tumult and with deafening screams and yells, that contrasted strangely with the silence inside the gates, with the noiseless, deserted streets, the closed windows of the houses, whose inhabitants scorned to be witnesses to the triumphal entry of the enemy. Only the ever-curious, ever-sight-loving, always-thoughtless populace, to whom the honor has at times been accorded of being called "the sovereign people," only this populace had hurried hither from all the streets of Berlin to see the entry of the Russians, and to hurrah to the conqueror, provided he paraded right handsomely and slowly in. And now a deep silence took place in the ranks of the enemy; the crowd opened and formed a lane, through which rode the Russian General Bachmann and his staff. As he reached the gate he drew in his horse and asked, in a loud, sonorous voice, in French, whether the magistrates and deputation of merchants were present.

The chief magistrate felt unable to answer; his knees tottered and his teeth chattered convulsively. He could only wag his head in silence and point with trembling hand to his companions.

"Is the merchant, John Gotzkowsky, one of your deputation?" asked the general.

Gotzkowsky stepped out of the crowd and approached the general with a proud step. "I am he, sir."

"I am glad to meet you," said the general, with a gracious smile. "I bring you greetings from General Sievers. He commissioned and ordered me to show you all possible favor. If I can be of service to you in any possible way, pray command me. I am General von Bachmann, and during our presence here have been appointed to the command of Berlin."

"Are you a friend of the noble Sievers?" cried Gotzkowsky, his countenance beaming with pleasure. "Oh, then, I need fear nothing for this unfortunate town, for only a noble, high-minded man can be a friend of Sievers. You will have pity on our distress!"

"Tell me wherein I can serve you, and how I can oblige you; my word has much influence on our general-in-chief, Count Tottleben."

Gotzkowsky was silent.

"Beg him to make the contribution as small as possible," whispered Kircheisen in Gotzkowsky's ear.

But Gotzkowsky took no notice of him. He fixed his dark eyes on the general, as if he wished to read his soul.

"Speak out," said the general. "If it is possible, your wish shall be granted."

"Well then, general," cried Gotzkowsky, "this is my request: Spare the poor and needy of this town. Order your soldiers to be humane, and do not forget mercy. Let your warriors neither murder nor plunder; let them not deride the defenceless and conquered. Give to the world the example of a generous and noble conqueror."

The general looked into Gotzkowsky's noble countenance with increasing astonishment, and his features assumed a more benevolent expression. "I give you my word that your petition shall be granted," said he; "I will give my soldiers strict orders, and woe be to him who does not obey them! But you have spoken for others, and I would like to oblige you personally. Have you no request to make for yourself?"

"Oh, yes, indeed!" cried Gotzkowsky, "I beg you to allow me to hasten to the Council-hall to report to the elders of the citizens your kind promise."

General Bachmann nodded affably to him. "Hasten then, and return soon."

But as Gotzkowsky turned to hasten away, Herr von Kircheisen seized him with a convulsive grasp and drew him back. "My God! you are not going to leave me?" he whined out. "Only think—"

"That the brave and noble citizens may lay the general's words as a balm to their wounds—that is what I am thinking of," cried Gotzkowsky, tearing himself loose and hurrying away with rapid strides.

"And now for you, most worthy burgomaster," said General Bachmann, sternly, "your name, if you please?"

Von Kircheisen looked at him gloomily, but made no answer.

The general repeated his question in a louder and sterner voice, but the burgomaster still maintained the same obstinate silence.

"Have you, by some unlucky chance, forgotten your name, sir?" asked the general with a lowering brow.

The angry, piercing look he fastened on him, seemed to awaken the burgomaster from his lethargy.

"My name is Kircheisen, Von Kircheisen," stammered he, with a heavy tongue.

"We came as conquerors, sir," said General Bachmann; "and it is usual for conquerors to dictate their terms before they enter a captured city. In the name of our general, Count Tottleben, I have to communicate to you what sum we demand from you as a war contribution. This demand amounts to four millions of dollars in good money."

The burgomaster stared at the general with glazed eyes, broke out into a loud laugh, and staggered back on the wall of the gate-warder's house.

"I implore you, collect yourself," whispered the second burgomaster, as he endeavored to support the reeling, staggering chief. "Remember our weal or woe depends upon you!"

Von Kircheisen grinned an idiotic laugh. "Four millions of dollars!" screamed he aloud. "Four millions of dollars! Hurrah! hurrah for the Russians!"

The countenance of the general became still more threatening, and an angry light flashed from his eye. "Do you dare to mock me?" asked he, in a harsh tone. "Beware, sir; and remember that you are the conquered, and in our power. I demand from you a decided answer. You understand my demand, do you not?"

But still he answered not. He stared at General Bachmann with a vacant smile, and his head wagged from side to side like the pendulum of a clock.

"This is disgraceful conduct," cried the general, "conduct which does little honor to the chief magistrate of Berlin. But I warn you, sir, to beware! I have promised the poor and suffering my protection, but I well know how to punish those who abuse our magnanimity. If you do not answer me this time, sir, by Heaven I will have you carried off under arrest and let a court-martial pronounce judgment on you!"

The chief magistrate continued dumb. The pale and terror-stricken countenances of those present were turned toward him. The members of the Council implored and besought him to put aside this unnatural stubbornness.

Von Kircheisen answered their pleadings with a loud-sounding laugh. He then stared at the general, his features worked and struggled, writhed, and finally he opened his mouth.

"Ah! God be praised, he is going to speak," cried the second burgomaster.

But no, he did not speak; he only distorted his face. A cry of dismay sounded from the lips of the deputation, a cry of anger from the Russian general, who, turning to his adjutant, ordered him immediately to arrest the burgomaster and carry him off. And now there arose an indescribable scene of confusion and terror. Pale with fright, the Council and deputation of merchants had flocked around Von Kircheisen to protect him from the advancing soldiers who sought to arrest him, while he, in the midst of all the horror and tumult, continued to giggle and make grimaces. The enraged soldiery had already commenced to push aside Kircheisen's defenders with blows from the butts of their muskets, when a man made his way through the crowd. It was Gotzkowsky, who, with a loud and full voice, demanded the cause of this singular uproar. A hundred voices were ready to answer him, and explain the scene in confused, unintelligible jargon.

But General Bachmann beckoned him to his side. "Tell me, sir, is this chief burgomaster a fool or a drunkard, or is he, indeed, so demented as to intend to mock us?"

As Gotzkowsky looked at the deathly pale, convulsed countenance of the magistrate, who renewed his shrill, screeching laugh, he comprehended the racking and terrible torture which the unfortunate man was suffering. He hastened to him, seized him by the arm, and led the tottering figure toward the general.

"This man is neither a fool nor a madman, your excellency; suffering has robbed him of speech, and he laughs, not in derision, but from the convulsion of intense sorrow."

And as the offended and angry general would not believe him, and commanded his soldiers anew to arrest the burgomaster, and the soldiers with renewed rage pressed on him, Gotzkowsky placed himself before him, and protected him with his proud and respect-inspiring person.

"General Bachmann," cried he, warmly, "I remind you of your oath. You vowed to me to protect the suffering. Well, then, this man is a sufferer, a sick man. I demand, from the noble friend of General Sievers, that he have compassion on the sick man, and allow him to be escorted safely and unmolested to his house."

"Can you give me your word that this man did not act thus out of arrogance?" asked the general, in a milder tone; "are you convinced that he is sick?"

"I swear to you, please your excellency, that the chief magistrate of Berlin has never been a healthy man; that, for many years, he has been subject to fits of convulsive laughter."

General Bachmann smiled. "This is an unfortunate disease for the chief magistrate of a city," said he, "and it seems to me as if the citizens of Berlin did wrong in choosing for their burgomaster a man who laughs and cries indifferently, and to whom the misfortunes of his fellow-citizens apparently serves only for a joke. But you reminded me of my promise, and you shall see that I will keep it."

He beckoned to his soldiers, and ordered them to fetch a litter on which to carry the sick burgomaster home. He then turned, with a smile, to Gotzkowsky, and said: "Sir, the Council of Berlin have cause to be grateful to you; you have saved their chief from death."

Herr von Kircheisen did not laugh now. His features jerked and distorted themselves still, but a stream of tears gushed from his eyes.

With an unspeakable expression he seized Gotzkowsky's hand, and pressed it to his lips, then sank unconscious in the arms of his deliverer.

* * * * *

CHAPTER III.

THE RUSSIAN, THE SAXON, AND THE AUSTRIAN, IN BERLIN.

Berlin was now given up to the enemy, and through the once cheerful and pleasant streets could be heard nothing but screams and shrieks of terror, mingled with the wild curses and boisterous laughter of the conqueror, who, not satisfied with attacking the trembling inhabitants to rob them of their possessions and property, ill treated them out of sheer cruelty, and took delight in hearing their screams and looking at the contortions caused by pain.

And who was this enemy, who, in scorn of all humanity and civilization, tortured the unfortunate and hunted them down?

They were not Russians, nor wild hordes of Cossacks. They were Austrians and Saxons, who, robbing and plundering, murdering and destroying, violating and burning, rushed through Berlin, filling all the inhabitants with terror and alarm.

General Bachmann kept faithfully the promise he had made to Gotzkowsky, and the Russian army at first not only preserved the strictest discipline, but even protected the inhabitants against the violence of the Austrians and Saxons.

The terrified citizens had one powerful and beneficent friend—this was John Gotzkowsky. Yielding to his urgent entreaty, General von Bachmann's adjutant, Von Brinck, had taken up his quarters in his house, and by his assistance and his own influence with the general, Gotzkowsky was enabled to afford material aid to all Berlin. For those citizens who were able to pay the soldiers he procured a Russian safeguard, and more than once this latter protected the inhabitants of the houses against the vandalism of the Austrians and Saxons.

Contrary to the wish of the Russians, the Austrians had forced themselves into the city, and, in spite of the terms of the capitulation agreed upon with the Russians, had quartered themselves upon the citizens, from whom, with the most savage cruelty and threats of ingenious torture, they extorted all the gold and jewels they possessed.

Berlin was now the open camping-ground of Croats and Austrian hussars, and Russian Cossacks, and all minds were filled with dread and anxiety.

It is true that even the Cossacks forgot the strict discipline which had been commanded them, and entered the houses, robbing and compelling the inhabitants, by blows of the knout, to give them all they wanted. But yet they were less cruel than the Saxons, less barbarous than the Austrians, who, with scoffing and derision, committed the greatest atrocities. Indeed, it was only necessary to complain to the Russian general in order to obtain justice immediately, and have the Cossacks punished. Eight of them were strung up in one day at the guard-house on the New Market square, as a warning and example to the others, and expiated their robberies by a summary death. But with the Austrians and Saxons it was the officers themselves who instigated the soldiers to acts of revolting barbarity, and who, forgetful of all humanity, by their laughter and applause excited their subordinates to fresh ill-treatment of the inhabitants. Disregarding the capitulation, and listening to their national enmity, and their love of plunder, they pressed forward with wild screams into the royal stables, driving away the safeguard of four-and-twenty men, which General von Tottleben had placed there for their protection, and with shameless insolence defiling the Prussian coat-of-arms pictured on the royal carriages. They then drew them out into the open street, and, after they had stripped them of their ornaments and decorations, piled them up in a great heap and set them on fire, in order to add to the fright and terror of the bewildered citizens by the threatening danger of conflagration.

High blazed the flames, consuming greedily these carriages which had once borne kings and princes. The screams and fright of the inmates of the nearest houses, and the crackling of the window-glass broken by the heat were drowned by the joyous shouts of the Austrians who danced round the fire with wild delight, and accompanied the roaring of the flames with insulting and licentious songs. And the fire seemed only to awaken their inventive powers, and excite them to fresh deeds of vandalism. After the fire had burnt out, and only a heap of ashes told of what were once magnificent royal vehicles, the Austrians rushed back again into the building with terrific outcry, to the apartments of the royal master of the horse, Schwerin, in order to build a new bonfire with his furniture, and fill their pockets with his gold and silver ware.

In the royal stalls a great uproar arose, as they fought with each other for the horses that were there. The strongest leaped on them and rode off furiously, to carry into other neighborhoods the terror and dismay which marked the track of the Austrians through Berlin. Even the hospitals were not safe from their brutal rage. They tore the sick from their beds, drove them with scoffs and insults into the streets, cut up their beds, and covered them over with the feathers. And all this was committed not by wild barbarians, but by the regular troops of a civilized state, by Austrians, who were spurred on, by their hatred of the Prussians, to deeds of rude cruelty and beastly barbarity. And this unlucky national hatred, which possessed the Austrian and made him forgetful of all humanity, was communicated, like an infectious plague, to the Saxons, and transformed these warriors, who were celebrated for being, next to the Prussians, the most orderly and best disciplined, into rude Jack Ketches and iconoclastic Vandals.

In the royal pleasure-palace at Charlottenburg, where Bruehl's (Saxon) dragoons had taken up their quarters by force, they set up a new species of dragoonade, which was directed not so much against the living as against marble statues and the sacred treasures of art. All the articles of splendor, brilliancy, and luxury which had been heaped up here, every thing which the royal love of the fine arts had collected of what was beautiful and rare, was sacrificed to their raging love of destruction. Gilded furniture, Venetian mirrors, large porcelain vases from Japan, were smashed to pieces. The silk tapestry was torn from the walls in shreds, the doors inlaid with beautiful wood-mosaic were broken up with clubs, the most masterly and costly paintings were cut in ribbons with knives. To be sure, it sometimes happened that the officers rescued from the soldiers some costly vase, some rare treasure or painting, and saved it from destruction, but this was not to save the King of Prussia's property, but to appropriate it to themselves, and carry it home with them.

Even the art-collection of Count Polignac, embracing the most splendid and rare treasures of art in the palace of Charlottenburg, did not escape this mania of destruction. This collection, containing among other things the most beautiful Greek statues, had been purchased in Rome by Gotzkowsky, and had afforded the king peculiar gratification, and was a source of much enjoyment to him. In the eyes of some Saxon officers, to whom this fact was known, it was sufficient reason for its condemnation. They themselves led the most violent and destructive of their soldiers into the halls where these magnificent treasures were exposed, even helped them to break the marble statues, to dash them down from their pedestals, to hew off their heads, arms, and legs, and even carried their systematic malice so far as to order the soldiers to grind into powder the fragments, so as to prevent any restoration of the statues at a subsequent period.

The unfortunate inhabitants of Charlottenburg witnessed all this abomination that was perpetrated in the royal palace with fear and trembling, and in order to save their own persons and property from similar outrage, they offered the enemy a contribution of fifteen thousand dollars. The Saxons accepted the money, but, regardless of every obligation usually considered sacredly binding, they only became more savage and ferocious. With yells of rage they rushed into the houses, and, when the money they demanded was refused them, they stripped the men of their clothes, lashed them until the blood flowed, or cruelly wounded or maimed them with sabre-cuts; and when the women fled from them, they followed them up, and forced them by brutal ill-treatment to yield themselves. No house in Charlottenburg escaped being plundered; and so cruel were the tortures which the inhabitants suffered, that four of the unfortunate men died a miserable death at the hands of the Saxon soldiers.

They were Germans who waged against their brother Germans, against their own countrymen, a brutality and barbarous love of destruction almost unequalled in the annals of modern history. Consequently it seemed but natural that the Russians should be excited by such examples of barbarity, so unstintedly set them by the Austrians and Saxons. No wonder that they, too, at last began to rob and plunder, to break into houses at night, and carry off women and maidens by force, in order to have them released next day by heavy ransom; and that even the severe punishments, inflicted on those whom the people had the courage to complain of to the generals lost their terror, and were no restraint on these sons of the steppes and ice-fields, led away as they were by the other ruffians.

Two hundred and eighty-two houses were destroyed and thoroughly plundered in Berlin by the Austrians; the Saxons had devastated the royal palace in Charlottenburg, and the whole town. Should not the Russians also leave a memorial of their vandalism? They did so in Schoenhausen, the pleasure-palace of the consort of Frederick the Great, who had left it a few days previous, by express command of the king, to take up her residence in Magdeburg. Eight Russian hussars forced themselves into the palace, and, with terrible threats, demanded the king's plate. Only the castellan and his wife, and a few of the royal servants, had been left behind to protect the place, and the only answer they could make to the furious soldiers was, that the booty which they were in search of had been carried with the royal party to Magdeburg. This information excited their fury to the highest pitch. Like the Saxon dragoons of Charlottenburg, they devastated the Schoenhausen palace, stripped the castellan and his wife, and, with shouts of wild laughter, whipped them and pinched their flesh with red-hot tongs. And, as if the sight of these bloody and torn human bodies had only increased their desire for blood and torture, they then attacked the two servants, stripped them of their clothes, cut one to pieces like a beast, and threw the other on the red-hot coals, roasting him alive, as formerly the warriors of her Most Christian Majesty of Spain did those whom, in the pride of their civilization, they denominated "the wild heathen."[1]

[Footnote 1: The account of all these cruelties and this vandalism is verified in the original, by reference to Von Archenholz: "History of the Seven Years' War," pp.194-198.—TRANSLATOR.]

* * * * *

CHAPTER IV.

THE CADETS.

The day following the occupation of Berlin, a strange and singular procession moved down the Linden Street through the Brandenburg Gate, and took the road to Charlottenburg. Bruehl's dragoons and De Lacy's chasseurs rode on each side of the line, which would have excited laughter, if pity and sorrow had not overcome the comical element. It was a procession of children decked in uniform, and having nothing military about them but their apparel, nothing manly but the dress-sword at their side.

This singular little regiment was the "Corps of Cadets," which had been made prisoners of war by the Austrians and Saxons.

The commandant, Von Rochow, did not imagine that the enemy would carry his hard-heartedness to such an extent as to consider these lads of tender age as part of the garrison, and make them prisoners of war in consequence. None of these boys exceeded the age of twelve years (the larger and older ones having been drafted into the army to supply the want of officers), and he presumed that their very helplessness and weakness would be their security, and therefore had omitted to mention them specially in the surrender. But the conqueror had no compassion on these little children in uniform, and pronounced them prisoners of war. Even Liliputian warriors might be dangerous! Remember the pangs suffered by Gulliver, as, lying quietly on the ground, he was suddenly awakened by a violent discharge poured into him from behind the high grass by the Liliputians. To be sure their weapons were only armed with needles—whence we may infer that the Liliputians are the original inventors of the modern Prussian needle-percussion rifles—but, one can be killed by needle-pricks. Count De Lacy feared, perhaps, the needle weapons of the little Liliputian cadets, and treated the poor, delicate, tender children as if they were tough old veterans, accustomed to all the hardships and privations of war. With coarse abuse and blows from the butt of the musket, they were driven out into the highway, and compelled to travel on the soft, muddy roads without cloaks, notwithstanding the severe weather, and only the short jackets of their uniforms. Heart-rending was the wail of the poor little ones from whom the war had taken their fathers, and poverty their mothers—torn from their home, the refuge of their orphaned childhood, to be driven like a flock of bleating lambs out into the desert wilderness of life.

And when their feet grew weary, when their little bodies, unaccustomed to fatigue, gave way, they were driven on with blows from sabres and the butts of muskets. When they begged for a piece of bread, or a drop of water for their parched lips, they were laughed at, and, instead of water, were told to drink their own tears, which ran in streams down their childish cheeks. They had already marched the whole day without food or refreshment of any kind, and they could hardly drag their bleeding feet along. With eyes bright with fever, and parched tongues, they still wandered on, looking in the distance for some friendly shelter, some refreshing spring.

At nightfall the little cadets were camped in an open field, on the wet ground. At first, they begged for a little food, a crust of bread; but when they saw that their sufferings gave pleasure to the dragoons, and that their groans were to them like a pleasant song, they were silent, and the spirit of their fathers reigned uppermost in the breasts of these little, forsaken, trembling lads. They dried their eyes, and kept their complaints in their little trembling hearts.

"We will not cry any more," said little Ramin, who though only twelve years of age, was yet the oldest of the captives, and recognized as their captain and leader. "We will not cry any more, for our tears give pleasure to our enemies. Let us be cheerful, and that perhaps will vex them. To spite them, and show how little we think of our hunger, let us sing a jolly song."

"Come on, let us do it!" cried the boys. "What song shall we sing?"

"*Prince Eugene*," cried young Ramin; and immediately with his childish treble struck up "Prince Eugene, the noble knight."

And all the lads joined in with a sort of desperate enthusiasm, and the song of the noble knight rose from their young lips like a peal of rejoicing.

But gradually one little trembling voice after another fell, by degrees the song grew lower and shriller, and became lost in a trembling whisper; then it would rise into an unnatural and terrified scream, or sink into a whining sob or trembling wail.

Suddenly little Ramin stopped, and a cry of pain, like the sound of a snapped string, burst from his breast. "I cannot sing any more," sighed he. "Hunger is killing me." And he sank down on his knees, and raised his little arms beseechingly to one of the Austrian soldiers, who was marching beside him, comfortably consuming a roast chicken.

"Oh! give me a bit of bread, only a mouthful, to keep me from starving to death."

"Have pity on us, do not let us starve!"

With similar piteous lamentations, the whole corps of trembling, weeping, starving little cadets threw themselves on their knees, and filled the air with their cries and prayers.

"Well, if you positively insist upon eating, you shall have something to appease your hunger," said the officer who commanded the chasseurs, and he whispered a few words to his corporal, who received them with a loud laugh, and then rode off.

"Now, be quiet, and wait," commanded the Austrian officer. "I have sent the corporal and some soldiers into the village to get food for you. Only wait now, and be satisfied." And the children dried their eyes, and comforted each other with encouraging words.

With what impatience, what painful longing, did they look forward to the promised food! How they thanked God, in the gladness of their hearts, that He had had pity on them, and had not allowed them to die of hunger!

They all seemed revived, and strained their hopeful eyes toward the quarter whence the corporal was to return. And now, with one voice, they broke out into a cry of joy; they had espied him returning, accompanied by soldiers who seemed to be bringing a heavy load.

They approached nearer and nearer. "Form a ring," commanded the officer, and they obeyed in expectant gladness; and around the thickly crowded ring the Austrian officers and the troop of soldiers took their stand. In silent waiting stood the cadets, and their hearts leaped for joy.

"Attention! your dinner is coming," cried the officer.

The ring opened. Ah! now the corporal and the soldiers are going to bring in the dinner.

But no! The dinner came walking along by itself. With a dignified step it marched in and gave utterance to an expressive bleat. It was a *live* sheep, which was to be given to the poor lads who were faint from hunger. An outburst of boisterous laughter from the Austrians greeted the dignified wether, and drowned the cries of the bitterly disappointed cadets.

"A sheep!" they cried, "and what are we to do with it?"—and they began to weep afresh.

"Kill him and roast him!" jeered the officer. "You are brave soldiers. Well, you will only have to do what we often do in camp. Be your own cook and butler; none of us will help you. We want to see what sort of practical soldiers you will make, and whether you are as good hands at cooking as at crying and blubbering."

And the Austrians folded their arms, and looked on idly and with derisive satisfaction at these poor children who stood there with their heads bowed down with helplessness and grief.

At length little Ramin arose. His eyes glistened with fierce defiance, and an expression of noble courage illuminated his pale countenance.

"If the sheep belongs to us," said he, "we will eat him."

"But he's alive," cried the boys.

"We will kill him," answered the little fellow.

"We? we ourselves? We are no butchers. We have never done such a thing!"

"Have we ever killed a man?" asked Ramin, rolling his large bright eyes around the circle of his comrades. "Have we ever deprived a man of his life?"

"No!"

"Well, then, we will have it yet to do! We hope to be able to kill many an enemy, and to do that we will have to begin with some one. Let us make believe, then, that this wether is the enemy, and that we have to attack him. Now, then, down upon him!"

"Ramin is right," cried the boys; "let us attack the enemy."

"Attention!" commanded Ramin.

The boys drew themselves up in military order right opposite the bleating sheep.

"Draw swords!"

In the twinkling of an eye they had drawn their little rapiers, which looked more like penknives than swords, and which the Austrians had left to their little prisoners of war.

"One, two, three!" commanded the little Ramin. "Attention! Forward!"

Down they charged upon the enemy, who was standing motionless, with staring eyes, bleating loudly. The Austrian soldiers roared and screamed with delight, and confessed, with tears in their eyes, that it was the best joke in the world, and no end of fun to see these poor boys made desperate by hunger.

The first feat of arms of the little cadets was completed, the wether was slain. But now came the question how to dress him, how to convert the dead beast into nice warm roast meat.

They were well aware that none of the laughing, mocking soldiers would help them, and therefore they disdained to ask for help. Wood, a roasting-pit, and a kettle were given them—means enough to prepare a good soup and roast. But how to begin and set about it they themselves hardly knew. But gnawing hunger made them inventive. Had they not often at home skinned many a cunningly caught mole—had they not often killed and drawn a rabbit? The only difference was that the sheep was somewhat larger than a mole or a rabbit.

Finally, after much toil and trouble, and under the approving laughter of the spectators, they accomplished it. The meat simmered in the kettle, watched by two cadets, two others turning the spit. The work was done; the sheep was converted into soup and roast.

And because they showed themselves so industrious and cheerful, one and another of the soldiers softened their hearts and threw them a piece of bread or a canteen; and the poor boys accepted these alms thrown at them with humble gratitude, and no feeling of resentment or defiance remained in their hearts, for hunger was appeased; but appeased only for the moment—only to encounter new sufferings, renewed hunger, fresh mockeries. For onward, farther onward must they wander. Every now and then one of them sank down, begging for pity and compassion. But what cared the soldiers, who only saw in the children the impersonation of the hated enemy, to be tortured and worried to death as a sport?

More than twenty of these little cadets succumbed to the sufferings of this journey, and died miserably, forsaken and alone, on the high road; and no mother was there to close their eyes, no father to lean over them and bless them with a tear. But over these poor martyr-children watched the love of God, and lulled them to sleep with happy dreams and gentle fancies about their distant homes, their little sister there, or the beautiful garden in which they had so often chased butterflies together. And amidst such fancies and smiling memories they dreamed away their childish souls, beyond the grave, to a holy and happy reawakening.

* * * * *

CHAPTER V.

THE EXPLOSION.

General von Tottleben was alone in his chamber—at least he had no visible company; but two invisible companions were there—Care and Sorrow. They whispered to him uncomfortable and melancholy thoughts, making his countenance serious and sad, and drawing deep and dark lines across his brow. He was a German, and was fighting in the ranks of the enemy against his German fatherland. Therein lay the secret of his care-worn features, the reading of the suppressed sighs; the broken, sorrowful words which he uttered, as with folded arms and bowed head he paced up and down his room. He was a German, and loved his country, which had repaid his love with that apathy and non-appreciation that have destroyed and killed some of the greatest and noblest men of Germany; while others have taken refuge in foreign countries, to find there that recognition which was denied them at home. General von Tottleben was only a German—why, then, should Germany take notice of him? Because he possessed information, talent, genius. Germany would have appreciated these if Von Tottleben had been a foreigner; but, as unfortunately he was only a German, Germany took no notice of him, and compelled him to seek in a foreign country the road to fame and distinction. He had gone to Russia. There his talents had been prized and employed. He was now a general in the Russian army, and the alliance between Russia and Austria compelled him to fight against his own country.

But the Russian general still preserved his German heart, this heart so strong in suffering, so unfaltering in its faith, so faithful in its love, so great in hope, humble in its obedience, modest in its desires; this German heart of his was the cause of much suffering to him, for it could not adapt itself to his Russian instructions, and despite his efforts to render it callous, would insist upon overflowing with pity and sympathy. He loved Berlin, for in this city he had passed the best years of his youth. And now he was called on to act as a cruel tyrant, an unfeeling barbarian, to sow broadcast death and destruction in this city, from which he yearned so to win a little love, a little sympathy for her rejected son.

But now his German heart was forced into silence by the exigencies of Russian discipline, and the general had to obey the orders of his superior officer, General von Fermore. His chief had ordered him to exercise the utmost severity and harshness, and imposed upon him the task of scourging Berlin like a demon of vengeance. And yet Berlin had committed no other crime than that of remaining faithful to her king, and of not wishing to surrender to the enemy.

A fresh dispatch had just arrived from General von Fermore, and its contents had darkened the brow of Tottleben with anxious care. He had received orders to blow up the arsenal in Berlin. This noble and handsome building, which rose in proud splendor in the midst of a populous town, was to be destroyed without reference to the fact that the blowing up of this colossal edifice would scatter death and ruin throughout unfortunate Berlin.

"I will not do it," said he, pacing up and down the room, and crushing the accursed paper which brought the cruel order in his clinched hand. "I cannot be such a barbarian. Fermore may command me to do barbarous actions, but I will not accept such commands! I will not obey! No one but myself knows of this order. I will ignore it. The Empress Elizabeth has always been very gracious toward me, and will forgive me for not executing an order which certainly never proceeded from her own kind heart." At this moment the door opened, and the adjutant entering, announced Count de Lacy.

Tottleben's countenance assumed a gloomy expression, and, as with hasty step he advanced toward the Austrian general, he muttered to himself, "I perceive the bloodhounds have got the scent, and are eager for blood." In the mean time Count de Lacy approached him with a friendly and gracious smile. He seemed not to be at all aware that Tottleben did not accept the hand which the Austrian general held out to him with a hearty greeting.

"I come to chat for a short quarter of an hour with your excellency," said Count de Lacy, in very fluent German, but with the hard foreign accent of a Hungarian. "After a battle won, I know nothing pleasanter than to recall with a comrade the past danger, and to revel again in memory the excitement of the fight."

"May I request your excellency to remember that the Austrians cannot count the conquest of Berlin in the list of their victories," cried Count Tottleben, with a sarcastic smile. "It was the Russian army which besieged Berlin, and Berlin surrendered *to us*."

"You are very kind to remind me of it," said Count de Lacy, with his unchangeable, pleasant smile. "In the mean time may I request a more particular explanation than this polite reminder?"

"You shall have it, sir," cried Tottleben, passionately. "I mean to say that Berlin is not Charlottenburg, and to request that the vandalism which the Austrian troops practised there, may not be transferred to Berlin. Be satisfied with the booty which your soldiers stowed away in their knapsacks at that place, and have the kindness to order the Austrian army to learn a little discipline and humanity from the Russians."

"From the Russians?" asked Count de Lacy, with ironical astonishment. "Truly one is not accustomed to learn humanity from that quarter. Does your excellency mean to say that the Austrians are to learn good manners from the Russians?"

"Yes, from the Russians," replied Tottleben—"from my soldiers, who neither plunder nor rob, but bear in mind that they are soldiers, and not thieves!"

"Sir," cried De Lacy, "what do these words mean?"

"They mean that I have promised my protection to the people of Berlin, and that I am prepared to afford it to them, even against our own allies. They mean that I have made myself sufficiently strong to bid you defiance, sir, and to defend Berlin against the cruelty and inhumanity of the Austrian army. The Russian army will compel it to be humane, and to pause in the cruel rage with which they have desolated unhappy Germany."

Count de Lacy shrugged his shoulders. "What is Germany to you, and why do you feel for her?" asked he jeeringly. "I beg you, count, let us not speak of Germany. What to us is this lachrymose, fantastic female Germania, which has been betrothed to so many lords and wooers, that she can remain faithful and true to none? Germania will then only be happy when one of her lovers has the boldness to kill off and tread under foot all his rivals and so build himself up an undisputed throne. That is Austria's mission, and our duty is to fulfil it. We are the heralds who go before Germania's Austrian bridegroom, and everywhere illuminate the heavens with the torches of our triumphs. If the torches now and then come too near some piece of humanity and set it on fire, what is that to us? Germany is our enemy, and if we have a puling compassion on our enemy, we become traitors to our own cause. That's all. But what is the use of this strife and these recriminations?" asked he, suddenly breaking into a smile. "I have only come to ask your excellency when you intend to light these new wedding-torches which are to redden the sky of Berlin?"

"What wedding-torches?" inquired Tottleben, turning pale.

"Well, those which are to burst out from the mint and factory buildings," said De Lacy, with a smile of indifference. "I anticipate with extraordinary pleasure this exhibition of fireworks which the town of Berlin is going to give in honor of our presence."

"You mean to say in disgrace of our presence," exclaimed Tottleben, ardently.

Count de Lacy looked at him with a compassionate shrug of the shoulders. "My dear count," said he, with cutting coldness, "when a man becomes a Russian general, he must have a Russian heart, and not allow himself to be influenced by any German softness or sympathy. Otherwise it might happen that they might make a mistake, and not being able to deprive you of your German heart, might take your German head instead."

General Tottleben drew back with astonishment, and stared at him.

Count de Lacy continued, smiling, and in a quiet tone: "I warn you to guard against your own mildness and your German heart. General Fermore is my friend, and often consults me about the meaning of German words. How would you like it if I should explain the word *treason* in a manner dangerous to yourself, and if this explanation should result in translating your excellency into Siberia?"

"General Fermore is neither my commander nor my master," cried Tottleben, proudly.

"But the lord and master of your lady and mistress, the high and mighty Empress Elizabeth—remember that. Will your excellency now condescend to inform me at what time the Berlin armory shall rise fluttering in the air like a bird?"

"And do you know that, too?" asked Tottleben, with painful astonishment.

"I have already told you that the Russians and Austrians are faithful allies, and have no secrets from each other, as far as their designs upon Germany are concerned. Oh, it will be a splendid *feu de joie* for the house of Austria, when the Prussian armory is blown into the air! When are we to enjoy this spectacle, general?"

General von Tottleben sank his head in silence on his breast. Count de Lacy regarded him with a cold and piercing glance. Tottleben felt this look, and understood its important significance. He knew that his whole future, his freedom, perhaps even his life, hung upon this moment.

"In three hours from now the spectacle will take place," said he, with a forced laugh. "In three hours the wedding-torches shall be lighted, and in order to make it the pleasanter, we will have the wails of the people of Berlin as a musical accompaniment."

"In three hours, then," said Count de Lacy, bowing low; "I hasten to announce it to my officers. I am burning with impatience to witness this rare spectacle."

Count de Lacy departed, and General Tottleben was again alone.

For a long time did he pace his room in abstract meditation, anger and pity, fear and terror struggling in his soul. He was perfectly aware of the danger which threatened him. He knew that Count Fermore hated him as a dangerous rival for the smiles of the empress, and only waited for a favorable opportunity to overthrow him. He was therefore obliged to yield to this cruel necessity; the Berlin armory must be sacrificed.

Suddenly his countenance lighted up, and his features assumed an expression of joy. He hastened rapidly to the door and summoned his body servant and slave, Ivan Petrowitsch. "Ivan," said he, with the stern and cold composure of a Russian— "Ivan, I have a commission for you, and if you are successful in its execution, I will not have your son Feodor hung, although I know that yesterday, contrary to my order, he was present at the plundering of a house."

"Speak, master, what am I to do? I will save my son, even if it cost my own life."

"It will cost your life, Ivan."

"I am your property, master, and my life belongs to you," said the serf, sadly. "You can have me whipped to death any time it pleases you. Say, then, what I must do to save my son."

"Fifty Cossacks are to ride immediately to the powder-mills to bring powder. You will accompany them."

Ivan looked at him with astonishment. "Is that all I have to do?" asked he.

Tottleben was not yet sufficiently Russian. His German heart would assert its rights. As he met the inquiring look of Ivan, he turned his eye away. He forgot that it was only a serf he was speaking to, and not a human being.

But he soon recalled it. "You will accompany these Cossacks to the powder-mills, I say, and as you do so you will smoke your pipe, and see that the tobacco burns well, and that you are burning tinder on top of it."

An expression of comprehension shone in Ivan's eyes. "I will smoke, master," said he, sadly.

"When you are in the powder-mills, and the Cossacks are loading the powder, you will help them, and in doing so you will let the pipe fall out of your mouth," said Tottleben, in an undertone, and his voice trembled ever so little. There was a pause—Ivan leaned, pale and trembling, against the wall. General Tottleben had turned away, as if afraid to encounter the pallid, terrified countenance of his slave.

"If you do not execute my command," said he, finally, "I will have your only son hung, as he deserves to be. If you betray to any one soever a word of my order, I will have your wife whipped to death. Now think of it."

Ivan shook as if in an ague. His teeth chattered together. "I will smoke, master," said he, at last, with an effort, "and I will drop my pipe in the powder-mills. Have pity on my son, master, and spare my wife!"

"I will do so, Ivan," said Tottleben. "I will give them both their freedom, and a pension."

Ivan dropped his head, and a convulsive groan burst from his breast.

"Time passes; make haste!" cried the general, with assumed harshness.

"I go, master," sighed Ivan. "You will not, then, string up my poor Feodor, nor have my wife whipped?"

"If you execute my order strictly and punctually, I will care for them."

122

Two tears coursed slowly down Ivan's brown cheek. "I will carry out your orders, master; I will smoke, and I will drop my pipe. Farewell, master!"

He approached his master with slavish humility, and kissed the seam of his garment. "Farewell, master. I thank you, for you have always been a kind master to me," said he, and his tears moistened the general's coat.

General Tottleben was as yet unable completely to convert his German heart into a Russian one. He felt himself touched by this humble and heroic submission of his slave. He felt as if he must give him some comfort on his fatal road.

"Ivan," said he, softly, "your death will save, perhaps, not only the property, but also the lives of many hundred other men."

Ivan kissed passionately his proffered hand. "I thank you, master. Farewell, and think sometimes of your poor Ivan."

A quarter of an hour afterward was seen a troop of fifty Cossacks, on their swift-footed little horses, racing down Frederick Street. Each man had a powder-sack with him, and seeing them ride by, people whispered to each other, "They are riding to the powder-mills. They have shot away all their own powder, and now, in true Cossack style, they are going to take our Prussian powder." At that time Frederick Street did not reach beyond the river Spree. On the other bank began the faubourgs and the gardens. Even Monbijou was then only a royal country seat, situated in the Oranienburg suburb. The powder-mills, which lay beyond the gardens, with a large sandy plain intervening, were sufficiently remote from the town to prevent all danger from their possible explosion.

Ivan, the serf of Count von Tottleben, rode by the side of the officer of the Cossacks. He pranced his pony about, and was cheerful and jolly like his comrades, the merry sons of the steppe. As they reached the gate they halted their horses, and gazed with evident pleasure on the desert, wild, sandy plain, which stretched out before them.

"How beautiful that is!" exclaimed Petrowitsch, the hetman of the Cossacks. "Just look—what a handsome steppe!"

"Just such a fine sand steppe as at home in our own country!" sighed one of the Cossacks, beginning to hum a song of his home.

"This is the finest scenery I have seen in Germany," cried another. "What a pleasure it would be to race over this steppe!"

"Come on, then, let us get up a race over this splendid steppe," said a fourth, "and let us sing one of the songs we are used to at home."

"Yes, agreed! let us!" cried all, ranging quickly their horses in line.

"Wait a moment," cried Ivan; "I can't sing, you all know, and I've only one sweetheart, and that's my pipe. Let me then light my pipe so that I can smoke." He struck fire with his steel, and lighting the tinder, placed it in the bowl of his pipe. No one saw the sad, shuddering look which he cast at the glowing tinder and his spark-scattering pipe. "Now forward, boys, and sing us a lively song from home," said Ivan.

"Hurrah! hurrah!"

They charge over the beautiful plain, and sing in a pealing chorus, the favorite song of the Cossack, at once so soft and sad:

"Lovely Minka! must I leave thee?"

Big tears ran down poor Ivan's cheek. No one saw them, no one observed him. He charged with the others over the Berlin steppe, and blew the smoke out of his pipe. No one heard the sad sighs which he uttered as he drew nearer and nearer to the powder-mills. No one heard the sad words of parting which he muttered to himself as his comrades sang:

"Lovely Minka! must I leave thee,
  Leave my happy, heather plains?
Ah! this parting does not grieve thee,
  Though still true my heart remains.
  Far from thee I roam,
Sadly see the sunbeams shining,
Lonely all the night I'm pining
  Far from thee alone."

They reach the powder-mills; the Cossacks halt their horses and spring from their saddles.

Slowly and hesitatingly does Ivan proceed; he passes about his pipe; he puffs at the tobacco to make it burn, and smoke more freely.

And now all's right. The pipe is alight. Like brilliant eyes of fire the burning tobacco shines out of the bowl. Ivan puts it back in his mouth and blows great clouds of smoke, as he and the Cossacks approach the gates of the powder-mills.

The Russian sentinels let them pass, and, joking and laughing merrily, the Cossacks carry their bags into the building to fill them with powder for the blowing up of the arsenal. How joyous and careless they are, these sons of the steppe! How calmly does Ivan continue to smoke his pipe, although they are now in the large hall, where casks of powder are ranged in endless rows!

124

And now a cask is opened, and merrily and jestingly the Cossacks begin to load the powder into their sacks.

What art thou staring at so wildly, Ivan Petrowitsch? Why do the big drops of sweat run down thy forehead? Why do thy limbs tremble, and why dost thou look so sadly and mournfully at thy comrades?

They sing so merrily, they chatter so gayly, all the while pouring the powder into their sacks nimbly and actively!

Ivan keeps on blowing furious clouds of smoke out of his pipe.

Suddenly he utters a cry, a heart-rending, pitiful cry. The burning pipe drops from his mouth!

Then rises a wild yell—an awful, horrible report!

The earth quakes and trembles, as if about to open, to vomit forth the burning stream of a thundering crater. The sky seems blackened by the fearful smoke which fills the air far and wide. Everywhere may be seen human bodies, single shattered limbs, ruins of the exploded building, flying through the air, and covering the groaning, trembling earth. But no syllable or sound of complaint, no death-rattle is now heard. All is over.

The powder-mills have flown into the air, and, though far distant from Berlin, yet this terrible explosion was felt in every part of the city.[1] In the Frederick Street the houses shook as if from an earthquake, and countless panes of glass were shattered.

With darkened brow and a burst of anger did General von Tottleben receive the news that the powder-mills had blown up, and fifty Cossacks had lost their lives thereby. He mourned for the unfortunate Cossacks and his poor serf, Ivan Petrowitsch. Still more did he lament that it was now impossible to blow up the arsenal in Berlin. But it was not his fault that the commands of his empress could not be executed. The Russians had shot away all their powder, and the stock in the powder-mills having been destroyed, there was none left to carry into execution this grand undertaking.

[Footnote 1: Archenholz: "History of the Seven Years' War," p. 194.]

* * * * *

CHAPTER VI.

JOHN GOTZKOWSKY.

A sad and anxious period had the unfortunate city of Berlin yet to pass through. With fear and trembling did the inhabitants await the approach of each morning, and in spiritless despondency they seemed to have lost all capacity for helping themselves.

There was but one man who, unterrified and unwavering, with the cheerful courage of a noble soul, exposed himself to danger, to suffering and grief, who proposed to himself but one object—to help others as far as lay in his power, and to avert fresh misfortune, additional care and anxiety from the too heavily laden inhabitants of Berlin.

This one man was John Gotzkowsky, the Merchant of Berlin. In this day of their trouble the inhabitants looked up to him as to a helping angel; the poor prayed to him, the rich fled to him with their treasures; with him the persecuted found refuge, the hungry shelter and food.

For Gotzkowsky there was no rest or leisure, nor did he feel care or sorrow. The tears he had shed about Elise he had buried in his heart, overcoming a father's grief by the power of his will. At this time he only remembered that he was called to the sacred duty of succoring his fellow-men, his suffering brothers—to be a father to the needy, a deliverer to the oppressed.

The doors of his house were open to all who sought refuge with him. The wives and children and aged parents of his workmen rushed there with screams and loud lamentations, and he received them all, and gave them beds in his splendid halls, and his gilt and silken ottomans served for refreshing places to hungry and freezing poverty.

But not the poor alone, the wealthy also found refuge in his house. They knew that Gotzkowsky's word had much influence, not only with General Bachmann, but also with General von Tottleben, and that this latter had ordered that Gotzkowsky should always have free admission to him. In their anxiety and need they put aside the proud bearing of their rank and dignity, and hastened to him to plead for help and rest, to hide their treasures and place their lives and fortunes under his guardianship.

But while hundreds sought refuge and safety there, Gotzkowsky himself was like a stranger in his own house. Day and night was he seen on the streets; where-ever danger and alarm prevailed, he appeared like a rescuing angel; he brought help when all else despaired, and the power of his eloquence and his pleading words silenced even the rough insolence of the enemy's soldiers. A hundred times did he expose his own life to save some unfortunate. In the New Frederick Street he rushed through the flames into a burning house to save a child which had been forgotten.

Elsewhere he fought singly against twenty Austrian soldiers, who were about to carry off two young girls in spite of their heart-rending shrieks and entreaties. The rescued maidens sank at his feet, and bathed his hand with their tears.

Gotzkowsky raised them to his heart, and said, with an indescribable expression: "Should I not have compassion on you? Am not I a father? Thank my daughter, for it was she who saved you."

But now, at last, exhausted Nature demanded her rights. After two days and nights without rest, Gotzkowsky tottered toward his own house. As he crossed the threshold he asked himself with an anxious heart—"Will Elise come to meet me? Has she cared for me?" And trembling with care and love, he went in.

Elise did not come to meet him. No one bade him welcome but his servant Peter. Gently at last, indeed almost timidly, he ventured to inquire after his daughter.

"She is in the large hall, busy nursing the wounded who have been carried there."

Gotzkowsky's countenance expressed great delight and relief at this report. Elise had not, then, buried herself in the solitude of her room in idle complaint, but had sought, like himself, comfort for her suffering in helping and sympathizing with others. In this moment he appreciated the infinity of his love. He yearned to take her to his heart, and pour out to her all his unappreciated, doubted love, and convince her that she, his daughter, the only child of his wife, was the true end and object of his life. But unhappy, oppressed Berlin left him no time to attend to the soft and gentle dictates of his father's heart. He had scarcely got into his house, when two messengers arrived from the town Council, bringing him six thousand dollars in cash, with the urgent request that he would take charge of this sum, which would be safe only with him. The town messengers had scarcely left him, when there arrived the rich manufacturers, Wegeli and Wuerst, with a wagon-load of gold and silver bars which Gotzkowsky had promised to keep in his fire-proof cellars.

His house had become the treasury of the whole of Berlin; and if it had been destroyed, with all these gold and silver ingots, these diamonds and silver ware, money and papers, all the Exchanges of Europe would have felt the disastrous consequences.

At last, all these treasures were stowed away, and Gotzkowsky addressed himself to rest, when the door of his room was suddenly opened, and General von Bachmann entered hastily.

"Gotzkowsky," said he, "I have come with important intelligence, and to redeem the promise I made to my friend Sievers." Approaching more closely to Gotzkowsky, he said to him in an undertone: "General von Tottleben has just received orders to destroy and burn all royal factories and mills."

Gotzkowsky turned pale, and inquired with horror, "Why this barbarous proceeding?"

General Bachmann shrugged his shoulders. "It is the order of the commander-in-chief, Count von Fermore," said he; "and Tottleben will have to be all the more particular from the fact that, instead of the arsenal, fifty of our soldiers were blown into the air. Here, in the mean while, take this paper, and see whether, among the factories to be destroyed, one of yours has been included by mistake."

Gotzkowsky looked over the list with dismay. "Did not your excellency say that only royal factories were to be destroyed?"

"Yes, so runs the order."

"But the factories that stand on this list are not royal institutions. The brass-works in Eberwalde, the gold and silver factories, and the warehouse in Berlin, do not belong to the king, and are they going to be so barbarous as to destroy them? That cannot be. I will hasten to General Tottleben, and entreat him to revoke this cruel order."

General Bachmann shook his head sadly. "I am afraid it will be in vain," said he. "Besides, you incur great risk in your undertaking. The general is in a very angry, excited mood, and your intercession will only increase his bitterness and anger."

"I fear not his anger," cried Gotzkowsky boldly. "If no one else dares to tell him the truth, I will do it; and with argument and entreaty compel him to be humane, and to respect the property of others. Come, sir, let us go to General Tottleben!"

"No, sir. I am not going with you," said Bachmann, laughing. "I am not a man to tremble on the eve of battle, and yet I fear to meet Tottleben's angry looks. In his wrath he is like a Jupiter Tonans, ready to launch his thunderbolts, and dash to pieces all who approach him."

"I am not afraid of his thunder!" cried Gotzkowsky, fervently. "The property and welfare of Berlin are in danger. I must go to the general!"

"Then go along," said Bachmann, "and may God give power to your words! I have warned you, and that is all I can do."

Gotzkowsky did not answer him. Trembling with eagerness and impatience, he dressed himself, and throwing his cloak around him, he once more left his house, with the alacrity of a young man.

General Bachmann looked after him, smiling thoughtfully. "He is a noble fellow," said he, "and Berlin has good reason to be grateful to him, and to love him. But who knows? perhaps, for that very reason, she will one day hate him. Noble-mindedness is so soon forgotten! It is the solid weight that sinks to the bottom, while light deeds float on top. Mankind is not fond of being grateful. I would like to know whether Berlin will ever show a due appreciation of this noble man?"

* * * * *

CHAPTER VII.

THE HORRORS OF WAR.

The Russians had at last allowed themselves to be carried away by the example set them by the Austrians and Saxons. Like them, they roamed through Berlin, robbing and plundering, unmindful of discipline, and forgetting the severe punishments which Tottleben inflicted on those whose misdeeds reached his ear.

Like the Austrians, the Cossacks entered houses with wanton arrogance, robbed, and ill-treated in the rudest manner those who opposed their demands. They had even managed to reduce their robbery and extortion to a kind of system, and to value the human person after a new fashion. It was a sort of mercantile transaction, and the Cossacks were the brokers in this new-fashioned business. Stealthily and unheard, they slipped into houses, fell upon the unsuspecting women and children, and dragged them out, not to capture them as the Romans did the Sabine women, but to hold them as so much merchandise, to be redeemed by their friends and relatives at high and often enormous ransoms.

But the Cossacks drew but small profit from this hunt after noble human game. They were only servants, acting under orders from their officers. These latter divided the booty, throwing to the Cossacks a small reward for their skill in robbing.

Thus, for some days, Berlin was not only subjugated by the enemy, but a prey to robbers and slave-dealers, and moans and lamentations were heard in every house. All the more merrily did the enemy's soldiers carouse and enjoy themselves, laugh and joke. For them Berlin was nothing more than an orange to be squeezed dry, whose life-blood was to be drawn out to add new zest to their own draught of life.

The young Russian officers were sitting together in the large room of their barracks. They were drinking and making merry, and striking their glasses noisily together; draining them to the health of the popular, handsome, and brilliant comrade who had just entered their circle, and who was no other than he whom Gotzkowsky's daughter, in the sorrow of her heart, was mourning as dead!—no one else than the Russian colonel, Count Feodor von Brenda.

He had been right, therefore, in trusting to Fortune. Fortune had favored him, as she always does those who boldly venture all to win all, and who sport with danger as with a toy. Indeed, it was an original and piquant adventure which the Russian colonel had experienced, the more piquant because it had threatened him with death, and at one moment his life had been in extreme danger. It had delighted him for once to experience all the horrors of death, the palpitation, the despair of a condemned culprit; to acquire in his own person a knowledge of the great and overpowering feelings, which he had read so much about in books, and which he had not felt in reality even in the midst of battle. But yet this bold playing with death had, toward the last, lost a little of its charm, and a moment arrived when his courage failed him, and his daring spirit was overpowered by his awed physical nature. There was not, as there is in battle, the excitement which conquers the fear of death, and drunk with victory, mocks one to his face; there was not the wild delight which possesses the soldier in the midst of a shower of balls, and makes him, as it were, rush toward eternity with a shout. No, indeed! It was something quite different which Colonel von Brenda, otherwise so brave and valiant, now felt.

When the Austrian soldiers had pronounced his sentence of death, when they formed a ring around him at the Gens-d'Armes Market, and loaded their pieces for his execution, then the haughty Russian colonel felt a sudden change take place; his blood curdled in his veins, and he felt as if thousands of small worms were creeping through them, gliding slowly, horribly to his heart. At length, in the very despair which oppressed him, he found strength to cast his incubus from his breast, and with a voice loud and powerful as thunder to cry out for help and succor. His voice was heard; it reached the ear of General Bachmann, who came in person to set free the wild young officer, the favorite of his empress, from the hands of the Austrians.

This adventure, which had terminated so famously, Count Brenda now related to his friends and comrades. To be sure, the general had punished the mad freak with an arrest of four-and-twenty hours. But after undergoing this punishment, he was more than ever the hero of the day, the idol of his comrades, who now celebrated his release from arrest with loud rejoicing and the cracking of champagne bottles. After they had laughed and joked to their satisfaction, they resorted to the dice.

"And what stake shall we play for?" asked Feodor, as he cast a look of ill-concealed contempt on his young companions, who so little understood the art of drinking the cup of pleasure with decency, and rolled about on their seats with lolling tongues and leering eyes.

Feodor alone had preserved the power of his mind; his brain alone was unclouded by the fumes of champagne, and that which had made the others mad had only served to make him sad and gloomy. The drunkenness of his comrades had sobered him, and, feeling satiated with all the so-called joys and delights of life, he asked himself, with a smile of contempt, whether the stammering, staggering fellows, who sat next to him, were fit and suitable companions and associates of a man who had made pleasure a study, and who considered enjoyment as a philosophical problem, difficult of solution.

"And for what stake shall we play?" he asked again, as with a powerful grip he woke his neighbor, Lieutenant von Matusch, out of the half sleep which had crept over him.

"For our share of the booty!" stammered the lieutenant.

Feodor looked at him with surprise. "What booty? Have we, then, become robbers and plunderers, that you speak of booty?"

131

His comrades burst into a wild laugh.

"Just listen to the sentimental dreamer, the cosmopolite," cried Major von Fritsch. "He looks upon it as dishonorable to take booty. I for my part maintain that there is no greater pleasure, and certainly none which is more profitable. Fill your glasses, friends, and let us drink to our hunting. 'Hurrah! hurrah for human game!'"

They struck their glasses together, and emptied them amidst an uproar of laughter.

"Colonel, you shall have your share of the booty!" said Lieutenant von Matusch, laying his heavy, shaky hand on Feodor's shoulder. "We never intended to cheat you out of your portion, but you were not here, and therefore up to this time you could have no share in it."

As Feodor pressed him with questions, he related how they had formed a compact, and pledged themselves to have their booty and captives in common.

"We have caught more than a dozen head, and they have ransomed themselves handsomely," cried Major von Fritsch. "We have just sent out ten of our men again on the chase."

"Oh! I hope they will bring in just such another handsome young girl as they did yesterday," cried Matusch, rubbing his hands with delight. "Ah, that was a pleasant evening! She offered us treasures, diamonds, and money; she promised us thousands if we would only release her at once! She wept like a Madonna, and wrung her snow-white hands, and all that only made her prettier still."

Colonel Feodor looked at him in anger. In contact with such coarse and debauched companions his more refined self rose powerful within him, and his originally noble nature turned with loathing from this barren waste of vulgarity and infamy.

"I hope," said he, warmly, "that you have behaved as becomes noble gentlemen."

Matusch shrugged his shoulders and laughed. "I do not know what you call so, colonel. She was very pretty, and she pleased me. I promised to set her free to-day, for the ransom agreed on, and I have kept my word."

As he spoke thus, he burst into a loud laugh, in which his friends joined with glee.

But Feodor von Brenda did not laugh. An inexplicable, prophetic dread overpowered him. What if this young girl, described to him with so much gusto, and who had been so shamefully ill-treated, should prove to be his Elise, his beloved!

At this thought, anger and distress took possession of him, and he never loved Elise more ardently and truly than he did at this moment when he trembled for her. "And

132

was there no one," cried he, with flashing eyes, "no one knightly and manly enough to take her part? How! even you, Major von Fritsch, allowed this thing to happen?"

"I was obliged to do so," replied the major. "We have made a law among ourselves, which we have all sworn to obey. It is established that the dice shall determine to which of the officers the booty shall belong; and he who throws the highest number becomes the owner of the person. He has to negotiate about the ransom. This, however, of course is divided among his comrades."

"But if the person is poor?" asked Feodor, indignantly, "if she cannot pay?"

"Then she belongs to him who has won her; he must decide on her fate. He is—"

The major stopped suddenly. The other officers raised themselves in their seats, and listened with breathless attention.

"I think I hear the signal," whispered the major. He had not deceived himself. A shrill, piercing whistle sounded a second time. The officers sprang from their seats, and broke into a loud cry of triumph:

"Our Cossacks are coming. They have caught something! Come, come, let us throw the dice."

With fierce eagerness, they all rushed to the table, and stretched out their hands for the bones. Immediately a deep, expectant silence ensued. Nothing was heard but the rattling of the dice, and the monotonous calling of the numbers thrown. Feodor alone remained at his place, lost in deep thought, and his tortured heart kept asking itself the question, "Could it be her whom the barbarians had captured and ill-used?" This question burnt in his brain like a red-hot dagger, upsetting his reason, and driving him almost mad with anger and grief. Still the rattling of the noisy dice went on—the calling of the numbers. No one took notice of the young man, who, in desperate distress, his clinched fist pressed against his breast, paced up and down the farther end of the room, uttering broken words of anger and grief. No one, as has been said, noticed him, nor did any one remark that at this moment the door in the background of the hall was opened, and six Cossacks entered, bearing a litter on their shoulders.

Feodor von Brenda saw them, and, with deep compassion, he regarded the veiled, inanimate figure lying on the litter, which was set down by the Cossacks.

"Colonel von Brenda," cried Major von Fritsch at this moment, "it is your turn."

"Oh, he is too sentimental!" laughed out Matusch. "Is not that the fact, colonel?"

Feodor remained musing and pensive. "It is a woman," said he to himself—"perhaps a young and handsome woman like Elise. How if I should try to save her? I have luck at the dice. Well, I will try." And with a firm step he approached the table. "Give me the bones," cried he. "I will throw with you for my share of the booty."

The dice rattled and tumbled merrily on the table.

"Eighteen spots!"

"The highest throw!"

"Colonel von Brenda has won!"

"The woman is mine!" cried Feodor, his countenance beaming with joy.

His comrades looked at him with astonishment. "A woman! How do you know beforehand that it is a woman?"

Feodor pointed silently to the back part of the room. There stood the Cossacks, next to the litter, waiting in solemn silence to be noticed.

"A woman! Yes, by Heavens! it is a woman," cried the officers. And, with boisterous laughter, they rushed toward the Cossacks.

"And where did you pick her up?" asked Major von Fritsch.

"Don't know," answered one of the Cossacks. "We crept along a wall, and when we had climbed to the top, we saw a garden. We got down slowly and carefully, and waited behind the trees, to see if any one would come down the long avenue. We did not have long to wait before this lady came by herself. We rushed on her, and all her struggles, of course, went for nothing. Luckily for her and us, she fainted, for if she had cried out, some one, perhaps, might have come, and then we would have been obliged to gag her."

The officers laughed. "Well," said the major, "Colonel Feodor can stop her mouth now with kisses." In the mean while, Lieutenant Matusch threw the Cossacks a few copper coins, and drove them out of the room, with scornful words of abuse.

"And now let us see what we have won," cried the officers, rushing to the litter. They were in the act of raising the cloth which concealed the figure, but Feodor stepped forward with determined countenance and flashing eyes.

"Let no one dare to raise this veil," said he haughtily. His comrades rushed, with easily aroused anger, on him, and attempted again to approach the veiled woman. "Be on your guard!" cried Feodor, and, drawing his sword from its scabbard, he placed himself before the litter, ready for the combat. The officers drew back. The determined, defiant countenance of the young warrior, his raised and ready sword, made them hesitate and yield.

"Feodor is right," said the major, after a pause; "he has fairly won the woman, and it is his business now to settle about the ransom."

The others cast their eyes down, perhaps ashamed of their own rudeness. "He is right, she belongs to him," murmured they, as they drew back and approached the door.

"Go, my friends, go," said Feodor. "I promise you that I will settle with her about her ransom, and give up beforehand all claim to my share!"

The countenances of the Russian officers brightened up. They nodded and smiled toward him as they left the room. Count Feodor von Brenda was now alone with the veiled and insensible woman.

* * * * *

CHAPTER VIII.

BY CHANCE.

As soon as the officers had left the room, Feodor hastened to close the door after them carefully, to prevent any importunate intrusion. He then searched thoroughly all the corners of the room, and behind the window-curtains, to make sure that no one was concealed there. He wished to be entirely undisturbed with the poor woman whose face he had not yet beheld, but toward whom he felt himself attracted by a singular, inexplicable sensation. As soon as he was convinced that he was quite alone, he went to her with flushed cheeks and a beating heart, and unveiled her.

But scarcely had he cast his eyes on her, when he uttered a cry, and staggered back with horror. This woman who lay there before him, lifeless and motionless, pale and beautiful as a broken flower, was none other than Elise Gotzkowsky, his beloved! He stood and stared at her; he pressed his hands to his forehead as if to rouse himself from this spell which had hold of him, as if to open his eyes to truth and reality. But it was no dream, no illusion. It was herself, his own Elise. He approached her, seized her hand, passed his hands over her glossy hair, and looked at her long and anxiously. His blood rushed like a stream of fire to his heart, it seethed and burned in his head, in his veins; and, quite overcome, he sank down before her.

"It is she," murmured he softly, "it is Elise. Now she is mine, and no one can take her from me. She belongs to me, my wife, my beloved. Fate itself bears her to my arms, and I were a fool to let her escape again."

With passionate impetuosity he pressed her to his heart, and covered her lips and face with his kisses. But the violence of his affection aroused Elise. Slowly and stunned she raised herself in his arms, and looked around, as if awakened from a dream. "Where am I?" asked she, languidly.

Feodor, still kneeling before her, drew her more closely to his heart. "You are with me," said he, passionately, and as he felt her trembling in his arms, he continued still more warmly: "Fear nothing; my Elise, look not so timidly and anxiously about you. Look upon me, me, who am lying at your feet, and who ask nothing more from Fortune than that this moment should last an eternity."

Elise scarcely understood him. She was still stunned—still confused by the dreams of her swoon. She passed her hand over her forehead, and let it drop again list-less and powerless. "My senses are confused," whispered she in a low voice, "I do not hear; what has happened to me?"

"Do not ask, do not inquire," cried Feodor, ardently. "Think only that love has sent an angel to you, on whose wings you have reposed on your passage hither to me. Why will you ask after the nature of the miracle, when the miracle itself brings delight to our eyes and hearts? Therefore, fear nothing, gentle, pure being. Like an

136

angel do you come to me through the deluge of sin. You bear the olive-branch of peace, and love and happiness are before us."

But as he was about to press her still more closely to his heart, a shudder pervaded her whole frame. "Oh, now, I recollect," she cried, vehemently; "now I know all! I was alone in the garden. There came those terrible men. They seized me with their rude hands. They wounded my heart with their horrible looks, which made me shudder. Whither have they brought me? where am I?"

"You are with me," said Feodor, carrying her hand to his lips.

For the first time, then, she looked at him—for the first time, she recognized him. A deep blush of joy suffused her cheeks, and an angelic smile beamed on her lips. She felt, she knew nothing further than that her lover was at her side, that he was not dead—that he was not lost to her. With an outcry of delight she threw herself into his arms, and greeted the lost, the found one, with warm and happy words of love. She raised her eyes and hands to heaven. "Oh, my God, he lives!" cried she, exultingly. "I thank Thee, God, I thank Thee. Thou hadst pity on my sufferings."

"Love protected me," said Feodor, gazing at her passionately. "Love saved me by a miracle. Still more miraculously, it brings you to my arms. Fear not, Elise. No other eye than mine has seen you. No one knows your name. That sweet secret, is only known to Love and ourselves."

Elise trembled. This imprudent speech woke her out of the stupor which had so long had possession of her; it recalled her to the world, and dispelled the charm which his presence, his looks, and his words had thrown around her. She was now aroused, and hurried from a state of dreamy delight to one of cruel and dread reality. The ray of joy faded from her cheek, the smile died on her lips, and, extricating herself forcibly from his arms, she stood before him in her pride and anger. "Feodor," said she, terrified, "you sent those fearful men! You caused me to be kidnapped!" With an angry, penetrating glance, she looked at Feodor, who sank his eyes in confusion to the ground.

As she saw this, she smiled contemptuously, and her injured maiden honor overcame her love and tenderness. "Ah! now I understand!" said she, with cutting scorn. "I have been told of the hunt after human beings which is carried on in the town. Colonel Feodor von Brenda plays a worthy part in this game!"

Feodor wished to approach her and take her hand, but she repulsed him sternly. "Do not touch me," cried she, haughtily; "do not seek to take my hand. You are no longer he whom I love. You are a kidnapper. But let me tell you, though you have compelled my body to suffer this dishonorable deed, yet my soul remains free, and that despises you!"

It was a splendid sight to see her in her noble wrath, which seemed to elevate her whole frame, and drive a deep glow to her cheeks.

Feodor looked at her with ardent gaze. Never had he seen her so fascinating, so charmingly beautiful. Even her wrath delighted him, for it was a token of her purity and innocence.

He wanted again to draw near to her, to take her to his heart, but she drew back in pride and anger. "Go," said she, "I have nothing to do with a man who violates the most sacred laws of human honor, and like a vile thief sneaks in to destroy innocence." Her voice failed her, her eyes filled with tears, but she shook them from her. "I weep," said she, "but not for grief, nor yet for love; anger it is alone which extorts tears from me, and they are bitter—far more bitter than death." And as she thus spoke, she pressed her hands to her face, and wept bitterly.

Feodor passed his arm gently around her trembling form. In the excess of her grief she did not feel it. "No, Elise," said he, "you weep because you love me. You weep because you think me unworthy of your love. But before you condemn me, listen to me. I swear to you by the memory of my mother, the only woman in whom, besides yourself, I ever believed, that I had no part in this treachery which has been committed toward you. You must believe me, Elise! Look at me, beloved one—I can bear your looks. I dare raise my eyes to you. I am not guilty of this crime."

Her hands glided slowly from her face, and she looked at him. Their looks met, and rested for a long time on each other. She read in his eyes that he was innocent, for love is confiding, and she loved him. With a charming smile she extended both hands toward him, and he read in her looks the words of love and tenderness which her timid lips did not dare give expression to.

Feodor drew her warmly to his heart. "You believe me," cried he, passionately; and as he raised her with irresistible strength in his arms, he murmured low, "Now let us enjoy the sacred hour of happiness without inquiring what divinity we have to thank for it."

But the instinct of modesty prevailed over love. "No," cried she, as she struggled out of his arms, trembling with excitement—"no, Feodor, it is no hour of happiness in which my honor and good name are to be buried—no hour of happiness when scandal can tell from mouth to mouth how a German maiden let herself be carried into the Russian camp, and shamelessly rushed into the arms of dishonor; for so will they tell it, Feodor. No one will believe that you had no hand in this outrage. The world never believes in innocence. Whoever is accused is already condemned, even if the judge's sentence should a thousand times pronounce him innocent, No, they will point at me with the finger of scorn, and with an exultant laugh will say to each other, 'Behold the barefaced woman who deserted to the Russians, and revelled with her lover, while her native town was groaning amidst blood and tears. Look at the rich man's child, who is so poor in honor!'"

Deeply moved by her own words, she drew herself up still more in the power of her dignity and innocence, and gazed at Feodor with flashing eyes. "Count Feodor von Brenda," cried she, firmly, "will you allow your bride to be suspected and defamed? that a stain should be allowed to rest upon the name of her who is to become your wife?"

In her proud excitement she did not perceive the rapid motion of his lips, nor the blush of shame which suffused his cheeks; she remarked not that he cast down his eyes and spoke to her with broken and trembling voice.

"Elise," said he, "you are beside yourself. Your excited fancy paints every thing to you in sombre colors. Who will dare to defame you? Who knows that you are here?"

"But the whole world will know it. Scandal has a thousand tongues to spread evil reports. Feodor, let me go. You say that no one knows that I am here; then no one will know that I go. Be merciful with me, let me go!"

"No," cried he, almost rudely. "I will not let you. You ask what is impossible. I were a fool if I were thus madly to cast the happiness away which I would fain purchase with my heart's blood. Twice have I risked my life to see you, to be able to kneel for one happy, undisturbed hour at your feet, and gaze on you, and intoxicate myself with that gaze. And now you ask that I shall voluntarily give up my happiness and you!"

"My happiness! my happiness! yes, even my life I ask you to preserve by letting me go hence, and return to my father's house," cried Elise, eagerly.

As she perceived that he shook his head in refusal, and met his wild, passionate looks, reading in them that she might expect no mercy from him, her anger flashed forth. Imploringly she raised her arms to heaven, and her voice sounded full and powerful: "Feodor, I swear to you by God in heaven, and the memory of my mother, that I will only become the wife of that man whom I follow of my free will out of the house of my father. I am capable of leaving my father's house; but it must be my own free choice, my free determination."

"No," said Feodor, wildly; "I will not let you go. You are mine, and you shall remain."

Elise drew nearer to him with bashful tenderness. "You must let me go now, in order one of these days to demand your pure wife from out her father's house," said she. There was something so touching, so confiding in her manner that Feodor, against his will, felt himself overcome by it; but even while submitting to this fascination he was almost ashamed of himself, and deep sadness filled his soul.

139

Silently they stood opposite to each other, Elise looking at him with tenderness, yet with fear—he his head bowed, wrestling with his own heart. Suddenly this silence was interrupted by a loud and violent knocking at the door. The voices of his wild companions and mad comrades were calling out loudly Feodor's name, and demanding, with vehement impetuosity, the opening of the closed door. Feodor turned pale. The thought that his Elise, this young, innocent, and modest girl, should be exposed to the insolent gaze of his riotous companions, irritated him.

Casting his angry glances around the room to seek for a hiding-place in which to conceal Elise, he perceived that this was in vain, that no escape was possible. Sadly he sank his head upon his breast, and sighed. Elise understood him; she comprehended her disconsolate and Desperate position.

"There is then no place where I can hide myself?" said she in despair. "Shame awaits me. The whole world will know that I am here!"

Outside the officers raged still louder, and demanded with more violent cries the opening of the door. Feodor still looked around him for a secret place. Nowhere was there a possibility of hiding her, or letting her escape unnoticed. His infuriated companions threatened to break the door in.

Feodor now with determination seized the large shawl which had previously enveloped Elise's form, and threw it over her face. "Well then," said he, "let them come; but woe to him who touches this cloth!"

He pressed the veiled maiden down in a chair, and, hastening to the door, drew back the bolt.

* * * * *

140

CHAPTER IX.

MISTRESS OR MAID.

As Feodor opened the door, his comrades rushed screaming and laughing uproariously into the room, spying round eagerly for the poor woman, the noble game which they had hunted down.

When they perceived Elise seated in a chair, veiled and motionless just as they had left her, they gave vent to a cry of delight, and began to explain to the colonel in a most confused jumble, often interrupted by bursts of laughter and merry ejaculations, the cause of their stormy interruption. A young man, they said, had just come inquiring after a young lady who had been carried off by the Cossacks. He had insisted upon seeing Colonel Feodor von Brenda, in order to offer a ransom for the captive lady.

"We have come to inform you of this," said Lieutenant von Matusch, "so that you may not let her go too cheap. This is the richest haul we have made yet."

"The daughter of the rich Gotzkowsky!" cried another officer.

"She'll have to pay a tremendous ransom," shouted Major von Fritsch.

Feodor exclaimed, with assumed astonishment, "That woman there the daughter of Gotzkowsky! Why, don't you know, my friends, that I lived for a long time in Berlin, and am intimately acquainted with the beautiful and brilliant daughter of the rich Gotzkowsky? I can assure you that they do not resemble each other in a single feature."

The officers looked at one another with amazement and incredulity. "She is not Gotzkowsky's daughter? But the young man told us that he came from Mr. Gotzkowsky."

"And from that you draw the conclusion that this is his daughter whom you have caught," cried Feodor, laughing. "Where is this man?"

Lieutenant von Matusch opened the door, and on the threshold appeared the serious figure of Bertram. He had fulfilled the vow which he had made to himself, and carefully and attentively watched and guarded every step of Elise; and while Gotzkowsky was absent from home night and day faithfully serving his country, Bertram had been a vigilant sentinel over his daughter. Indeed, Gotzkowsky's house had been, to all appearance, perfectly safe; it was the sanctuary and refuge of all the unfortunate, the only secure place where they could bestow their valuables. Russian sentinels stood before the house, and Tottleben's adjutant had his residence in it. But this security only applied to the *house*. As long as Elise kept herself within-doors, Bertram had no fear. But there was the large garden in which she loved to roam for hours together, and especially her favorite resort at the extreme end of the same, not far from the wall, which was so easy to climb.

Bertram had not ventured to restrain Elise from visiting this solitary and secluded spot, but he had followed her on her visits to it. There, hidden behind some tree he had, with the patience and perseverance of which love alone is capable, watched the young girl, who was neither desirous of nor grateful for guardianship. This very day he had followed her softly and unperceived into the garden. Then, when he had ascertained whither she directed her steps, he had returned into the house to complete some important business of Gotzkowsky. But impelled by anxious and unaccountable restlessness, he had hastened back into the garden; at a distance he heard Elise's cry for help, and, rushing forward, had come up just in time to see her raised over the wall by the Cossacks.

Stunned by horror at this sight, Bertram stood for a moment motionless. He then felt but one desire, one resolve, and that was—to rescue her. He hurried to the house for the purpose of proceeding to General Tottleben and invoking his assistance and support. But a sudden and painful thought arrested his steps.

Suppose that Elise had not gone against her will? Suppose that this had been a preconcerted abduction to which the semblance of violence had only been given in order, in case of failure, to maintain Elise's reputation free from stain?

With a sigh of anguish he recalled to mind when Elise had hidden her lover in her bedchamber that night when Gotzkowsky had delivered Feodor over to the Austrians. Since then father and daughter had not met, and no word of reproach had passed Elise's lips. But Bertram understood that Gotzkowsky's cruel and relentless sacrifice of her lover had forever estranged the heart of his daughter from him; that this hard though just deed had torn asunder the last link which bound her to him.

Elise could have learned just as well as Bertram had that Feodor had been accidentally saved. Her lover himself could have sent her this information, and she, who in the bitterness of her grief had torn herself loose from her father, might not have had the strength to withstand his ardent prayers. Perhaps in her sense of bereavement, trusting to her love, she might have found the sad courage to brave not only her father, but the judgment and scorn of the world, in order to be united to her lover.

Such thoughts as these arrested Bertram's steps, and compelled him to reflection. Only one thing was positive—he must save her at every hazard, even against her will, even if he should reap, as the sole reward of his devoted love, her aversion; he must save her from her own passionate, foolish heart, or from the wild lust of the unprincipled man to whom she trusted her innocence, her youth, and beauty.

But this duty he had to perform alone; he dared not trust any one with his secret, for fear of thereby defeating the object he had in view, and, instead of saving, bringing disgrace upon her. His resolve was formed. He must seek her out. He must penetrate to where she was, even if hid behind a wall of Russian soldiers. Faithful and unselfish as ever, she should find him at her side, ready to protect her against every attack, every danger, even from her own inexperience or the reckless passion of her lover. Especially above all things, her abduction must remain a secret. To her maidens, therefore, Bertram said, that their young mistress had withdrawn into her room, and shut herself in, in order, after so many sleepless nights, to enjoy a little rest. The same information he left behind for Gotzkowsky, and, providing himself with weapons, he betook himself to the search for Elise. In the first place, he naturally directed his steps to the dwelling of Colonel von Brenda. Here he learned that the latter was not at home, but had gone to an entertainment at the mess-room of his regiment. Thither he hastened, firmly resolved to overcome all obstacles, and in spite of every refusal to see the colonel, and read in his countenance whether he were an accomplice of the crime committed, or whether Elise had followed him of her own free will.

At first, he had been obstinately refused admittance; then in his despair and anguish he had made use of Gotzkowsky's name, a golden key to open the doors, as he well knew. In fact, scarcely had the gold-greedy Russian officers ascertained that the young stranger came as a messenger from Gotzkowsky and wished to inquire of Count von Brenda, after a young lady who had been carried off by the Cossacks, than with a yell of delight they rushed toward the door of the room in which were Feodor and the captured maiden. Bertram had, therefore, to thank the avarice of the Russian officers that the door was opened and he was allowed to enter.

As Bertram appeared on the threshold of the room a scream escaped the lips of the female, and he was enabled, notwithstanding the concealment, to recognize her whom he sought. His heart was convulsed with pain, and his impulse for a moment was, to rush upon this audacious, dissolute young man who stood next to Elise, to murder him, and revenge in his blood the disgrace he had brought upon her. But remembering the sacred duty he had undertaken of protecting Elise and concealing her flight as far as possible, he controlled his anger and grief, and forced himself to appear calm and collected.

Elise, in the mean while, with joyful emotion recognized Bertram. His unexpected and unlooked-for appearance did not surprise her, it seemed so natural to her that whenever danger threatened he should appear as her protector and savior. She had such confidence in Bertram's appearance whenever she stood in need of him, that when she saw him, she looked upon herself as saved, and protected from every danger which threatened her. She motioned Feodor to her side, and with a touch of triumphant pride, said to him, "It is Bertram, the friend of my youth. He has risked his life to save me from dishonor." Feodor felt the reproof which lay in the intonation of these words, and his brow grew dark. But he overcame this momentary irritation, and turning to Bertram, who was approaching him with a firm and determined step, asked him, "Well, sir, whom do you seek?"

"A young girl who has been carried off by force," replied Bertram, and he regarded the young man with angry looks. But Feodor met his glance with firmness and composure. "It is true," said he, "such an outrage has been committed; some Cossacks kidnapped a young girl in a garden and brought her here. I myself will inform the general of this dishonorable deed, for you understand, sir, that this outrage is an insult to us as well as to yourself. I have promised my protection to this young person, and I am ready to defend her against any one who dares to touch her honor or to doubt her virtue. Come, now, sir, and see whether this he the same young girl whom you seek."

He stepped toward Bertram, and as he led him to Elise, he whispered rapidly in a low tone. "Be silent, and do not betray her name, for Elise's honor is at stake."

He raised the veil, and, pointing to Elise's abashed and blushing countenance, he asked, with a derisive laugh, "Well, now, do you recognize her? Will you swear that this is Gotzkowsky's daughter?"

Bertram looked at him with assumed surprise. "Gotzkowsky's daughter?" asked he, shrugging his shoulders. "Why, it is the young lady herself who sent me, and no one is looking for her."

Colonel Feodor turned with a laugh of triumph toward his comrades. "Did I not tell you so?" cried he. "You credulous fools were hoping to get half a million ransom, and I have been bargaining with her for the last hour for a hundred dollars. She swears, with tears in her eyes, that she is not worth a hundred pence. Gotzkowsky's daughter, indeed! Do you imagine that she goes about in a plain white dress, without any ornament or any thing elegant about her? She is just as fond of dress as our own princesses and pretty women, and, like them, the daughter of the rich Gotzkowsky is never visible except in silk and velvet, with pearls diamonds. Oh! I would like myself to catch the millionnaire's daughter, for then we might bargain for a decent ransom."

"But who, then, is this woman?" roared the disappointed officers. "Why does the rich Gotzkowsky send after her, if she is not his daughter?"

"Who is she?" cried Feodor, laughing. "Well, I will tell you, as you attack so much importance to it. You have been served like the seekers after hidden treasure. You have been seeking for gold, and, instead, you have only found coals to burn your fingers. You sought after the millionnaire, the rich heiress, and, instead of her, you have only caught her—chambermaid."

"A chambermaid!" growled out his comrades, and turning their dark, lowering looks on Bertram, they inquired of him whether this woman were only a chambermaid in Gotzkowsky's house, and assailed him with reproaches and curses because he had deluded them into the belief that Gotzkowsky's daughter had been captured.

"If we had not thought so, we would not have let you in," cried Lieutenant von Matusch. "It was not worth while making so much fuss about a little chambermaid."

"It was just for that very reason," replied Bertram, "and because I knew that you would not otherwise help me, that I let you believe it was Gotzkowsky's daughter whom you had captured; otherwise you would never have let me come near Colonel von Brenda. And Mademoiselle Gotzkowsky had expressly directed me to apply to that gentleman, and I did so. You can understand my doing so, when I inform you that this young girl is my sister!"

Feodor turned himself to Elise with an expression of anger on his countenance. "Is this true?"

"It is true!" cried she, reaching her hand out to Bertram, with a look of heartfelt gratitude. "He is my brother, my faithful brother!"

But, as she read in Feeder's darkened countenance the marks of ill-concealed anger and jealousy, she turned toward her lover with a rare, sweet smile. "Oh," said she, "there is nothing nobler, nothing more sacred and unselfish, than the love of a brother."

Feodor's searching look seemed to penetrate into the inmost recesses of her heart. Perhaps he read all the love, innocence, and strength that lay therein, for his brow cleared up, and his looks resumed their open cheerfulness. Quickly he took Bertram's hand and laid it in Elise's. "Well, then," said he, "you happy pair, take each other's hands, and thank God that the danger is over. We have nothing to do with young and pretty girls—we only want rich ones. Go!"

"No, no," cried the officers, "not at all, not without ransom!" Saying which, they pressed noisily and angrily nearer, raising their clinched fists. "She must pay, or we will keep her!"

"Dare one of you touch her?" cried Feodor, drawing his sword, and placing himself in front of Elise.

"I have come to fetch my sister," said Bertram, turning to the officers, "but I knew very well that you would not let her go unless her ransom were paid. I therefore brought all my little portion with me. Take this purse full of ducats, and let it pay for her."

A cry of triumph was the answer from the soldiers as they drew Bertram toward the table that he might count out the money. While they were dividing it among themselves, talking loudly and laughing merrily, Feodor remained standing at Elise's side, neither daring to break the impressive silence. Their souls communed with each other, and they needed not words nor outward signs. At last, after a long pause, Feodor asked—

"Are you satisfied now, Elise?"

145

She answered him with a sweet smile, "I am thine forever!"

"And will you never forget this hour?"

"I will not forget it. I will remember that I have sworn to follow you voluntarily from my father's house, even against his will." And letting her blushing face droop upon her breast, she whispered, in a voice scarcely audible—"I await you!"

But these words, low as they had been spoken, reached the ears of two men at the same time. Not only Colonel Feodor, but also Bertram, who had drawn close up to Elise again, had overheard them. The first they filled with emotions of delight, the other with painful anguish. Bertram, however, was accustomed to wrestle with his love, and smother the expression of his pain, under the appearance of quiet composure. He approached Elise, and offered her his hand, said, "Come sister, let us go."

"Yes, go," said the colonel, with the proud superiority of a preferred rival. He extended his hand to Bertram, and continued, "Be a good brother to her, and conduct her safely home."

Bertram's countenance, usually so quiet and calm, assumed for an instant an offended and almost contemptuous air, and bitter words were on his tongue; but his angry eye accidentally met Elise's, anxiously and imploringly directed toward him. He could not master himself sufficiently to accept Feodor's hand, but at least he could control his anger. "Come, sister," said he, gently leading Elise toward the door which the colonel indicated to him by a silent nod.

Elise had not the courage to leave her lover without a word of farewell; or rather, she was cruel enough to inflict this torture on Bertram. Stretching both hands toward him, she said softly, "I thank you, Feodor; God and love will reward you for having greatly and nobly conquered yourself."

Feodor whispered to her, "And will you remember your vow?"

"Ever and always!"

In bending over to kiss her hand, he murmured, "Expect me, then, to-morrow."

"I will expect you," said she, as she passed him on her way to the door.

No word of their whispered conversation escaped the attentive ear of Bertram; and he understood it, for he loved her, and knew how to read her thoughts in her looks and her eyes. As he followed her through the long corridor, and her light, graceful figure floated before him like a vision, a deep, despairing melancholy settled on his heart, and he murmured to himself, "To-morrow she expects him!" But with

146

desperate determination he continued to himself, "Well, then, woe to him if I find him going astray!"

* * * * *

CHAPTER X.

AN UNEXPECTED ALLY.

Thanks to Bertram's forethought and caution, he had succeeded in restoring Elise to her father's house, without her absence having been remarked, or having occasioned any surmise. In the close carriage in which they performed the journey home, they had not exchanged a word; but leaning hack on the cushions, each had rest and repose after the stormy and exciting scenes they had just passed through. Elise's hand still rested on Bertram's, perhaps unconsciously, perhaps because she had not the courage to withdraw it from him to whom she owed so much gratitude.

Bertram felt the feverish warmth of this trembling hand, and as he looked at her and remarked the paleness of her cheeks, the painful twitching of her lips, he was overcome by a feeling of deep wretchedness, of pitying sadness, and was obliged to turn his head away to conceal his tears from her.

When the carriage stopped, and he accompanied her into the house, Elise pressed his hand more firmly, and turned her gaze upon him with a look of deep gratitude, which made his heart palpitate with a mixture of delight and anguish. He wished to withdraw, he wished to let her hand go, but she held his still more firmly clasped, and drew him gently up the steps. Powerless with emotion, he followed her.

As they entered the hall which led to her room, she cast a searching look around to see if any one were present, and perceiving that they two were alone, she turned toward Bertram with an indescribable expression. She tried to speak, but the words died on her lips, a deep glow suffused her cheeks, and completely overpowered, and giddy from the tumult of her feelings, she leaned her head on her friend's shoulder.

Gently he passed his arm around her delicate, trembling figure, and his eyes beamed with a pure emotion. In the depth of his heart he renewed to God and himself his vow of fidelity and self-sacrificing love to this poor girl who lay on his bosom like a drooping flower.

Suddenly she raised her head, her face wet with tears and convulsed with deep feeling. "Bertram," she said, "I know that I am not worthy of your noble, generous love, but yet, in my crushed heart, I thank God that I possess it. A time may come when all the thoughts and feelings which now fill my soul will appear as vain dreams and illusions. It may be that some day I will look upon life as a grand delusion, a fruitless striving after happiness and repose. But never, my brother, never will that time come when I can doubt your faithful, pure affection. No power, no other feeling, will ever succeed in supplanting the deep and boundless gratitude which pervades my whole soul and binds me to you forever."

And then it seemed to him as if he felt the breath of an angel wave over his face; as if the dream and desire of his whole life had closed his lips in unexpected bliss; as if the wishes and hopes of his ardent but resigned heart had been fulfilled, and become a delightful reality.

When he recovered from this sweet dream, which for a moment robbed him of his consciousness, Elise had disappeared. But her kiss still glowed on his lips, and seemed to bless and sanctify his whole life.

This stream of happiness lasted but for a short time, and Bertram soon awoke, with a sad sigh, from his delightful fancies, to recall the painful hours he had just gone through, and to say to himself that Elise was lost to him forever, that he never could hope to rescue that heart from the lover to whom she had yielded it with all the devotion of her ardent nature. With a sorrowing heart did he remember the last words of the lovers. She had appointed a meeting for him on the morrow, she expected him, and, braving the anger of her father, had giving him a rendezvous in his house.

As Bertram thought over this, he paced the room up and down, panting with excitement, and wringing his hands. "If Gotzkowsky knew this, he would kill her, or die himself of grief. Die of grief!" continued he, after a pause, completely buried in his sad and bitter thoughts—"it is not so easy to die of grief. The sad heart is tenacious of life, and sorrow is but a slow grave-digger. I have heard that one could die of joy, and it seemed to me just now, when Elise rewarded me with a kiss, that I could understand this. If she only loved me, it were a blessing of God to die, conscious of her love."

Completely overcome by his painful thoughts, he remained for a while motionless and sad. But he soon recovered himself, and shook off the dark cloud which overshadowed his soul. "I am not born to die such a death. It is my destiny not to be happy myself, but to save others from unhappiness. I feel and know that Elise cannot be happy in this love. A loving heart is gifted with prophetic second sight to read the future. Elise can never be happy without her father's blessing, and Gotzkowsky will never give his sanction to this love. How can I lead her past this abyss which threatens to engulf her? May God, who sees my heart, help me! He knows how hopeless and disinterested it is. Help me, Father in heaven! show me some way of saving her noble father from the grief which lies before him."

It seemed as if God had heard his prayer, and taken compassion on his pure, unselfish spirit, and sent him assistance. A loud knocking at the door aroused him suddenly from his gloomy thoughts, and he hastened to open it.

A veiled lady stood there, wrapped in furs, and attended by a servant in rich livery. In fluent French, which it could be perceived, however, was not her native tongue, she inquired whether, as she had been told, Herr von Brink, Tottleben's adjutant, resided there. As Bertram answered this question in the affirmative, but added, that Herr von Brink was in the habit of not returning from the general's quarters before evening, she added, in a decided tone, "Well, then, I will wait for him."

Without deeming Bertram's consent necessary, she entered the hall and motioned to her servant to remain at the door.

After a pause, there ensued between the two one of those superficial, ceremonious conversations, the usual refuge of those who have nothing to say to each other; but the evident uneasiness and confusion of the young lady prevented her from joining freely in it. Her large, bright eyes strayed restlessly around the room. A hectic flush alternated on her cheeks with deathly pallor, and the smile, which occasionally played around her lips, seemed but a painful expression of mental suffering. Suddenly she raised her head, as if determined no longer to bear this constraint, or submit to the fetters of conventionality.

"Sir," said she, in a tone vibrating with excitement and anxiety, "you will excuse my asking you a question, on the answer to which depends my future happiness, my life, indeed—to obtain which I have travelled from St. Petersburg here. I have just left my carriage in which I performed the journey from that city. You can therefore judge how important the cause of this undertaking is to me, and what an influence it may have on my whole existence. Its object lies in the question I am about to put to you."

Bertram took pity on her painful agitation. "Ask" he said, "and, on the honor of a gentleman, I assure you that your question shall be answered truly, and that I am ready to serve you as far as it lies in my power."

"Are you acquainted with General Bachmann's adjutant?" asked she, shortly and hurriedly.

"I am," replied Bertram.

She trembled as in an ague. "I am come to inquire after a man of whom I have not heard for six months. I wish to know whether he is alive, or only dead to me."

"His name?" asked Bertram, with painful misgiving.

Her voice was scarcely audible as she replied: "Colonel Count Feodor von Brenda, of the regiment Bachmann."

Bertram was quite taken aback by this unexpected turn of the conversation, and she continued with great excitement, "You do not answer! oh, have compassion on me, and speak! Is he alive?"

"He is alive, and is here," answered Bertram sadly.

A cry of delight escaped the lips of the lady. "He lives," she exclaimed loudly. "God has then heard my prayer, and preserved him to me."

150

But suddenly the cheerful smile on her lips died away, and, dropping her head on her breast, she cried, "He is alive, and only dead to me. He is alive, and did not write me!" For a moment she stood in this position, silent and depressed; then drawing herself up erect, her eyes sparkling with passionate warmth, she said: "Sir, I crave your pardon for a poor stranger, who hardly knows what she is doing or saying. I am not acquainted with you, or even your name, but there is something in your noble, calm countenance which inspires confidence."

Bertram smiled sadly. "Fellow-sufferers always feel attracted to each other by a community of feeling. I, too am a sufferer, and it is God's will that our sorrows should spring from a common source. The name you have uttered is but too well known to me."

"You know Colonel Brenda?" she asked.

"I do know him," answered Bertram.

"The count was at one time a prisoner of war," continued the lady. "He visited this house frequently, for I have been told that it belongs to Mr. Gotzkowsky, of whom the colonel wrote me, in the commencement of his captivity, that he received him most hospitably."

"Did he write you any word of Gotzkowsky's handsome daughter?" asked Bertram, looking inquiringly into the countenance of the stranger.

She shuddered, and turned pale. "O Heaven!" she murmured low, "I have betrayed myself!"

Bertram seized her hand, his features evincing deep emotion. "Will you answer me one question?" he asked, and as she bowed her head in silence, he proceeded—"is the Count von Brenda your brother?"

"Oh, sir," she said, with a faint smile, "one does not suffer for a brother as I have suffered for Feodor. I am the Countess Sandomir, and Count Feodor is my betrothed. The good empress herself joined our hands, and blessed our union. A short time after our marriage the war broke out, and deprived me of my lover and husband. For six months I have had no tidings of him, and, tortured by anxiety and apprehension, I resolved to come myself to Germany to seek my betrothed, either to bury or nurse him, for I believed he must be sick or dead, as he did not return to me."

Bertram offered in his heart a prayer of gratitude to God. With feelings of sympathy, he then turned his eyes on the quivering features of the stranger. "Listen to me," said he, gently. "As you entered, I had just prayed to God, in the suffering and sadness of my heart, to show me some way and means of escape from the labyrinth in which Count Brenda has placed us. It would seem as if He has had compassion on us all, for at the very moment he sends you, the affianced bride of the count, and through you alone can we be saved. We must be open and candid toward each other. Therefore, listen to me. I love Gotzkowsky's daughter—I love her without hope, for she loves another."

"And this other?" asked she breathlessly.

"She loves Count Feodor von Brenda, and is about to escape with him."

"Escape!" cried the lady, and her voice sounded threatening and angry, and her eyes flashed. "Oh!" said she, gnashing her teeth, "I will prevent this, even if I kill this girl!"

Bertram shook his head sadly. "Let us rather try to kill this love in her heart. Let us contrive some means of bringing your lover back to you."

"Are there any such means?" asked she, anxiously.

Bertram did not answer immediately. His brow was clouded with deep thought, and a heavy sigh escaped him. He then asked quickly, "Will you follow me and enter into my plot?"

"I will," she said firmly.

"Above all things, then, let us be cautious. Count Feodor must have no suspicion that you are here, for your presence would drive him to some desperate resolve, and I fear Elise loves him sufficiently not to draw back from any thing."

"You are very cruel," murmured the lady. "You know not what torture you are preparing for me."

"If I did not know it, I would not undertake the enterprise that is to serve us both. I have told you that I love Elise, but I have not told you how deep and sacred this love is. I would cheerfully venture my life for her, but now I dare to interfere with her love, and earn her hatred."

"You have, then, already made your plan?"

"I have made my plan, and if you will allow me to escort you to your hotel, I will disclose it to you, so that we may arrange the particulars together."

"Come, then," said she, grasping his hand warmly, "and may God assist us, and restore to you your bride, and to me my lover!"

* * * * *

152

CHAPTER XI.

THE JEW EPHRAIM.

Much sorrow and tribulation were suffered during this time by the inhabitants of Berlin. But the saddest lot of all fell to the Jews, who were threatened with the greatest danger. In Berlin, as everywhere else, they only led a tolerated, reviled, and derided existence. They possessed no rights, only duties; no honor, only insults; no dignities, but humiliation and disgrace. Now they were called on to give up the last and only thing which shed some gleam of brightness on their poor, down-trodden existence—their gold and their treasures.

The Russian commander had imposed upon the Jewish community in Berlin a special tax; and as they hesitated about paying it, and declared themselves incapable of raising such a large sum, General von Tottleben had the three elders of the Jews arrested and strictly guarded in the Vincenti House in Brueder Street.

But who could despise or blame the poor Jews for not wishing to give up their gold? Gold was to them a condition of existence, their future, their happiness, their family. Gold enabled some of them to raise themselves from the dust and degradation to which the cruel severity of *Christian charity* had condemned them, and to indulge in human aspirations, human happiness, and human feelings. Only those among them who possessed wealth were tolerated, and dared hope by strenuous industry, ceaseless activity, and fortunate speculation, to amass sufficient fortune to found a family or beget children. The happiness of domestic life was only allowed to them on condition of their being rich.

Frederick the Great had learned with indignation that the Jewish families in Berlin far exceeded the number of one hundred and fifty-two allowed by law, and that there were fifty-one too many. Consequently a stringent decree was issued that they should no longer be counted by families, but by heads, and that when the poll exceeded the permitted number, the poorest and lowest of them should be shipped off.[1] Gold was therefore to the rich Jew a certificate of naturalization, while the poorer ones had no certainty of a home. They could at any moment be turned off, driven out of Berlin, if a richer one should by his wealth and trading acquire the right to take to himself a wife, and by her have a child. But even he, the rich one, could only have one child; only one child was allowed to him by law. For one child only could he obtain legal protection, and only in exceptional cases, as when their factories and firms succeeded remarkably well, did the king, in the fulness of his grace, allow a second child to inherit its guardianship.[2]

Of what avail, then, was it to the poor Jews to have toiled and worked so hard, driven by the necessity of paying the hateful *Jewish poll-tax,* and thereby procuring for themselves a temporary toleration? At any moment they could be driven off in case the rich Ephraim or the rich David Itzig, in the arrogance of their wealth, should venture to give to the world more than one child, and purchase for the sum of three thousand dollars another certificate of protection for the second! Of what avail was their wealth even to the rich Jews Ephraim and Itzig? They were nevertheless under the ban of their proscribed race. No privileges, no offices existed for them. They could only build factories or carry on commerce. All other paths of life, even agriculture and horticulture, were forbidden to them. And now they were called on to give up to the Russians their very life, the nerve of their existence, the heart which carried blood and warmth to their entire organization—their money.

Ephraim and Itzig were rich and powerful in Berlin; they could build houses, found factories, and even determine the value of money, for the mint was in their hands. They had farmed it from the king, and paid him an enormous rent for the same, which had increased each year, and in 1760 amounted to seven millions. But, thanks to this farming, the value of money had increased exorbitantly. Twenty dollars were paid for a Frederick d'or, and five-and-thirty for the mark of fine silver. Owing to the labors of these Jewish lessees, there were many millions of light money, many millions of bad eight-groschen pieces, which, to this day, are known by the name of *Ephraimites*, and whose repudiation at a later period ruined many thousands of honest, worthy tradesmen, while Ephraim and Itzig became wealthy and powerful thereby. Yet it was now this same money which brought misfortune to them, and was the cause of their suffering and mortal anxiety; for General Tottleben had threatened that if the Jews could not pay the tax imposed on them, he would take the mint farmers with him as hostages, and destroy their factories. Besides this, he had, as we said before, arrested their elders and sworn to send them to Siberia, if the Jews did not pay.

The payment was to be made in three days. But the three days had elapsed, and they had not been able to raise the money which was demanded of them. In this dire extremity, the two mint-contractors remembered the man whom they had hitherto most cordially hated, and whose ruin was the cherished wish of their life. They now recollected that John Gotzkowsky was the only man who, in the generosity and kindness of his heart, was capable of forgetting their former insults and injuries, and of remembering only their need and misery. They determined, therefore, to apply to him, and request his intercession and assistance, but they did this with a bitter sigh, for they felt the hatred and grudge which they nursed in their hearts toward him become only more intense and stronger.

"Who would have thought it?" said Ephraim, as, by the side of Itzig, and accompanied by some of the most wealthy Jewish merchants, he took the road to Gotzkowsky's dwelling—"who would have thought it? The powerful Russian General von Tottleben is the friend of Gotzkowsky, and the greatest men among our people are now obliged to go to Gotzkowsky's house to implore his influence and protection."

"Yes," sighed the rich merchant David, "we are obliged to apply to him to befriend us, and yet what is he compared to you? You are much richer than he is."

"Silence, unfortunate man!" cried Ephraim with a shudder, as he looked shyly around. "I am poor, and for that reason can pay nothing. I am poor, as all of us wretched Jews are. Have we not to contribute the greater portion of the war-tax? Are not all our means exhausted? Is that not enough?"

"Too much!" groaned Itzig, who till now had walked in melancholy contemplation at Ephraim's other side. "It is too much. Are we then treated like human beings? Have we any rights? Only when we have to pay, do they remember that we have the right of giving up our hard-earned property. If the Jew has no money, is he not at least a man, say I?"

"Pshaw! a man!" cried Ephraim. "Whoever is without money is no man, be he Jew or Christian. If Gotzkowsky had no money, he would be no better than we are. Why does the Russian general have any thing to do with him? Because he is rich. Why do the counts and lords pay court to him? For the same reason. Why do they call his daughter an angel, and swear she is the handsomest woman in Berlin? Because her father is the richest Christian merchant in the town. The whole world knows and admires him. And why? Because he is rich."

"No one is rich," said Itzig, shaking his head. "He who has not every thing is not rich. There is no such thing as riches, for he who has much has to give much."

"God knows we will have to give much!" whimpered Ephraim, and all his companions joined in with groans and sighs as a chorus to his speech. "They mean to take every thing from us that we own, and Itzig is right; if the Jew has not money, he is nobody. Have we not suffered as much as others? Have we not protected our people, and fed and housed our poor? No one talks about these things, but the whole town talks about Gotzkowsky. They praise him, they exalt him; they cry out his name everywhere, so that one's heart actually burns for vexation. And yet at the highest calculation he is not worth more than a million."

"He is worth more than ourselves; he is worth much more, for he has the favor of the Russian general. For this reason we must bow down before him, and flatter him, and assure him of our eternal gratitude, for it is a question not of life, but what is more precious than life—money."

With deep-drawn sighs they whined out, "Yes, we must bow to him, and flatter him, and yet we are richer than he is."

As long as they were on the street they maintained an air of pride and vexation; but as soon as they entered Gotzkowsky's house and stood in his presence, they were all gentleness, humility, and friendliness. With tears they implored Gotzkowsky to have pity, and to beg General Tottleben to have compassion on them. They vowed eternal gratitude to him, and swore with solemn oaths that if he succeeded in relieving the Jews from the special impost, they would love him forever, and be everlastingly thankful to him.

Gotzkowsky smiled in pity. "That means that you would feel yourselves under obligations to me, and, if ever you got me in your power, you would take the opportunity to ruin me. But that is of no consequence to me. This impost is a crying injustice, and therefore will I plead for you, for it never shall be said that Gotzkowsky suffered an injustice to be done when he could prevent it. Go home in peace, for, if I can, I will help you."

"How arrogant this man is!" said Itzig, when they had left the house. "One would suppose that he had all virtue and honor on lease, just as we have the mint."

"And if he has," said Ephraim with a laugh, "if he has the monopoly of virtue and honor, it is only to trade on. No doubt his speculation will turn out just as profitably as ours with the mint. No doubt he will coin it into light eight-groschen pieces, cheat the people with them, and make more than his expenses, as we have done."

"But woe be unto him," growled Itzig, "if any light coin of his virtue come into my hands! I will throw them back into his face till blood flows, and I will never forgive him that this day we have had to stand before him begging and pleading. If he ever comes to grief, I will remember it. If the Jew has no money, he is nobody. Well, we will see what Gotzkowsky is worth without money. Let me tell you we will all of us live to see that day. He has too much stupid generosity, which some day or other will run away with his purse, and then there will be a grand blow-up, honor and virtue and all, sky high. Then there will be no more talk about the great Gotzkowsky and his virtue and all that. Oh! I do so rejoice over that time a-coming. But in the mean time I am so very glad that Gotzkowsky can be of some service to us!"

[Footnote 1: Buesching's Travels, 1780.]

[Footnote 2: "Annals of the Jews in the Prussian States," Berlin.—UNGER.]

* * * * *

156

CHAPTER XII.

THE RUSSIAN GENERAL AND THE GERMAN MAN.

Scarcely had the Jewish deputation left Gotzkowsky's house, before he betook himself, full of the important information received from General Bachmann, to General Tottleben's residence, fully determined to venture every thing to prevent the execution of the cruel order which threatened the factories and other branches of industry. But this was not the sole object which led him there. He went there as a representative of the whole town. Every one who needed assistance applied to him, and to each one he had promised to intercede for him. Laden with petitions and commissions from the magistracy, the merchants, and the citizens of Berlin, he entered the Russian general's quarters. Deeply inspired with the importance of his commission, he traversed the halls which led to the general's private apartments, saying to himself, "This is the most important mission I have ever undertaken, for the welfare of the whole town depends upon it—a million dollars depend upon every word I may utter. Many a struggle have I had in these days, but this is the hardest of them all, and victory hangs on my tongue."

With beaming countenance and sparkling eyes, with his whole being animated with the sacredness of his office, he entered the cabinet of the Russian general. Tottleben did not offer him, as heretofore, a friendly welcome. He did not even raise his eyes from the dispatches which he was in the act of reading, and his contracted brows and the whole expression of his countenance was such as to discourage any petition or pleading. At this moment General von Tottleben was a true Russian, and, thanks to General Fermore's dispatches, he had succeeded in suppressing his German sympathy. At least he flattered himself that he had, and for that reason he avoided meeting Gotzkowsky's clear, bright eye.

Without taking any notice, he finished reading the papers, and then rose and walked about the room. After a while he seemed as if by accident to perceive Gotzkowsky's presence, and stopped short. "Have you come back already?" he asked in a sullen, grumbling tone. "I know very well that you have returned to beg for all sorts of useless trash; I can't bear such eternal begging and whining—a pitiful rabble that is all the time creeping to our feet."

"Yes, your excellency, it is nothing but a poor, pitiful rabble," said Gotzkowsky with a smile; "and for this very reason the Russians are despised all over Europe. Toward the high and mighty they behave like fawning hounds, and toward the low and humble they are rude and arrogant."

"I am not speaking of the Russians," cried the general, as he turned his lowering countenance toward Gotzkowsky, "I am speaking of *you*. All day long you have done nothing but beg and demand."

But Gotzkowsky met him with quiet and smiling composure. "Pardon, your excellency, it is you who demand; and because you are all the time demanding, I must all the time be begging. And, in fact, I am only begging for yourself."

Tottleben looked at him in inquiring astonishment, but in silence. "I am not begging for favor," continued Gotzkowsky, "but for justice; and if you grant this, why, it is so much gained for you. Then, indeed, the world will esteem you as not only brave, but just; and then only will history honor you as truly great—the equitable and humane conqueror. The Vandals, too conquered by the sword; and if it only depended on mere brute strength, wild bulls would be the greatest generals."

Tottleben cast a fierce, angry look toward him "For that reason," cried he, threateningly, "he is a fool who irritates a wild bull."

Gotzkowsky bowed and smiled. "It is true one should never show him a red cloak. A firm, unterrified countenance is the only way to tame him. The bull is powerless against the mind which beams out of the human eye."

It was very probably the very boldness of this answer which pleased the general, accustomed as he was to Russian servility. His features assumed a softer expression, and he said, in a milder tone: "You are an extraordinary man, and there is no use in contending with you. One is obliged to do whatever you wish. Well, now—quick, out with it—what do you want of me?"

"Justice," said Gotzkowsky. "You gave me your word that your soldiers should not rob nor plunder, and, notwithstanding, they do it."

"That is not true!" thundered the general.

"It is true," replied Gotzkowsky, calmly.

"Who dares to contradict me?" cried Tottleben, trembling with rage, and striding toward Gotzkowsky.

"I dare," answered the latter, "if you call that 'to dare' which is only convincing you of your error. I, myself, have seen your soldiers striking down the flying women with the butts of their muskets, robbing and plundering the houses. Your orders have been but poorly obeyed; and your soldiers *almost* equal the Austrians in rudeness and violence."

A light smile played over Tottleben's countenance. Gotzkowsky had understood how to soften his anger. "*Almost*—only," said he, "woe be to my soldiers if they equal the Austrians in rudeness!" With hasty steps he traversed the apartment, and called his adjutant. "Send patrols through the whole town," was his order to the officer as he entered, "and give orders to all the soldiers to maintain strict discipline. Whoever dares to plunder, is guilty of disobedience to military orders, and shall be

158

tried by military law. The gallows for thieves and marauders—say so to my men; they know that General Tottleben keeps his word. Are you satisfied now?" he asked Gotzkowsky, as the adjutant left the room.

"I thank your excellency," said Gotzkowsky, hesitating.

"Thank God that at last you are satisfied, and have nothing more to ask!" cried Tottleben, almost cheerfully.

"But indeed I have a great deal yet to ask, and if you allow me I will ask your excellency a question. You have just issued an order. How high up does this order reach?"

"How high up?" asked the general, surprised.

"I mean does this order which forbids the soldiers from robbing and plundering under pain of death, affect only the common private, or must the higher officers also obey it?"

"I would advise every one to do so," cried Tottleben, with a harsh laugh. "The order is for all."

"Even the highest officers?"

"Not even the generals are excepted." "Then, sir," said Gotzkowsky, drawing himself up and advancing a step toward the general, "I accuse before you an officer who has had the presumption to disobey your general order. You forbid, under severe penalty, robbery and plundering, and yet he is intent on them. You have strictly ordered the army to preserve discipline, and not to ill-treat nor abuse the defenceless, and yet a general is about to do it."

"Who dares that? Give me the name of this general!"

"It is General von Tottleben," answered Gotzkowsky, quietly.

Count Tottleben stepped back and gazed at him in amazement.

Gotzkowsky did not lower his eyes, but met his flashing glance firmly. "Are you beside yourself?" asked the general, after a long pause. "Is your life such a burden to you that you are determined to lose it?"

"If my head were to fall, it would only be a confirmation of what I have asserted—- that General von Tottleben issues an order, and does not respect it himself; that while he forbids his soldiers to rob and steal, under penalty of death, even *he* commits those very offences."

The excess of this boldness had the effect upon the general on which Gotzkowsky had calculated. He had speculated somewhat on the leonine nature of Tottleben's character.

The general, instead of annihilating his foolhardy antagonist, found pleasure in his presumption, and it flattered him that he was esteemed too magnanimous to revenge himself for a few words of insult.

"Look here, my friend, you are so outrageously bold that you make me laugh. For the sake of its rarity, I will hear you out, and try to remain cool. Speak on, then. Accuse me—but woe to you if I justify myself! Fail not to prove what you say."

"The proverb says, 'Small thieves are hung, while great ones go free,'" replied Gotzkowsky, shrugging his shoulders. "You wish to prove the truth of this proverb. The soldier who enters the house for theft and plunder, you condemn; but you acquit the general who devastates a whole town, and in the arrogance of his victory wishes to make himself, like Erostratos, immortal by incendiarism and arson."

"Do not presume too much on my forbearance," interrupted Tottleben, stretching his arm out threateningly toward the bold speaker. "Erostratos was a violator of temples."

"You are not less one!" cried Gotzkowsky; "you mean, with impious hand, to cast a firebrand into the holy temple of labor. Erostratos only destroyed the temple of an imaginary deity; but you, sir, are worse—you wish to destroy factories!"

"Do you know what that means?"

"It means to deprive the poor man of the morsel of bread which, by the sweat of his brow, he has earned for his wife and children! It means to rob him who possesses nothing but the craft of his hands and his body, of his only right—the right to work. You are going to destroy the gold and silver manufactories, to burn the warehouse, to tear down the brass works in the New Town Eberswald! And why all this? Why do you intend to leave behind you this memorial of your vandalism? Because your empress is angry with our king!"

"Because enemies wish to revenge themselves on enemies," interrupted the general.

"Do that!" cried Gotzkowsky, warmly. "Revenge yourself on your enemy, if you consider the destruction of his property a noble revenge. Destroy the king's palaces; rob him, if you choose, of his most ennobling enjoyment! Rob him of his pictures; do like the Saxons, who yesterday destroyed Charlottenburg. Send your soldiers to my house; there hang splendid paintings bought by me in Italy by the king's order. I know that our noble king anticipates much pleasure in carrying them some day to Sans Souci. But revenge yourself, take these pictures, set fire to these noble works of art, but spare what belongs to the poor man!"

160

He spoke with noble warmth, with glowing eloquence, and against his will Tottleben's German heart was touched, and moved him to clemency and compassion. But he would not listen to it. General Fermore's dispatches lay before him, and compelled him to be harsh.

"You think you speak wisely, and yet you talk nothing but impudent nonsense," said he, with assumed severity. "Who thinks of destroying the poor man's property? The royal property shall be destroyed, and nothing else."

"But the gold and silver manufactories and the warehouse are not the property of the king," said Gotzkowsky quickly. "Not a penny goes thence into the king's treasury."

The general's countenance brightened up considerably. "Not into the king's treasury?" said he; "where, then, does it go?"

"The money, your excellency, which is earned at the gold and silver factories and at the warehouse is devoted to a praiseworthy and touching purpose. Perhaps you are a father—have children; and when you go into battle you think of them, and utter a silent prayer, intrusting them to God's care, and praying that they may not be left orphans."

Count Tottleben muttered some untelligible words, and stretched out his hand deprecatingly. His lips trembled, and to conceal his agitation he turned away.

Gotzkowsky cried out joyously: "Oh, I see in your eyes that you are vainly trying to compel yourself to look at me in anger. Yes, you are a father. Well, then, father, spare the orphans! From the proceeds of the gold and silver factories, and the warehouse, the new, large orphan-house in Potsdam is supported. Oh, you cannot be so cruel as to deprive the poor children, whom the pitiless war has rendered fatherless, of their last support, of their last refuge!"

The general stepped up to him, and grasped his hand. "God be my witness that I will not! But is this so certainly? Do you speak the truth?"

"Yes, it is the truth!"

"Can you swear to it?"

"Yes, with the most sacred oath."

The general paced the room in silence several times, and then, pausing before Gotzkowsky, laid his hand on his shoulder. "Listen," said he. "I have often been reproached at home for being too soft and pitiful. But never mind! I will once more follow my own inclination, and act in spite of the orders which I have received. You must help me. Put all that you have just stated down on paper. Write down that these buildings are not the property of the king, but of the orphan-house. Swear to it with a sacred oath, and affix your signature and seal. Will you do this?"

"Gladly will I do it," cried Gotzkowsky, his face radiant. "Never have I signed my name with a happier heart than I will have when I sign it to this affidavit, which will procure for us both the heart-felt blessings of so many children."

He stepped to the general's writing-table, and, following his direction, seated himself and wrote.

Tottleben in the mean while walked up and down pensively, his arms folded. His features wore a thoughtful and mild expression. No trace of the late angry storm was visible. Once he stopped, and murmured in a low voice: "Orphans one dare not plunder. Elizabeth has a tender heart, and if she learns the reason of my disobedience, she will be content. Yes, my course is the right one."

"I have finished, sir," said Gotzkowsky, standing up and handing him the paper on which he had written.

Tottleben read it over carefully, and laid it alongside of the dispatches to his empress. He then called to his adjutant and ordered him immediately to place strong safeguards over the gold and silver manufactories and the warehouse, and to protect these against any attack.

Gotzkowsky clasped his hands, and directed his eyes to heaven with joyful gratitude, and in the deep emotion of his heart he did not perceive that the general again stood before him, and was looking at him with inquiring sympathy. His voice first awakened him from his reverie. "Are you contented now?" asked Tottleben, in a friendly tone.

"Content, general," said Gotzkowsky, shaking his head, "only belongs to him who lies in his coffin."

Again the general's brow grew dark. "What is troubling you now? Don't hesitate—"

"To speak on, your excellency?" inquired Gotzkowsky, with a gentle smile.

"No—to put yourself in your coffin," answered the other, rudely.

"I have not time for that, as yet," replied Gotzkowsky, sadly. "Both of us, general, have still too much to do. You have to add fresh laurels to your old ones—I have to clear thistles and thorns from the path of my fellow-men."

162

"Ah! there are more thorns, then?" asked Tottleben, as he sank down into a chair, and regarded Gotzkowsky with evident benevolence.

"A great many yet, sir," answered Gotzkowsky, sighing. "Our whole body is bloody from them."

"Then call on the regimental surgeon to cure you," said Tottleben, with a coarse laugh.

"You only can cure us," said Gotzkowsky, seriously, "for only you are able to inflict such severe wounds. You are not satisfied with having conquered and humiliated us, but you wish to tread us in the dust, and make our cheeks, which were pale with sadness, now redden with shame. You have ordered that the citizens of Berlin should be disarmed. You are a brave soldier, sir, and honor courage above all things. Now, let me ask you, how could you bear to exhibit the certificate of your cowardice? Could you survive it? You look at me in anger—the very question makes you indignant; and if that is your feeling, why would you subject the citizens of Berlin to such disgrace? With our weapons we have fought for our just rights and our liberty. God has willed it that we should be subdued nevertheless, and that you should be the conquerors. But methinks it would redound more to your honor to be the conquerors of honorable men than of cowardly slaves! And when you require of us, the conquered, that we shall give up our manly honor, our weapons, you convert us into abject cowards, and deprive yourselves of all honor in having conquered us. Let us then, sir, keep our weapons; leave us this one consolation, that on our tombstones can be inscribed: 'Freedom died, but with arms in her hand!'" and Gotzkowsky, quite overcome by his painful emotions, leaned back against the wall, breathless, his imploring looks fixed upon the general.

But the latter avoided meeting his eyes, and directed his own darkly toward the ground.

Gotzkowsky perceived the indecision, the wavering of the general, and he felt that he must now risk every thing to overcome his resistance. "Leave us our weapons. Oh, you are a German! spare your German brethren."

Tottleben sprang from his seat as if a venomous snake had stung him. Dark and terrible were his features, his eyes flashed fire, and raising his right hand threateningly, he cried out: "You remind me in an evil hour that I am a German. Germany drove me out to find in a foreign land the appreciation which my own country refused me! Had I been a foreigner, Germany would long ago have proclaimed my fame; but, being the son of the family, the mother drives me out among strangers—and that they call German good-nature!" and he broke out into a bitter, scornful laugh.

"It is but too true," said Gotzkowsky, sadly. "Our mother Germany is fond of sending her greatest sons out from home on their pilgrimage to fame. For her great men she has but the cradle and the grave. But show your unfeeling mother that you are better than she is; prove to her how unjust she has been. Be magnanimous, and leave us our weapons!"

"I cannot, by Heaven! I cannot do it," said Tottleben, sadly, in a low tone. "I must obey the higher authorities above me—the empress and the commander-in-chief, General Fermore. My orders are very strict, and I have already yielded too much. It is written in these dispatches that the arms must be given up."

"The arms?" said Gotzkowsky, hastily. "Yes, but not *all* arms. Take some of them—we have three hundred inferior rifles—take them, sir, and fulfil the letter of your orders, and save our honor."

General von Tottleben did not answer immediately. Again he paced the room, from time to time casting sharp, piercing glances at Gotzkowsky, whose firmness and animation seemed to please him. He stopped suddenly, and asked in a voice so low that Gotzkowsky was scarcely able to distinguish the words—"Do you think the Germans will praise me, if I do this thing?"

"All Germany will say, 'He was great in victory, still greater in his clemency toward the conquered,'" cried Gotzkowsky, warmly.

The general dropped his head upon his breast in deep meditation. When he raised it again, there was a pleasant smile upon his face. "Well, then, I will do it. I will once more remember that I am a German. Where are the three hundred rifles?"

"In the armory, sir."

The general made no reply, but stepped toward his writing-table hastily. He wrote off a few lines, and then with a loud voice called his adjutant again to him. As the latter entered, he handed him the writing. "Let the disarming take place. There are not more than three hundred muskets. Let the citizens bring them to the Palace Square. There they will be broken up, and thrown into the river."

"O general!" cried Gotzkowsky, his countenance radiant with delight, when the adjutant had left the room, "how I do wish at this moment that you were a woman!"

"I a woman!" cried Count Tottleben, laughing, "why should I be a woman?"

"That I might kiss your hand. Believe me, I never thanked any man so truly and sincerely as I now do you! I am so proud to be able to say, 'Berlin is conquered, but not dishonored!'"

Tottleben bowed amicably toward him. "Now, after this proof of my generosity, the town will hasten to pay its war-tax, will it not?" Then seeing the dark cloud which gathered on Gotzkowsky's brow, he continued with more vehemence, "You are very dilatory in paying. Be careful how you exhaust my patience."

"Pray let me know, sir, when it is exhausted," said Gotzkowsky. "It is cruel to drive an exhausted animal beyond his strength. Do you not think so?"

The general nodded his assent in silence.

"You are of my opinion," cried Gotzkowsky. "Well, then, you will be just, and not exact of this exhausted city, wearied unto death, more than she can perform."

With glowing words and persuasive eloquence he explained to the general how impossible it was for the city to pay the demanded war contribution of four millions.

Tottleben let himself again be persuaded. In the presence of this ardent, eloquent German patriot, his German heart resumed its power, and compelled him to mercy and charitableness. He consented to reduce the tax to two millions of dollars, if Gotzkowsky would guarantee the punctual payment of the bonds given by the body of merchants, and give two hundred thousand of it in cash down, as hush-money to the Austrians.

The latter declared himself gladly willing to accept the orders, and to stand security with his whole fortune for their payment. Both then remained silent, as if fatigued by the long and severe war of words, from which Gotzkowsky had always come out victorious.

The general stood at the window, looking into the street. Perhaps he was waiting for Gotzkowsky to give vent to his warm and delighted gratitude before he took leave. But Gotzkowsky did neither the one nor the other. He remained with folded arms, his countenance full of earnest courage and bold determination.

"I will finish what I have commenced," said he to himself. "I will keep my word, and not move from the spot before I have pleaded for all those to whom I promised my assistance. The general is at liberty to curse my importunity, if I only do my duty toward my fellow-citizens." As he still remained silent, Tottleben turned toward him laughingly.

"What," said he, "are you dumb? Is your eloquence exhausted? Indeed, when I think of all that you have got out of me to-day, it almost makes me smile." And he broke out into a merry, good-natured laugh.

"Well, laugh, sir," said Gotzkowsky, "I know you are fond of a laugh. For example, you have just played a little joke on the Jews, and made them believe that they have to pay an imposition—"

"Made believe?" interrupted Tottleben, hastily. "Man! be satisfied that I have remitted two millions to the citizens. Don't speak up now for the Jews."

"But the Jews are a part of the citizens."

"Are you crazy, man?" cried Tottleben, violently. "Is the Jew a citizen with you?"

"Yes," answered Gotzkowsky, "as far as paying goes. The Jew is obliged honestly to contribute his proportion of the war-tax. How can you, with any semblance of justice, require of him another further tax, when he has already, in common with us, given up all he possesses?"

"Sir," cried Tottleben, with suppressed vexation "this is enough, and more than enough!"

"No," said Gotzkowsky, smiling. "It is too much. The Jews are not able to pay it—"

"I will remit their contribution," cried the general, stamping violently on the floor, "to please you—just to get rid of you—but now—"

"But now," interrupted Gotzkowsky, insinuatingly, "one more favor."

The general stepped back astounded, and looked at Gotzkowsky with a species of comical terror. "Do you know that I am almost afraid of you, and will thank God when you are gone?"

"Then you think of me as the whole town of Berlin thinks of you," said Gotzkowsky.

The general laughed. "Your impudence is astonishing. Well, quick, what is your last request?"

"They are preparing at the New Market a rare and unheard-of spectacle—a spectacle, general, as yet unknown in Germany. You have brought it with you from Russia. You are going to make two men run the gantlet of rods—not two soldiers convicted of crime, but two writers, who have only sinned in spirit against you, who have only exercised the free and highest right of man—*the right to say what they think.* You are going to have two newspaper writers scourged, because they drew their quills against you. Is not that taking a barbarous revenge for a small offence?"

"A small offence," cried the general, whose countenance had resumed its dark, fierce expression. "Come, that's enough. Stop, if you do not wish me to take back all that I have granted you. Do you call that a small offence? Why, sir, the editor of *Spener's Journal* called me an adventurer, a renegade. Ah! he at least shall feel that I have the power of punishing."

"Why," said Gotzkowsky calmly, "that would only prove to him that he had hit you on a tender spot."

"And the scribbler of the *Vossian Gazette*, did he not venture even to attack my gracious empress?" continued Tottleben, perfectly carried away by his indignation.

166

"He wrote a conversation between peasants, and in it he made fun of the empress. He even went so far as to make his own king join in the dirty talk, in the character of a peasant. Sir, I am very much surprised that you should defend a man who carries his impudence so far as to canvass and scandalize the conduct of his own king in such a disrespectful and audacious manner."

"The king is great enough to be able to bear this calumny of little minds. Whosoever is truly great, is not afraid of free speaking nor of calumny. Have you never heard the story of how the king was riding by, where the people were collected at the corner of a street, stretching out their necks to read a pasquinade which had been hung on the wall, and was directed against the king himself? The king reigned in his horse, and read the hand-bill. The people stood in silent terror, for the paper contained a sharp abuse of the king, and a libel on him in verse. What does your excellency think the king did when he had read this most treasonable placard?"

"He had the mob cut it down, as it deserved to be, and the author strung up on the gallows," cried Tottleben.

"Not at all, sir," replied Gotzkowsky. "He said, 'Let the paper be hung lower; the people can't see to read it up so high.' He then saluted the crowd, and rode off, laughing."

"Did the *great Fritz* do that?" said Tottleben, unconsciously using the epithet which the Prussian people had applied to their king.

"He did it *because* he is great," replied Gotzkowsky.

"Strange, hard to believe," muttered the general, folding his arms, and striding up and down. After a pause, Gotzkowsky inquired, "Would you not like to emulate the great king, general?"

Count Tottleben awoke from his reverie. Approaching Gotzkowsky, he laid his hand upon his shoulder; his expression was indescribably mild and gentle, and a melancholy smile played around his lips. "Hark'ee, I believe it would do me good if we could be always together. Come with me. Settle in Russia. The empress has heard of you, and I know that she would be rejoiced if you came to Petersburg. Do it. You can make a large fortune there. The empress's favor will elevate you, and she will not let you want for orders or a title."

Gotzkowsky could hardly suppress a smile of contempt. "Orders for me! A title! What would I do with them? Sir, I am more powerful than all your counts, for the greatness of the nobility lies in the past, in mouldering ancestors; but the greatness of the manufacturer lies in the future, and the future belongs to industry. I founded the first large factories here in Berlin, and the manufacturers who come after me can call me their ancestor. No other nobility do I desire, count."

"You would then be capable of refusing a count's title?" asked Tottleben, in astonishment.

Gotzkowsky shrugged his shoulders. "If I had wished for nobility I could long ago have bought a countship of the holy German empire, for such things are for sale, and thirty thousand ducats is the highest price for a count's title; and as for the orders, my own ribbon-factory turns out the ribbons for them."

General Tottleben looked at him for a long time in mild astonishment. "You are a wonderful man, and I wish I were like you. If I had thought as you do, my life would have been a less stormy one, and less tossed by care and restlessness. I would have—"

The general was interrupted by the hasty entrance of the adjutant. He was the bearer of dispatches brought by a courier who had just arrived. The courier, he said, had ridden so hard, that his horse had fallen dead on his arrival.

Tottleben tore open the dispatches and read them rapidly. His countenance immediately lost its former expression of mildness and gentleness. His German heart was silenced by the will of the Russian general.

He seemed to forget Gotzkowsky's presence, and turning to his adjutant, with proud military bearing, he said: "These dispatches contain important and surprising information. They announce that the Prussian army is drawing on in forced marches, with the king at its head. We cannot give him battle here, and must, in consequence, arrange for a rapid retreat from Berlin. Call all the generals and staff-officers together. Let the alarm be sounded. In three hours the whole army must have left the city. And, further, summon the Town Council to the New Market, that we may take our leave, for we must not leave Berlin as fugitives, but as conquerors, who are proceeding on their march."

"And the poor editors who are to be flogged?" asked Gotzkowsky, when the adjutant had left.

The general smiled, as he took Gotzkowsky amicably by the hand. "We will hang them a little lower," said he, significantly. "Come, accompany us to the market-place!"

NOTE.—Count von Tottleben expiated his clemency toward Berlin very dearly. A few months later he was sent to Petersburg under arrest, accused principally of having behaved too leniently and too much in the German interest for a Russian general.

* * * * *

168

CHAPTER XIII.

THE EXECUTION.

The morning was cold and rainy, the wind howled down the empty streets, rattling the windows, and slamming the open house-doors. Surely the weather was but little suited for going out, and yet the Berlin citizens were to be seen flocking toward the New Market in crowds, regardless of wind and rain.

The Berliners have, from time immemorial, been an inquisitive race, and where any thing is to be seen, there they rush. But this day there was to be a rare spectacle at the New Market.

The editors of the two newspapers were to run the gantlet; and besides, General von Tottleben had summoned the Town Council and Jews thither, to receive his last orders and resolutions before he left Berlin. People were, therefore, very much excited, and curious to witness this double show, and in their eagerness they forgave the hostile general, who had prepared such a delightful entertainment for them, all the terrors of the last few days. Two gentlemen—two learned men—were to be flogged. That was, indeed, a precious and delightful sight for cold, hungry, ragged poverty, which always takes delight in seeing those whom fortune has favored, suffer and smart.

How often had these shoemakers and tailors worried and fretted themselves over their pot of beer, that the newspaper writers should have had the hardihood and stupidity to write so violently against the Russians, without taking into account that the Russians would one day occupy Berlin, and take revenge on its innocent citizens! It served these newspaper writers quite right that they should be punished for their arrogance. And, besides, the good people would see the Russian general and his staff, and the grand Town Council and the chief magistrate, who, in his golden chain and his robes of office, was to hand over to the hostile general a present of ten thousand ducats. The Berliners were, therefore, quite happy, and delighted to hear the hollow sound of the drum, and the Russian word of command.

A regiment of Russian soldiers marched past the corner of the Bishop Street, toward the market-place. They ranged themselves in two long lines, leaving a lane between them, just wide enough for a man to pass through. Then came two provost-marshals, and walked slowly down the lane, delivering to each soldier one of the long slender rods they carried under their arms.

The Russian soldiers were now armed, and awaited the victims they were to chastise. These were dragged out of the guard-house. First came tottering the gray-headed Mr. Krause, slowly and sadly; then came Mr. Kretschmer, formerly the brave, undaunted hero of the quill—now a poor, trembling, crushed piece of humanity. They stood in the middle of the square, and, bewildered with terror, their help-imploring looks swept over the gaping, silent multitude, who gazed at them with eager countenances and malicious joy, and would have been outrageously mad if they had been denied the enjoyment of seeing two of their brother-citizens scourged by the enemy's soldiers.

"I cannot believe it!" whimpered Mr. Krause; "it is impossible that this is meant in earnest. They cannot intend to execute so cruel a sentence. What would the world, what would mankind say, if two writers were scourged for the articles they had written? Will the town of Berlin suffer it? Will no one take pity on our distress?"

"No one," said Mr. Kretschmer, mournfully. "Look at the crowd which is staring at us with pitiless curiosity. They would sooner have pity on a murderer than on a writer who is going to be flogged. The whole town has enjoyed and laughed over our articles, and now there is not one who would dare to beg for us."

At this moment another solemn procession came down the Bishop Street toward the square. This was the Town Council of Berlin. Foremost came the chief burgomaster Von Kircheisen, who had recovered his speech and his mind, and was memorizing the well-set speech in which he was to offer to the general the thanks of the town and the ten thousand ducats, which a page bore alongside of him on a silken pillow.

Behind the Council tottered trembling and broken-hearted the elders of the Jews, including those of the mint, in order to receive their final condemnation or release from General Tottleben.

The people took no notice of the Council or of the Jews. They were busy staring with cruel delight at the journalists, who were being stripped by the provost-marshals of their outer clothing, and prepared for the bloody exhibition. With a species of barbarous pleasure they listened to the loud wailing of the trembling, weeping Krause, who was wringing his hands and imploring the Russian officer who had charge of the execution, for pity, for mercy.

The Russian officer was touched by the tears of sorrow of the editor; he did have pity on the gray hairs and bowed form of the old man, or perhaps he only acted on instructions received from General Tottleben. He motioned to the provosts to lead the other editor to the lane first, and to spare Mr. Krause until Mr. Kretschmer had been chastised. The provost seized hold of Mr. Kretschmer and dragged him to the terrible lane; they pushed him in between the rows of soldiers, who, with rude laughter, were flourishing the rods in their hands.

Already the first, the second, the third blow has fallen on the back of the editor of the *Vossian Gazette*, when suddenly there sounds a powerful "Halt!" and General Count von Tottleben appears, with Gotzkowsky at his side, and followed by his brilliant staff.

With a wild scream Kretschmer tears himself loose from the hands of the provost-marshals, and rushes toward the general, crying out aloud; Mr. Krause awakens from his heavy, despairing brooding, and both editors sink down before the Russian general.

With a mischievous smile, Tottleben looked at Mr. Kretschmer's bleeding back, and asked, "Who are you?"

"I am the *Vossian Gazette*" whined out Mr. Kretschmer, "whom you have accused of such cruel things. Ah! we have suffered great injustice, and we have been represented as worse than we really are. Oh, believe me, your excellency, I have been belied. I never hated Russia!"

"You are both of you accused of libel," said Tottleben, sternly.

"If we are guilty of libel, it is without our knowledge," said Mr. Krause. "Besides, we are very willing to recall every thing. I confess we were in error. We did not know you and your army, and we spoke ignorantly, as the blind man does about colors. Now we are better able to judge. You are the noblest among noble men, and finer soldiers than the Russians, and a chaster woman than the Empress Elizabeth, are not to be found anywhere. Oh, yes, your excellency, *Spener's Journal* is ready to eat its words. Only don't let me be flogged, sir, and I will sing your praises everlastingly, and proclaim to all the world that the Prussian has no better friend than the Russian, and that God has ordained them to be brothers."

"Only don't let us be flogged," implored Mr. Kretschmer, rubbing his sore back, "I promise your excellency that the *Vossian Gazette* shall be as tame as a new-born infant. It shall never indulge in bold, outspoken language; never have any decided color. I swear for myself and my heirs, that we will draw its fangs. Have, therefore, mercy on us!"

The general turned away with a smile of contempt. "Enough, gentlemen," said he, roughly, and laying his hand on Gotzkowsky's shoulder, he continued: "I pardon you, not in consequence of your idle talk, but for the sake of this noble gentleman, who has begged for you. You are free, sirs!" As the two editors were about to break out into expressions of gratefulness, Tottleben said to them, "It is Gotzkowsky alone that you have to thank for your liberty."

They threw themselves into Gotzkowsky's arms; with solemn oaths they vowed him eternal, inviolable gratitude; they called him their savior, their liberator from shame and disgrace.

Gotzkowsky smiled at their glowing protestations of friendship, and withdrew himself gently from their ardent embraces. "I did not do it for the sake of your thanks, and personally you owe me therefore no gratitude."

"Gotzkowsky, have you entirely forgotten us?" said a plaintive voice near him. It was Itzig, one of the rich Jews of the mint, to whom Gotzkowsky had promised assistance.

"Ask the general," said the latter, smiling.

"He has spoken for you, and his intercession has freed you from the special tax," said Count Tottleben.

"He has saved us, the great Gotzkowsky has had pity on our wretchedness," cried the Jews, crowding around Gotzkowsky to press his hand, to embrace him, and with tears of grateful emotion to promise him their unalterable attachment.

"You have saved my life," said Itzig, "for I had determined to die rather than pay any more money. For what is life to me without money? If the Jew has not money, he is nobody. In saving my money you saved my life. If ever you should be without money, Gotzkowsky, come to me; I will lend you some at very low interest."

"I will lend it to you gratis," said Ephraim, pressing his hand affectionately in his own.

Gotzkowsky answered sadly: "If it ever came to pass that I were obliged to borrow, you would not remember this day, and I would not be the man to remind you of it."

"Remind us of it," protested Ephraim, "and you shall see that we keep our word. Come to us and say, 'Remember the tax that I freed you from,' and you shall see all that you desire shall be fulfilled."

"God grant that I may never have need to remind you of it!" said Gotzkowsky, pressing back the excited Jews, and approaching General Tottleben.

"You forget, sir, that you summoned the honorable Council of Berlin hither, and that these gentlemen are awaiting your orders."

The general seemed to awaken out of a deep reverie. "Yes," said he, as if to himself, "the German dream is finished, and now I must be a Russian again." He then turned quickly to Gotzkowsky and offered him his hand. "Gotzkowsky," said he, gently and persuasively, "consider it once more—come with me and be my teacher."

"What I can teach you is but little. It is an easy lesson for him who has a heart, an impossible one for him who has none. Learn to love mankind. That is all my wisdom, and my farewell."

The general sighed. "You will not go with me? Well, then, farewell!" And as if to disperse the painful and bitter feelings which assailed his German heart, he turned away and called, in Russian, to his adjutant: "Let us break up, gentlemen. To horse, to horse!"

But in the midst of the confusion of the soldiers, and the tramping of horses, the chief burgomaster made a way for himself. He had to sustain the honor of the Council, and pronounce the beautifully worded oration which had cost him two sleepless nights to compose; he had to place in the hands of the general the offering of Berlin gratitude.

At last he succeeded in reaching the general, and he began his speech. Full and powerful did his voice sound through the New Market, and the delighted people rejoiced over the oratorical talent of their chief magistrate, and gazed with pride and admiration at his golden chain of office—that chain which had gone through so much, had endured so much, without growing pale or dim.

But General Tottleben did not accept the present which the city of Berlin offered him. He said: "If the town believed that its fate was rendered more tolerable by my discipline than it otherwise would have been, let it thank the express orders of my empress. The honor of having been commander of Berlin for three days is sufficient reward for me."

Three hours later Berlin was freed from Russians and Austrians. Gotzkowsky, who had finally succeeded in freeing himself from the tumultuous expressions of gratitude of the Council, the editors, and the Jews, returned to his home, of which he himself says: "My house resembled more a cow-house than a dwelling, having been filled for a while, night and day, with Russians."

* * * * *

CHAPTER XIV.

BRIDE AND DAUGHTER.

At the mere announcement of the approach of the king toward Berlin, the Russian army had left the city and withdrawn to Frankfort. But no inconsiderable number of officers had stayed behind; some of them to organize the withdrawal of the troops, while others, detained by personal affairs, had merely obtained short leave of absence. To the latter belonged Colonel Feodor von Brenda. General Bachmann had given him two days' leave, under the impression that he would avail himself of the time to enjoy, undisturbed, the society of his bride, the Countess Lodoiska von Sandomir.

The general knew nothing of the difference between the colonel and his betrothed. He did not know that, according to her agreement with Bertram, Lodoiska had not informed Feodor of her arrival in Berlin. But, nevertheless, Feeder had heard of it. The countess's own chambermaid, knowing the liberality of the young count, had gone to him, and for a golden bribe had betrayed to him her presence, and communicated all that she knew of her plans and intentions.

This news detained the colonel in Berlin. The unexpected arrival of his affianced pressed upon him the necessity of a decision, for he was aware of the impossibility of tearing asunder the firm and heart-felt bond which attached him to Elise, to unite himself to a wife to whom he was only engaged by a given promise, a pledged word.

Feodor would probably have given up his whole fortune to pay a debt of honor; would have unhesitatingly thrown his life into the scale if it had been necessary to redeem his word. But he was not ashamed to break the vow of fidelity which he had made to a woman, and to desert her to whom he had promised eternal love. Besides, his pride was wounded by the advent of the countess, which appeared to him as a restraint on his liberty and an espionage on his actions.

She had concealed her arrival from him, and he consequently concluded that she was acquainted with his faithlessness, and nursed some plan of removing the obstacles which lay between her and her lover. His pride was irritated by the thought that he should be compelled to maintain an engagement which he could no longer fulfil from love, but only from a sense of duty. Such a restraint on his free will seemed to him an unparalleled hardship. He felt a burning hatred toward the woman who thus forcibly insisted on fastening herself upon him, and an equally ardent love toward the young girl of whom they wished to deprive him.

Doubly charming and desirable did this young, innocent, lovely girl appear to him when he compared her with the mature, self-possessed, worldly woman of whom he could only hope that he might be her last love, while he knew that he was Elise's first.

174

"If I must positively be chained, and my hands bound," said he to himself, "let it be at least with this fresh young girl, who can conceal the thorny crown of wedlock under freshly-blown rosebuds. My heart has nothing more to do with this old love; it has grown young again under the influence of new feelings, and I will not let this youthfulness be destroyed by the icy-cold smiles of duty. Elise has promised to be mine, and she must redeem her promise."

Still full of the passionate and defiant thoughts which the vicinity of his affianced bride had provoked, he had gone out to seek Elise. But to find her had become not only difficult, but almost impossible.

Bertram, who had not thought fit to reveal to Gotzkowsky the forcible abduction of his daughter, had yet quietly arranged his precautions that a repetition of the attempt from any quarter, or at any time, should be impossible.

Under the pretence that the withdrawal of the troops rendered the city unsafe, and filled it with marauders and plundering stragglers, Bertram, secure of Gotzkowsky's approval beforehand, had armed a number of the factory workmen, and placed them as sentinels on the wall, in the court, and on the ground-floor. These had orders not to let any one enter who was not able to tell the object and purpose of his coming. By this precaution Bertram prevented any attempt of Feodor to climb the wall; and, furthermore he obtained the advantage that Elise, to whom the presence of the sentinels was unpleasant and objectionable, not only did not visit the dangerous, solitary parts of the garden, but withdrew into her own room. In this manner Bertram had rendered any meeting between Feodor and Elise impossible, but he could not prevent his servant, Petrowitsch, from meeting his sweetheart, Elise's chambermaid, on the street.

By means of these a letter of Feodor reached Elise's hand. In this Feodor reminded her solemnly and earnestly of her promise; he now called upon her to fulfil her vow, and to follow him from the house of her father. He adjured her to unite herself to him at the altar as his wife, and to give him the right to carry her abroad with him as his own.

Elise received this letter of her beloved, and her heart during its perusal was moved by unfamiliar emotions. She could not herself determine whether it was joy or dread which caused it to beat so convulsively, and almost deprived her of consciousness. She could have screamed aloud with joy, that at last she would be united to her lover, wholly, sacredly as his own; and yet she was filled with deep grief that the path to the altar would not be hallowed by her father's blessing. Even love, which spoke so loudly and powerfully in her heart, could not silence the warning voice of conscience—that voice which again and again threatened her with sin and sorrow, disgrace and shame. Yet Elise, in the warmth and passion of her heart, sought to excuse herself, and in the pride of her wounded filial love said to herself: "My father does not regard me; he will not weep for my loss, for I am superfluous here, and he will hardly perceive that I am gone. He has his millions and his friends, and the whole multitude of those to whom he does good. He is so rich—he has much on which his heart hangs! But I am quite poor; I have nothing but the heart of my beloved. His love is my only possession. Would it not be wicked in me to cast this away, and lead here a lonesome, desolate life, without pity or sympathy? If my father loved me, would he have left me during these days so full of danger? After the terrible scene in which I, in the desperation of my heart, offended him, he would at least have given me some opportunity of asking his pardon, of begging him for forbearance and pity. But he seems purposely to have secluded himself, and avoided any meeting with me. He has shut me out from his heart, and withdrawn his love from me forever. And so I am forced to carry my heart full of boundless affection over to my lover. He will never repulse, neglect, or forget me; he will adore me, and I will be his most cherished possession."

As these thoughts passed through her mind, she pressed his note to her lips, each word seeming to greet her, and with Feodor's imploring looks to entreat her to fulfil the vow she had made him. There was no longer any hesitation or wavering in her, for she had come to a determined resolution, and with glowing cheeks and panting breast she hastened to the writing-table, in order to clothe it in words, and answer Feodor's note.

"You remind me of my pledged word," she wrote. "I am ready to redeem it. Come, then, and lead me from my father's house to the altar, and I will be your wife; and wherever you go I will be with you. Hence-forth I will have no other home than your heart. But while I cheerfully elect this home, at the same time I am shutting myself out from my father's heart forever. May God forgive the sins that love causes me to commit!"

But when this note had been sent, when she knew that her lover had received it, and that her decision was irrevocable, she was seized with trembling faintness, with the oppression of conscious guilt; and it seemed to her as if a new spring of love had suddenly burst forth in her heart, and as if she had never loved her father so sincerely, so devotedly, so tenderly, as now that she was on the point of leaving him.

But it was too late to draw back; for in the mean, time she had received a second letter from Feodor, imparting the details of a plan for their joint flight, and she had approved of this plan.

Every thing was prepared, and all that she had to do was to remain in her room, and await the concerted signal with which Feodor was to summon her.

As soon as she heard this signal she was to leave the house with her maid, who had determined to accompany her, come out into the street, where Feodor would be in waiting with his carriage, and drive in the first place to the church. There a priest, heavily bribed, would meet them, and, with the blessing of the Church, justify Feodor in carrying his young wife out into the world, and Elise in "leaving father and home, and clinging only unto her husband."

176

Some hours were yet wanting to the appointed time. Elise, condemned to the idleness of waiting, experienced all the anxiety and pains which the expectation of the decisive moment usually carries with it.

With painful desire she thought of her father, and, although she repeated to herself that he would not miss her, that her absence would not be noticed, yet her excited imagination kept painting to her melancholy fancy, pictures of his astonishment, his anxiety, his painful search after her.

She seemed, for the first time, to remember that she was about to leave him, without having been reconciled to him; that she was to part from him forever, without having begged his forgiveness, without even having felt his fatherly kiss on her brow. At least she would write to him, at least send him one loving word of farewell. This determination she now carried out, and poured out all her love, her suffering, her suppressed tenderness, the reproaches of her conscience, in burning and eloquent words, on the paper which she offered to her father as the olive-branch of peace.

When she had written this letter, she folded it, and hid it carefully in her bosom, in order to carry it unnoticed to her father's room. He would not be there—for two days he had not been at home; she could, therefore, venture to go there without fear of meeting him. She felt as if she would not be able to bear his gaze—the full, bright look of his eye.

Carefully and softly, with the secret fear of meeting Bertram, whose sad, reproachful looks she dreaded even more, perhaps, than the eye of her father, she crept along the corridor, and finally reached the antechamber, breathing more freely, and glad to have met no one. Every thing here was quiet and silent; her father, therefore, had not yet returned, and she was quite safe from any surprise by him.

She now entered his private room, and crossing this, was in the act of opening the desk of his writing-table in order to deposit the letter therein, when she heard the door of the antechamber open. It was too late for flight, and she had only time to conceal the letter in her bosom, when the door of the room itself was opened.

It was her father who now entered the apartment. Speechless and motionless they both stood, confounded at this unexpected meeting, each waiting for a word of greeting of reconciliation from the other. But however earnestly their hearts yearned toward each other, their lips remained silent, and their looks avoided one another.

"She shuns me. This is my reception after so many toilsome days of absence," thought Gotzkowsky, and his heart was full of sadness and sorrow.

"He will not look at me, his eye avoids me, he has not yet forgiven me," thought Elise, as she regarded her father's pale, care-worn countenance. "No, he does not wish to see me. For the last time, therefore, I will show him obedience, and leave the room." Sadly and softly, with her looks cast on the ground, she took her way to the door on the opposite side.

Gotzkowsky followed her with his eyes. If she had only ventured to raise her looks once more to him, she would have perceived all his love, all the forgiving affection of a father, in his face. But she did not, and Gotzkowsky said to himself, in the bitterness of his heart, "Why should I speak to her?—she would only misunderstand me. I will lie down and sleep, to forget my cares and my sorrows. I will not speak to her, for I am exhausted, and tired to death. I must have rest and composure, to be able to come to an understanding with her."

And yet he regarded her with longing looks as she directed her sad steps toward the door. Now she stands on the threshold; now her trembling hand clasps the bright handle of the lock, but still she hesitates to open it; she still hopes for a word, if even an angry one, from her father.

And now she hears it. Like an angel's voice does it sound in her ear. He calls her name, he reaches his hand out to her, and says with infinite, touching gentleness, "Give me your hand, Elise. Come here to me, my child—it is so long since I have seen you!"

She turned to him, and yet she dared not look upon him. Seizing his offered hand, she pressed it to her lips. "And do you remember that you have been so long absent? You have not then forgotten me?"

"Forgot you!" cried her father tenderly; and then immediately, as if ashamed of this outburst of fatherly love, he added calmly and almost sternly—"I have much to talk with you, Elise. You have accused me."

Elise interrupted him with anxious haste: "I was beside myself," said she, confused and bashfully. "Forgive me, my father; passion made me unjust."

"No, it only developed what lay hidden in your heart," said Gotzkowsky; and the recollection of that unhappy hour roughened his voice, and filled his heart with sadness. "For the first time, you were candid with me. I may have been guilty of it all, but still it hurts!" For a moment he was silent, and sank his head on his breast, completely overpowered by painful reminiscences.

Elise answered nothing, but the sight of his pale and visibly exhausted countenance moved her to tears.

When Gotzkowsky raised his head again, his face had resumed its usual determination and energy. "We will talk over these things another time," said he seriously. "Only this one thing, remember. I will not restrain you in any way, and I have never done so. You are mistress of every thing that belongs to me except my honor. This I myself must keep unsullied. As a German gentleman I cannot bring

178

the dishonor upon me of seeing my daughter unite herself to the enemy of my country—to a Russian. Choose some German man: whoever he may he, I will welcome him whom you love as my son, and renounce the wishes and plans I have so long entertained. But never will I give my consent to the union of my only child with a Russian."

While he spoke the expression of the countenance of both changed surprisingly. Both evinced determination, defiance, and anger, and the charm which love had laid for a moment on their antagonistic souls was destroyed. Gotzkowsky was no longer the tender father, easily appeased by a word, but the patriot injured in his holiest right, his most delicate sense of honor. Elise was no longer the humble, penitent daughter, but a bride threatened with the loss of her lover.

"You would, then, never give your consent?" asked she, passionately. "But if this war were ended, if Russia were no longer the enemy of Germany; if—"

"Russia remains ever the enemy of Germany, even if she does not appear against her in the open field. It is the antagonism of despotic power against culture and civilization. Never can the free German be the friend of the barbarous Sclavonian. Let us hear nothing more of this—you know my mind; I cannot change it, even if you should, for that reason, doubt my love. True love does not consist only in granting, but still more in denying."

Elise stood with bowed head, and murmured some low, unintelligible words. Gotzkowsky felt that it would be better for both to break off this conversation before it had reached a point of bitterness and irritation. At the same time he felt that, after so much excitement, his body needed rest. He, therefore, approached his daughter and extended his hand toward her for a friendly farewell. Elise seized it, and pressed it with passionate feeling to her lips. He then turned round and traversed the room on the way to his bedchamber.

Elise looked after him with painful longing, which increased with each step he took. As he was in the act of leaving the room she rushed after him, and uttered in a tone of gentle pleading, the single word, "Father!"

Gotzkowsky felt the innermost chord of his heart touched. He turned round and opened his arms to her. With a loud cry of joy she threw herself on his breast, and rested there for a moment in happy, self-forgetting delight. They looked at one another, and smilingly bade each other good-by. Again Gotzkowsky turned his steps toward his bedroom. And now he was gone; she saw him no more. Father and daughter were separated.

But Elise felt an unutterable grief in her heart, a boundless terror seized her. It seemed as if she could not leave her father; as if it would be a disgrace for her, so secretly, like a criminal, to sneak out of her father's house, were it even to follow her lover to the altar. She felt as if she must call her father back, cling to his knees, and implore him to save her, to save her from her own desires. Already had she opened her lips, and stretched forth her arms, when she suddenly let them fall, with a shudder.

She had heard the loud rolling of a carriage, and she knew what it meant. This carriage which stopped at her door—could it be the one in which Feodor had come to take her? "It is too late—I cannot go back," muttered she low, and with drooping head she slowly left her father's room in order to repair to her own chamber.

* * * * *

CHAPTER XV.

THE RIVALS.

Elise, immediately on reaching her room, hurried to the window and looked into the street, already darkened by the shades of evening. She was not mistaken—a carriage stood at the door; but to her surprise, she did not perceive the signal agreed on, she did not hear the post-horn blow the Russian air, "Lovely Minka, I must leave thee." Nor was it the appointed hour; neither did her chambermaid, who waited in the lower story, come to seek her. She still stood at the window, and involuntarily she felt herself worried by this equipage. A sharp knocking at the door was heard. Before she had time to come to any determination, it was hastily opened, and Bertram entered with a lady, deeply veiled, on his arm.

"Bertram!" cried Elise, drawing back shyly. "What do you wish here?"

"What do I wish here?" answered Bertram, earnestly. "I come to ask a favor of my sister. I have promised this lady that she shall see and speak with you. Will my sister fulfil her brother's promise?"

"What does the lady wish with me?" asked Elise, casting a timid look toward the mysterious veiled figure.

"She will herself tell you. She requested me, with tears, to bring her to Elise Gotzkowsky, for, she assured me, the happiness of her life depended on it."

Elise felt an icy shudder run through her. She laid her hand on her heart, as if to protect it against the terrible danger which she felt threatened her, and with trembling lip she repeated, "What does the lady wish with me?"

Bertram did not answer her, but letting go the arm of the unknown, he bowed low. "Countess," said he, "this is Mademoiselle Elise Gotzkowsky. I have fulfilled my promise: allow me now to leave you, and may God impart convincing power to your words!"

He greeted the ladies respectfully, and left the room quickly. The two ladies were now alone together. A pause ensued. Both trembled, and neither ventured to break the silence.

"You desired to speak to me," said Elise, finally, in a low, languid voice. "May I now beg of you—"

The lady threw back her veil, and allowed Elise to see a handsome countenance, moistened with tears. "It is I who have to beg," said she, with a touching foreign accent, while seizing Elise's hand, she pressed it warmly to her breast. "Forgive me;

since I have seen you, I have forgotten what I had to say. At sight of you, all my words, and even my anger have left me. You are very beautiful. Be as noble as you are beautiful. My fate lies in your hands. You can restore me to happiness."

"God alone can do that," said Elise, solemnly.

"At this moment you are the divinity who has the disposal of my fate. You alone can restore me to happiness, for you have deprived me of it—yes, you, so young, so handsome, and apparently so innocent. You are the murderess of my happiness." Her eyes sparkled, and a bright blush suffused her hitherto pale cheeks. "Yes," cried she, with a triumphant laugh, "now I am myself again. My hesitation has vanished, and anger is again supreme. I am once more the lioness, and ready to defend the happiness of my life."

Elise drew herself up, and she, too, felt a change in her heart. With the instinct of love, she felt that this handsome woman who stood opposite to her was her rival, her enemy with whom she had to struggle for her most precious property. Passion filled her whole being, and she vowed to herself not to yield a single step to this proud beauty. With an expression of unspeakable disdain, she fixed her eyes upon the countess. Their flashing looks crossed each other like the bright blades of two combatants in a duel.

"I do not understand you," said Elise, with angry coldness. "You must speak more plainly, if you wish to be understood."

"You do not wish to understand me," cried the countess. "You wish to avoid me, but I will not let you. I have suffered so much that I will not suffer any longer. We stand here opposite each other as two women engaged in a combat for life and death."

Elise suppressed the cry of pain which rose in her breast, and compelled herself to assume a proud and impassible composure. "I still do not understand you, nor do I desire to contend with an unknown person. But if you will not leave my room, you will allow me to do so."

She turned to go, but the countess seized her hand, and held her back. "No! you cannot go!" cried she, passionately. "You cannot go, for I know that you are going to him, to him whom I love, and I come to demand this man of you."

These half-threatening, half-commanding words, at last drove Elise from the assumed tranquillity she had maintained with so much difficulty. "I know not of whom you speak," cried she, in a loud voice.

But the countess was tired of dealing in these half-concealed meanings, these mysterious allusions. "You know of whom I speak," cried she, vehemently. "You know that I have come to demand the restoration of my holiest possession, the heart

182

of my beloved. Oh! give him back to me, give me back my betrothed, for he belongs to me, and cannot be another's. Let my tears persuade you. You are young, rich, handsome; you have every thing that makes life happy. I have nothing but him. Leave him to me."

Elise felt furious. Like a tigress, she could have strangled this woman, who came to destroy her happiness. A wild, angry laugh rang from her lips: "You say that you love him," exclaimed she. "Well, then, go to him and ask him for his heart. Why do you demand it of *me*? Win it from him, if you can."

"In order to be able to win it, you must first release him from the fetters with which you have bound him."

An angry flush overspread Elise's pale face. "You become insulting," she said.

The countess paid no attention to these words, but continued still more vehemently: "Make him free. Loose the bands which fetter him, and then, I am sure, he will return to me and be mine again."

Elise stared terrified at the face of the countess, excited and streaming with tears. She had heard but one little word, but this word had pierced her heart like a dagger.

"*Return* to you?" asked she, breathlessly. "Be yours *again*? He was then *once* yours?"

"I yielded to him what is most sacred in life, and yet you ask if he was mine!" said the countess, smiling sadly.

Elise uttered a loud, piercing shriek, and covered her face with her hands. Her emotion was so expressive and painful that it touched the heart even of her rival. Almost lovingly she passed her arm around Elise's waist and drew her down gently to her on the sofa. "Come," said she, "let us sit by each other like two sisters. Come, and listen to me. I will disclose a picture which will make your soul shudder!"

Elise yielded to her mechanically. She let herself involuntarily glide down on the sofa, and suffered the countess to take her hand. "Feodor once belonged to her," she murmured. "His heart was once given to another."

"Will you listen to me?" asked the countess; and, seeing Elise still lost in silent reverie, she continued: "I will relate to you the history of Feodor von Brenda, and his unhappy, forsaken bride." Elise shuddered, and cast a wandering, despairing look around.

"Will you listen to me?" repeated the countess.

"Speak—I am listening," whispered Elise, languidly. And then, the Countess Lodoiska von Sandomir, often interrupted by Elise's plaintive sighs, her outbursts of heartfelt sympathy, related to the young girl the sad and painful story of her love and her betrayal.

She was a young girl, scarcely sixteen, the daughter of a prince, impoverished by his own fault and prodigality, when she became the victim of her father's avarice. Without compassion for her tears, her timid youth, he had sold her for a million. With the cruel selfishness of a spendthrift miser, he had sold his young, fresh, beautiful daughter for dead, shining metal, to a man of sixty years, fit to be her grandfather, and who persecuted the innocent girl with the ardent passion of a stripling. She had been dragged to the altar, and the priest had been deaf to the "No!" she had uttered, when falling unconscious at his feet. Thus she had become the wife of the rich Count Sandomir—a miserable woman who stood, amidst the splendor of life, without hope, without joy, as in a desert.

But one day this desert had changed, and spring bloomed in her soul, for love had come to warm her chilled heart with the sunbeam of happiness. She did not reproach herself, nor did she feel any scruples of conscience, that it was not her husband whom she loved. What respect could she have for marriage, when for her it had been only a matter of sale and purchase? She had been traded off like a slave, and with happy exultation she said to herself, "Love has come to make me free, and, as a free and happy woman, I will tear this contract by which I have been sold." And she had torn it. She had had no compassion on the gray hairs and devoted heart of her noble husband. She had been sacrificed, and now pitilessly did she sacrifice her husband to her lover. She saw but one duty before her—to reward the love of the man she adored with boundless devotion. No concealment, no disguise would she allow. Any attempt at equivocation she regarded as an act of treason to the great and holy feeling which possessed her whole soul.

Usually all the world is acquainted with the treachery and infidelity of a woman, while it is yet a secret to her husband. But the countess took care that her husband should be the first to learn of his injured honor, her broken faith. She had hoped that he would turn from her in anger, and break the marriage-bond which united her to him. But her husband did not liberate her. He challenged the betrayer of his honor, whose treachery was the blacker, because the count himself had introduced him into his house, as the son of the friend of his youth. They fought. It was a deadly combat, and the old man of sixty, already bowed down by rage and grief, could not stand against the strength of his young and practised adversary. He was overcome. The dying husband had been brought to Countess Lodoiska, his head supported by his murderer, her lover. Even in this terrible moment she felt no anger against him, and as the eyes of her husband grew dull in death, she could only remember that she was now free to become his wife. She had thrown herself at the feet of the empress to implore her consent to this marriage, on which depended the hope and happiness, the honor and atonement of her life. The empress had not refused her consent, had herself appointed the wedding day which should unite her favorite with the young countess.

But a short time before the arrival of this day, so ardently longed for, looked forward to with so many prayers, such secret anxiety and gnawing self-reproaches, the war broke out, and Lodoiska did not dare to keep back her lover, as with glowing zeal he hastened to his colors. He had sworn to her never to forget her; to return faithful to her, and she had believed him.

* * * * *

CHAPTER XVI.

THE PUNISHMENT.

Elise had followed the countess in her narration with intense attention and warm sympathy. Her face had become pale as marble, her countenance sad, and her eyes filled with tears. A fearful anticipation dawned in her heart, but she turned away from it. She would not listen to this secret voice which whispered to her that this sad tale of the countess had reference to her own fate.

"Your lover did not deceive your trust?" asked she. "With such a bloody seal upon your love he dare not break his faith."

"He did break it," answered the countess, painfully. "I was nothing more to him than a guilty woman, and he went forth to seek an angel. He forgot his vows, his obligations, and cast me away, for I was a burden to him."

Both were silent in the bitterness of their sorrow. The countess fastened her large, bright eyes upon the young girl, who stared before her, pale, motionless, absorbed in her own grief.

This anxious silence was finally broken by the countess. "I have not yet told you the name of my lover. Shall I name him to you?"

Elise awoke as if from a heavy dream. "No," cried she, eagerly, "no, do not name him. What have I to do with him? I do not know him. What do I care to hear the name of a man who has committed so great a crime?"

"You must hear it," said the countess, solemnly. "You must learn the name of the man who chained me to him by a bloody, guilt-stained past, and then deserted me. It is Colonel Count Feodor von Brenda!"

Elise uttered a cry, and sank, half fainting, back on the cushions of the sofa. But this dejection did not last long. Her heart, which for a moment seemed to stop, resumed again its tumultuous beating; her blood coursed wildly through her veins, and her soul, unused to the despair of sorrow, resolved to make one last effort to free itself from the fetters with which her evil fate wished to encompass her. She drew herself up with glowing cheeks and flashing eyes. "This is false," she cried; "a miserable invention, concocted to separate me from Feodor. Oh! I see through it all. I understand now my father's solemn asseverations, and why Bertram brought you to me. But you are all mistaken in me. Go, countess, and tell your friends, 'Elise offers up every thing and gives every thing to him whom she loves, in whom she believes, even if the whole world testifies against him.'" And with a triumphant smile, throwing back her head, she stood up and was about to leave the room.

The countess shrugged her shoulders as if in pity. "You do not believe me, then?" said she; "but you will believe this witness?" and she drew a letter from her bosom and handed it to Elise.

"It is his handwriting," cried the young girl, terrified, as she took the letter.

"Ah! you know his handwriting, then? He has written to you, too?" sighed the countess. "Well, then, read it. It is a letter he wrote me from Berlin at the commencement of his captivity. Read it!"

"Yes, I will read it," murmured Elise. "These written words pierce my eyes like daggers, but I will not mind the pain. I will read it."

She read the letter, which annihilated her whole happiness, slowly and with terrible composure. Drop by drop did she let the poison of these words of love, directed to another, fall into her soul. When she had finished reading it, she repeated to herself the last cruel words, the warm protestations, with which Feodor assured his bride of his unalterable love and fidelity, with which he swore to her that he looked upon his love to her not only as a happiness, but as a sacred obligation; that he owed her not only his heart but his honor. Then long and carefully she considered the signature of his name, and folding up the paper, she handed it back, with a slight inclination to the countess.

"Oh, my God! I have loved him beyond bounds," muttered she, low; and then, unable to restrain her tears, she put her hands to her face and wept aloud.

"Poor, unhappy girl!" exclaimed the countess, laying her arm tenderly around her neck.

Elise drew back violently and regarded her almost in anger. "Do not commiserate me. I will not be pitied by you! I—"

She suddenly stopped, and an electric shock passed through her whole frame. She heard the concerted signal; and the tones of the post-horn, which slowly and heavily sounded the notes of the sad Russian melody, grated on her ear like a terrible message of misfortune.

The two women stood for a moment silent and motionless. They both listened to the dirge of their love and their happiness, and this simple, hearty song sounded to them horrible and awful in the boundless desolation of their hearts. At last the song ceased, and a voice, too well known and loved, cried, "Elise! Elise!"

The maiden started up, shuddering and terrified. "His voice frightens me."

But still she seemed not to be able to withstand the call; for she approached the window, and looked down hesitatingly.

187

The countess observed her jealously, and a fearful thought suddenly entered her mind. How, if this young girl loved him as much as she did? If she were ready to forgive him every thing, to blot out the whole past with the hand of love and commence a new existence with him? If she felt no compassion for Feodor's forsaken bride, and were willing to trample triumphantly on her broken heart at the call of her lover, and follow him to the altar? Her whole soul writhed in pain, "Follow his call," cried she, with a derisive smile. "Leave your father, whom you have betrayed, for the sake of a traitor! You have vowed to love him. Go and keep your vow."

Outside Feodor's voice called Elise's name louder and more pressingly. A moment she listened, then rushed to the window, threw it open, and called out, "I come, I come!"

Lodoiska flew to her; drew back the young girl violently from the window, and throwing both arms firmly around her, said, almost breathlessly, "Traitress! You shall not cross this threshold! I will call your father. I will call the whole household together! I will—"

"You will call no one," interrupted Elise, and her proud, cold composure awed even the countess. "You will call no one, for I stay, and you—you go in my stead."

"What say you?" asked Lodoiska.

Elise raised her arm and pointed solemnly to the window. "I say," cried she, "that your bridegroom is waiting down there for you. Go, then."

With an exclamation of joy the countess pressed her in her arms. "You renounce him, then?"

"I have no part in him," said Elise coldly. "He belongs to you; he is bound to you by your disgrace and his crime. Go to him," cried she more violently, as she saw that the countess looked at her doubtingly. "Hasten, for he is waiting for you."

"But he will recognize me; he will drive me from him."

Elise pointed to her clothes, which were placed ready for her departure. "There lie my hat and cloak," said she haughtily. "Take them; drop the veil. He knows this dress, and he will think it is me."

At this moment the door was torn open, and Bertram burst in. "Make haste," he cried, "or all is lost. Count Feodor is becoming impatient, and may himself venture to come for Elise. Gotzkowsky, too, has been awakened by the unaccustomed sound of the post-horn."

"Help the countess to prepare for the journey," cried Elise, standing still, motionless, and as if paralyzed.

Bertram looked at her, astonished and inquiringly; but in a few rapid words the countess explained to him Elise's intention and determination, to allow her to take the journey in her stead, and with her clothes.

Bertram cast on Elise a look which mirrored forth the admiration he felt for this young girl, who had so heroically gained the victory over herself. His reliance on her maiden pride, her sense of right and honor, had not been deceived.

The countess had now finished her toilet, and donned Elise's hat and cloak.

Bertram called on her to hasten, and she approached Elise to bid her farewell, and express her gratitude for the sacrifice she had made for her. But Elise waved her back proudly and coldly, and seemed to shudder at her touch.

"Go to your husband, countess," cried she, and her voice was hoarse and cold.

Lodoiska's eyes filled with tears. Once more she attempted to take Elise's hand, but the latter firmly crossed her arms and looked at her almost threateningly. "Go!" said she, in a loud, commanding voice.

Bertram took the arm of the countess and drew her to the door. "Hasten!" said he; "there is no time to lose."

The door closed behind them. Elise was alone. She stood and listened to their departing steps; she heard the house door open; she heard the post-horn once more sound out merrily, and then cease. "I am alone!" she screamed, with a heart-rending cry. "They are gone; I am alone!" And stretching her arms despairingly to heaven, and almost beside herself, she cried out, "O God! will no one have compassion on me? will no one pity me?"

"Elise," said her father, opening the room door.

She sprang toward him with a loud exclamation, she rushed into his arms, embraced him, and, nestling in his bosom, she exclaimed faintly, "Have pity on me, my father; do not drive me from you! You are my only refuge in this world."

Gotzkowsky pressed her firmly to his breast and looked gratefully to heaven. "Oh! I well knew my daughter's heart would return to her father."

He kissed ardently her beautiful, glossy hair, and her head that was resting on his breast. "Do not weep, my child, do not weep," whispered he, tenderly.

"Let me weep," she answered, languidly; "you do no know how much sorrow and grief pass off with these tears."

The sound of the post-horn was now heard from the street below and then the rapid rolling of a carriage.

Elise clung still more closely to her father. "Save me," she cried. "Press me firmly to your heart. I am quite forsaken in this world."

The door was thrown open and Bertram rushed in, out of breath, exclaiming: "She is gone! he did not recognize her, and took her for you. The countess—"

He stopped suddenly and looked at Gotzkowsky, of whose presence he had just become aware.

Gotzkowsky inquired in astonishment, "Who is gone? What does all this mean?"

Elise raised herself from his arms and gazed at him with flashing eyes. "It means," she answered, "that the happiness of my life is broken, that all is deception and falsehood where I looked for love, and faith, and happiness!" With a touching cry of suffering, she fell fainting in her father's arms.

"Do not rouse her, father," said Bertram, bending over her; "grant her this short respite, for she has a great sorrow to overcome. When she comes to herself again, she will love none but you, her father."

Gotzkowsky pressed his lips on her brow, and blessed her in his thoughts. "She will find in me a father," said he, with deep emotion, "who, if necessary, can weep with her. My eyes are unused to tears, but a father may be allowed to weep with his daughter when she is suffering."

* * * * *

190

CHAPTER XVII.

THE BANQUET OF GRATITUDE.

Berlin had recovered from the terrors it had undergone. It was eight days since the enemy had left, and every thing was quiet and calm. But on this day the quiet was to be interrupted by a public merry-making. Berlin, which had suffered so much, was to rejoice again.

The festival which was to be celebrated, was intended for none else than John Gotzkowsky, the Merchant of Berlin, the man whom all looked upon as their guardian angel and savior. He had cheerfully borne hardship and toil, danger and injustice, for the good of his fellow-men; he had always been found helping and ready to serve, unselfish and considerate. The whole town was under obligation to him; he had served all classes of society, and they all wished to evince their gratitude to him.

Gotzkowsky had been requested to remain at home on the morning of the festal day, but to hold himself in readiness to receive several deputations. They were to be succeeded by a grand dinner, given by the citizens of Berlin in his honor. They were to eat and drink, be merry, and enjoy themselves to his glorification; they were to drink his health in foaming glasses of champagne, and Gotzkowsky was to look upon it all as a grand festival with which the good citizens of Berlin were glorifying him, while they themselves were enjoying the luscious viands and fragrant wines.

In vain did Gotzkowsky refuse to accept the proffered festival. At first he tried to excuse himself on the plea of his daughter's illness, alleging that he could not leave her bedside. But information had been obtained from her physician, who reported her out of danger, and that Gotzkowsky might leave her for several hours without risk. Gotzkowsky being able to find no other excuse, was obliged to accept. Elise was indeed sick. The grief and despair of her betrayed and deceived heart had prostrated her; and her wild, fever-dreams, her desponding complaints, the reproachful conversations she carried on with her lover—unseen but nevertheless present in her delirium—had betrayed her secret to her father. Full of emotion, he thanked God for her happy escape, and felt no resentment against this poor, misguided child, who had taken refuge from the loneliness of her heart, in his love, as in a haven of shelter. He only reproached his own want of discernment, as he said to himself: "Elise had cause to be angry with me and to doubt my affection. I bore solitude and the constant separation from my daughter because I thought I was working for her, but I forgot that at the same time she was solitary and alone, that she missed a father's tenderness as I did my child's love. I wished to make her rich, and I have only made her poor and wretched."

He kissed her burning, feverish forehead, he bedewed it with tears, and forgave her, from the bottom of his heart, her misplaced love, her errors and transgressions. She was with him; she had returned to his heart. In her despair she had fled to the bosom of her father, and sought support and assistance from him.

The dark clouds had all rolled over, and the heavens were again bright and clear. Berlin was freed from the enemy. Elise was convalescent, and the town of Berlin, was preparing for her noblest citizen a banquet of gratitude.

The appointed hour had arrived for Gotzkowsky to receive the deputations, and he betook himself to the hall next the garden. A thundering hurrah received him. It proceeded from his workmen, who had come in procession through the garden, and were waving their hats and caps. They were followed by a multitude of women in black. This day they had laid aside the tears and griefs for their husbands and sons fallen in battle, in order to thank Gotzkowsky with a smile for the magnanimous kindness with which he had taken their part and secured their future.

Following these women came the poor orphans, with mourning-crape on their arms. They rushed forward joyously toward Gotzkowsky, stretching out their little hands to him, and, at a word from the head operative, Balthazar, they stretched open their small mouths, and gave out such a shrill and crashing hurrah that the windows rattled, and many a stout workman stopped his ears and felt a ringing in his head.

"One more hurrah!" cried the enthusiastic Balthazar; and "hurrah!" screamed and squeaked the children.

"And now for a third—"

But Gotzkowsky seized hold of Balthazar's arm which he was about to move again, and with a look of comical terror, exclaimed: "But, man, don't you know that I have further use for my ears to-day? You deafen me with your screaming. That's enough."

Balthazar struggled himself free from the strong grasp of his master, and placed himself in a theatrical position opposite to him. He was able this day to indulge in his passion for eloquence, for the workmen had chosen him for their orator, and he had a right to speak. As he spoke, it could be seen by his sparkling eyes, and by his fiery enthusiasm, that his words had not been learned by rote, but proceeded from his heart.

"Sir, allow me to speak and express my joy, for it is a joy to have a noble master. Look at these children, dear master. Three days ago they had fathers who could work and care for them. But the cannon-balls deprived them of their fathers, and God sent them a father, and you are he. You adopted these children when they were forsaken by all else. You said: 'God forbid that the children of these brave men, who had fallen in defence of the liberty of Berlin, should be orphans! I will be their father.' Yes, sir, that is what you said, and all the weeping mothers and all your workmen heard it and wrote it down in their hearts. Ask these widows for whom they pray to God. Ask the poor who were without bread and whom you fed. Ask the whole town who it is whom they bless and praise. They will all name the name of Gotzkowsky; with one voice they will all cry out: "Long live our friend and father! Long live Gotzkowsky!"

192

Unanimously did all join in this cry, shouting out, "Long live Gotzkowsky!"

Deeply moved, Gotzkowsky stretched out his hands to the workmen, and accepted, with cordial gratification, the flowers offered by the children. "Thank you, thank you," cried he, in a voice of deep emotion. "You have richly recompensed me, for I perceive that you love me, and nothing can be more beautiful than love."

"Diamonds!" cried out Ephraim, as he made his way through the crowd with Itzig and a deputation of the Jews, toward the hero of the day—"diamonds are more valuable than love, Gotzkowsky. Look at this brilliant, which sparkles and shines more brightly than ever did a look of love from any human eye."

He presented to Gotzkowsky a costly *solitaire* diamond, and continued: "Be so kind and grant us the favor of accepting this present. It is a diamond of the first water."

"It is a petrified tear of joy," interrupted Itzig, "shed by us on our delivery by you from taxation. You are our greatest benefactor, our best friend. You have proved yourself the savior of the Jews, for you freed us from the tax, and saved us what is more precious than honor, and rank, and happiness—our money; for, without money, the Jew is nobody. Accept, therefore, the ring, and wear it for our sakes."

"Accept it, we pray you," cried Ephraim, and the Jews took up the cry.

Gotzkowsky took the ring, and placed it on his finger, thanking the givers for the costly present, and assuring them he would wear it with pleasure in honor of them.

Itzig's brow was clouded with a slight frown, and stepping back to Ephraim and his friends, he muttered, "He accepts it. I was in hopes he would refuse it, for it cost much money, and we could have made very good use of it."

The solemn advance of the honorable gentlemen of the Berlin Town Council interrupted Itzig's private soliloquy, and drew his attention toward the chief burgomaster, Herr von Kircheisen, who, in all the splendor and dignity of his golden chain and of his office, accompanied by the senators and town officers, strode pompously through the crowd, and presented his hand to Gotzkowsky, who was respectfully advancing to meet him.

"The Council of Berlin has come to thank you. For it is an unparalleled example for a man to undertake and go through what you have done for us, without any interest, without any ulterior object."

"You make me out better than I am," replied Gotzkowsky, smiling at Herr von Kircheisen's pompous words. "I had an ulterior object. I wished to gain the love of my fellow-citizens. If I have succeeded, I am more than rewarded, and I pray you say no more on the subject."

The chief burgomaster shook his head majestically. "You have exercised toward us the virtue of philanthropy. Allow us to exercise toward you in return the virtue of gratitude." He took from the hands of the assistant burgomaster a dark-red *etui*, from which he a wreath of oak-leaves, worked in silver, which he presented to Gotzkowsky. "John Gotzkowsky," said he, solemnly, "the Council and citizens of Berlin request you, through me, to accept this memorial of their love and gratitude. It is the civic crown of your magnanimity. Receive it from our hands, and accept also our vow that we will never forget what you have done for the town of Berlin."

Tears of delight, of heart-felt joy stood in Gotzkowsky's eyes as he took the oaken crown from his hands, and glowing words of gratitude poured from his lips.

Not far off, in a niche of a window of the hall, stood Messrs. Krause and Kretschmer, with sullen looks, witnessing the homage paid to Gotzkowsky, their souls filled with envy and rage. They, too, had come to thank him, but with unwilling hearts, because they could not be well absent from the festivities which the whole town offered him. But they were vexed to see this man, whom they hated from the bottom of their hearts, because of their obligations to him, so universally honored and beloved. It annoyed them to see the pleasant and affable smile with which the otherwise proud burgomaster conversed with him; to see with what cordial friendship the senators and councilmen surrounded him.

"I came hither," said Mr. Krause, softly, "to thank Gotzkowsky for saving us, but I must confess it worries me to see him so glorified."

Mr. Kretschmer shrugged his shoulders contemptuously. "Let them praise him," said he; "the *Vossian Gazette* will not notice it, and I will not write the smallest article on this occasion. As for the service he rendered us—well, certainly, it would have been unpleasant to have been flogged, but then we would have been martyrs to our liberal opinions; the whole world would have admired and pitied us, and the king would not have refused us a pension."

"Certainly," whispered Mr. Krause, "he would have granted us a pension, and the whipping would have made us famous. It has never been forgotten of the English poet, Payne, that King Charles the First had his ears cut off, because he wrote against him. He is not celebrated for his writings, but for his chopped ears. We, too, might have become famous if this Gotzkowsky had not, in the most uncalled-for manner, interfered, and—but look!" cried he, interrupting himself, "the interview with the Council is finished, and it is now our turn to thank him."

The two editors hastened toward him in order, in well-arranged speech, and with assurances of eternal gratitude, to offer their thanks.

* * * * *

CHAPTER XVIII.

A ROYAL LETTER.

Mr. Krause had not yet finished the declamation of the poem which his inspiration had produced in honor of Gotzkowsky, when a loud noise was heard at the door of the hall, and Gotzkowsky's body-servant rushed in. A messenger of the Council was without, he announced; a letter had just arrived from the king, and, as he was to deliver it to the burgomaster in person, the messenger had brought him here. He handed Herr von Kircheisen a letter, and the latter broke the seal with majestic composure.

A pause of anxious expectation ensued. Each one inquired of himself with trembling heart what could be the meaning of this royal letter.

The countenance of the chief magistrate grew more and more cheerful, and suddenly he called aloud: "This is indeed a message of gladness for our poor town. The king, our gracious lord, releases us from our obligation to pay the promised war-tax of a million and a half. He wishes to retaliate for the Wurzburg and Bamberg bonds captured from the Aulic Council. For which reason his majesty's order is that we do not pay."

A single cry of joy sounded from the lips of all present. Gotzkowsky alone was silent, with downcast eyes, and his earnest, pensive expression contrasted strongly with the bright, joyous countenances which were illuminated by the order of the king to keep their money.

Among the happiest and most radiant, however, were the rich mint farmers Ephraim and Itzig, and the chief burgomaster.

"The royal decree relieves our town of a horrible burden," said Herr von Kircheisen, with a happy smile.

"The whole mercantile community must be grateful to the king," cried Ephraim. "Berlin saves a million and a half, and the Russian is sold."

Suddenly Gotzkowsky drew himself up erect, and his eagle eye ran over the whole assembly with a bold, beaming glance. "The Russian is not sold," cried he, "for Berlin will pay him the balance of a million and a half. Berlin has pledged her word, and she will redeem it."

The countenances of those around grew dark again, and here and there were heard words of anger and wild resentment.

"How!" cried Itzig, "do you require of the merchants to pay what they can keep for themselves? The king has said, 'You shall not pay!'"

"And I say, we will pay," cried Gotzkowsky. "What is written is written, and what is promised must be performed, for this our honor requires. The king possesses not the power of annulling a promise or revoking an oath! He who does not fulfil his word of honor is not a man of honor, were he even a king."

"But," said Herr von Kircheisen, pathetically, "there are nevertheless circumstances which render impossible the fulfilment of an obligation."

Gotzkowsky answered ardently: "If such do occur, the man of honor dies when he cannot fulfil his word. But you—you do not wish to die. Oh no! You wish to break your word in order to live pleasantly. You wish to profit by your breach of promise. You wish to declare yourselves insolvent and cheat your creditors of their money, and thereby amass wealth."

A general storm of indignation interrupted Gotzkowsky, and the very men who had come for the purpose of making a formal demonstration of their gratitude now approached him with angry gestures and threatening words.

"A million and a half is no child's play," screamed Ephraim. "Money is more precious than honor."

"I say money is honor," cried Itzig. "As long as we keep our millions, we keep our honor."

"You are very generous," sneered Kretschmer. "Like a gentleman, you pay your debts out of other people's pockets, and the citizens will have to pay millions to enable you to keep your word."

Gotzkowsky cast one look of contemptuous pity on him, and replied: "You forget, sir, that I did not act in my own name, but in that of the magistracy and merchants of Berlin. Not I alone would be faithless to my word, but the whole town of Berlin."

"But I repeat," said the chief burgomaster, "that the king has released us from the obligation of keeping our word."

"No king can do that," interrupted Gotzkowsky. "A man of honor must keep his word, and no one, not even a king, can absolve him from it."

"Let us not quarrel about matters of opinion," said Kircheisen, shrugging his shoulders. "My opinion is, that we do not pay this sum."

196

"No, we will not pay it!" cried all in tumultuous excitement, as they surrounded the burgomaster, discussing in cheerful conversation the advantages of non-payment.

Gotzkowsky stood listening to them alone, unobserved, and forgotten. His heart was heavy with sadness, and painfully did he reflect: "This is the unholy influence of money, hardening the heart and silencing the voice of honor. For a few millions of dollars do they sell their good name. One final attempt let me make. I will see what their cowardice will do."

Again did he enter their midst, and with convincing words and ardent eloquence portray the danger which would ensue from the non-payment of the bonds.

The Russian was not very far from Berlin: if he had retired in forced marches he could return thither with equal rapidity in order, in the wantonness of his wrath, to take vengeance on the faithless town.

"In an unlucky moment," said he, "the Russians might gain a victory over our king. He would then return and rend us like a tiger. I would then no longer have the power of protecting you, for General Tottleben's anger would be turned principally against me, who guaranteed the payment of the contribution. God himself does not protect him who breaks his word. He is an outlaw."

A deep silence followed Gotzkowsky's speech. All the faces were again overcast, and in the contracted brow and anxious countenances could be read the fact that his words had painfully convinced them that it was necessary to pay.

Even Herr von Kircheisen in his fear of the return of the Russians, forgot the enormous amount of the sums to be paid, and said, with a melancholy sigh: "Gotzkowsky is, I am afraid, right. It is very hard to pay the money, but it is very dangerous not to do it."

"It might cost us our heads," confirmed the first councilman.

Ephraim stood with his head cast down, and muttered to himself, "Money is very dear, but life is still dearer."

Itzig cried out in despair: "Let us keep our money. Without money the Jew is nobody."

But the chief burgomaster, who had consulted the councilmen, now approached Gotzkowsky, and, with a smile, offered him his hand. "We thank you," said he, "for you have spoken wisely, and your advice shall be followed. We will pay, for we cannot help ourselves. But we must beg you to do us another important service. Go to the king and beg him not to be angry with us if we do not obey his order."

"Yes, do so, do so, Gotzkowsky!" cried all the others. "Go to the king, he is friendly toward you—beg for us."

Gotzkowsky's countenance beamed with generous satisfaction. "Very well," said he; "I will go to the king and beg him to allow the town of Berlin to preserve its honor immaculate, and pay the promised sum."

"Use all your eloquence, that the king may remain favorably inclined toward us, and not become angry with us for acting this once against his orders," admonished the chief burgomaster.

"The king is a high-minded and noble man," said Gotzkowsky, enthusiastically. "He looks upon a man's word as sacred, and will understand us and honor us for not wishing to break ours."

An hour later the chief citizens and merchants of Berlin repaired to the spacious town-hall, where an elegant banquet had been prepared, and merriment prevailed, and glasses sounded; and Berlin, rescued, celebrated the first day of joy and happiness.

But John Gotzkowsky, to whom this feast was given, whom Berlin called her deliverer and benefactor, was not present at this banquet. Deeply buried in furs he had just entered his carriage, and braving danger and toil, in the cold and darkness he drove away toward Meissen, where the king had established his headquarters.

* * * * *

BOOK III.

CHAPTER I.

The great battle of Torgau had been fought, and the Prussian army, after so many combats and such a bloody victory, was contemplating with lively satisfaction the going into winter quarters, which, it hoped, this time would be in Saxony. The Prussian headquarters were, for the time being, in Meissen, and in the palace there, for a short resting-spell, dwelt the king, who for many years had only experienced the troubles and dangers of his position; the king who had often struggled with hunger and care, daily privation and mortal danger, and who one day, wearied out by sleeping night after night on the cold ground, commissioned his adjutant to provide a bundle of straw for the comfort of his royal person. The king had for a long time spared Saxony. He was sorry for this beautiful, afflicted land. But Saxony was finally to be treated as an enemy's country, as she would not appreciate Frederick's noble forbearance and clemency, and had allied herself to his enemies with fanatical zeal. And now her devastated fields, her paralyzed factories, her impoverished towns and deserted villages, testified to her distress and the calamities of war. But at this time quiet and tranquillity reigned in the hostile camps. On both sides they were too tired to be able to carry on a fresh conflict, and the strength of both parties being exhausted, they were obliged to allow each other time for rest. Besides, the winter had set in early with unusual severity, and, to all appearances, put an end to the campaign of 1760.

The only contest now was for winter quarters; and it had been, therefore, after the victory of Torgau, the king's first endeavor to cut off the retreat of the Austrians to Dresden, or at least to drive them out of this town. But, as the king wrote to Countess Camas, "They laughed at us from the top of the hills—I withdrew immediately, and, like a little boy, have stuck myself down in pure disgust in one of the accursed Saxon villages. I assure you I lead a perfect dog's life, such as no one else, except Don Quixote, has ever led."

In the mean while Frederick had left this "accursed Saxon village" (Neustadt) and had gone to Meissen, and his "dog's life" had given place to ease and comfort. He had, therefore, for some quiet weeks laid aside the sword, and the gentleman had become again the royal poet and *savant*, who divided his time between music and poetry, between serious studies and writing to his friends, to whom he sent letters, in which his great and elevated manner of thinking, his soul above prejudice, were displayed in all their beauty and power.

The king was alone in his study. He had just finished a letter to the Marquis d'Argens, calling upon him to give some news of his gallery at Sans-Souci, and to inform him of its progress. The king laid down his pen, and leaned back in his chair for a moment. His usually sharp, bright eye had now a soft, gentle expression, and a light smile played around his thin, nobly-formed lips. He has forgotten for the time the care and bustle of war, and fancied himself in his beloved paradise, his Sans-Souci, where it was allowed the hero to be a poet, and where he could for some genial hours put aside his dignity, and, instead of the enthroned ruler, be the cheerful sage, the smiling son of the Muses.

The king, pleased by these memories of happy days, rose and seized his flute, which, by his express orders, always lay on his writing-table. He put it to his lips, and began an *adagio*, in the execution of which he was acknowledged to be one of the first *virtuosos* of his day, and the sounds, as they poured forth, rose plaintively, and floated around him in bewitching melody. No one could listen to this beautifully-executed, deeply-felt music of the royal performer, without being impressed in his inmost soul, and feeling his heart swell with powerful emotions. Outside, in the antechamber, were standing the stern generals, the heroic warriors, Zeithen, and the brave Schwerin, and General von Saldern, and their scarred, austere features assumed a soft, touching expression, as they leaned against the wall and listened in breathless silence to the performance of the king. But suddenly the playing ceased.

To these brave warriors, unaccustomed to music, the execution had seemed superb; but the king was not satisfied with it. He, who had in his memory the royal *artiste* of Sans-Souci, exacted of the king, driven about by the hardships and necessities of war, that he should have lost nothing of the fulness of tone or the power and energy of execution. It worried him that the notes no longer flowed so clearly; it vexed him to hear a sharp, whistling sound, that seemed to accompany the melody as with a painful sigh. He threw the flute aside, and stepped to a looking-glass, which he took up with evident unwillingness.

It was very seldom that the king held it worth his while to consult the mirror about his personal appearance, and when he did so, it was usually to inquire for some failing or evidence of frailty which restricted him in the freedom of his being. And while he thus looked at himself, his features assumed a sad expression, and his eyebrows became contracted.

What was it, which thus put out of humor the brave hero, the victory-crowned king?

He became aware that his second front tooth had broken off. The gap thus caused was the natural explanation of the want of clearness in his playing. He threw the mirror angrily aside, and with a frown on his brow paced rapidly up and down the room two or three times.

But gradually another expression succeeded, and a sarcastic smile played around his mouth. Again he stepped to the writing-table, on which lay several unfinished letters. Looking for the one he had commenced to the Countess Camas, he said to himself: "The good countess inquires after my personal appearance. Well, now that I am in the humor, I will draw my portrait for her."

Again he took up the hand-glass and regarded himself long and attentively; but this time not with vexation or ill-humor, but with the cheerful smile and dignified calm of a philosopher. He then applied himself to his writing: "You ask how I look, dear mother. The disorder of war has made me so old, that you would hardly recognize me. My hair is quite gray on the right side of my head; my teeth break off and fall out; my face is as full of wrinkles as the furbelow of a woman's frock; my back as bent as that of a monk of La Trappe. Only my heart is unchanged; and, as long as I have breath, will preserve feelings of esteem and the most tender friendship toward you, good mamma."[1]

As the king read over this description of his appearance once more, he broke into a loud, merry laugh. He then pushed the letter aside, and took up another piece of paper, and a drawing-pencil.

Silence prevailed now in the cabinet of the king. Outside was heard the monotonous tread of the sentinel, sometimes the sound of a trumpet, the neighing of a horse, or the order of some officer. The king paid no attention to all this. His ear was so accustomed to these noises, that it seemed like perfect silence to him. He was so buried in his work, that even the unwonted tumult which now arose was unperceived by him; nor did he notice that a carriage drove into the palace-yard, its post-horn sounding loud and merrily. The generals and courtiers, who were in the antechamber, noticed it all the more, because any thing was welcome to them which broke in upon the prevailing quiet; for so accustomed were they to the varied business of war, that any thing which departed from it was insupportably tedious. They drew to the window and looked with pleasure on the dusty, dirty travelling carriage, which, with its four panting post-horses, had drawn up at the entrance to the palace, and out of which descended a tall, manly figure, who went in at the palace door.

The gentlemen in the antechamber amused themselves guessing who the stranger who had just arrived could be; and they had all arrived at the unanimous conclusion that it must be the Marquis d'Argens, as the door opened, and the stranger entered. He asked for the adjutant on duty, and, as the latter was pointed out to him, he stepped toward him with an air of quiet dignity.

"I pray you announce me immediately to his majesty. Have the kindness to say to him, that I have not come hither on my private affairs, but as a delegate from the city of Berlin, with full powers from the Council and citizens, to request the honor of an audience with the king, and that I am obliged to return as speedily as possible to the capital."

"Your name, sir?"

"I am the merchant, John Gotzkowsky."

The serious and proud features of the aristocratic adjutant immediately relaxed, and assumed a more polite and obliging expression.

"Ah! Gotzkowsky, the rich and magnanimous merchant of Berlin—the special *protege* of the king. I will announce you immediately to his majesty." And the adjutant hurried through the halls and entered the boudoir of the king.

In the mean while, the generals drew near Gotzkowsky, who related to them all about the siege of Berlin, and the cruel and relentless conduct of the enemy; pressing him with questions, whether on his journey thither he had encountered or come into the vicinity of any portion of the enemy.

"You will find the king very much out of humor," said General von Saldern; "he has not left his study to-day, and doubtless he is occupied with very serious plans."

"Perhaps even with the plan of a battle," said another of the gentlemen, "for it is said that Lacy has advanced his army, and even that Landon has left Dresden. A battle is therefore imminent, and the king is evidently drawing up his plan."

At this moment the door of the study was opened, and the adjutant motioned to Gotzkowsky to enter. As the latter was traversing the hall, the generals cast an eager glance through the open door, anxious to see the countenance of the king, and find out from its expression whether this intolerable armistice was to be interrupted by the violent clash of arms.

In the mean time, Gotzkowsky entered the chamber of the king, and the door closed after him. He was now alone in the presence of the monarch, who was still sitting at his writing-table, making rapid strokes with his drawing-pencil on the paper before him.

"He is writing," said Gotzkowsky to himself, "and is perhaps in the act of drawing out the plan of the battle which the generals out there are awaiting with such joyous impatience. Yes, he is writing, and perhaps each stroke of the pen may cost the lives of hundreds of human beings." And he did not venture by a single word or a loud breath to draw attention to his presence. On his entrance, the king had cast on him one of his sharp, penetrating glances, before whose commanding power many a general and many a brave man had quailed, and had then bent his head again over the paper.

Absolute silence prevailed for a while. Suddenly the king interrupted it, and motioned to Gotzkowsky with his hand to draw near. "Just look and see whether that pleases you," said he, in a friendly tone. "You are known as a connoisseur in art, and you have proved to me that you understand painting. Look at that, and tell me whether you like it."

What was it that the king had drawn on the paper? Was it really, as his brave generals wished, the plan of a battle soon to be fought, was it a philosophical treatise, or one of those witty and piquant epistles to which the king treated his friends? None of all these.

"A nosegay!" cried Gotzkowsky, as with unconcealed astonishment he looked now on the paper, now on the king. "Your majesty is drawing a bouquet of flowers, and out there the gentlemen have just told me in confidence that you were busied with a plan of battle, and that the Austrians were approaching."

"Nonsense!" said the king, shrugging his shoulders, "that rough set out there are always anxious for war, and to be cutting and slashing at each other. Don't you listen to them, but rather tell me how you like this drawing. Don't you think these roses mixed with lilies look well? But I see you wish to know what it is intended for. Well, it is for a set of porcelain which I wish to have painted for the Marquis d'Argens." And, as he met Gotzkowsky's looks, he continued with a friendly smile: "Yes, you see, you are rich; you can make others presents. But the king of Prussia is a poor man; he has only his coat, his sword, and his porcelain. And this last even," continued he, with a slight frown, "I am obliged to get from Meissen."

"That your majesty need not do in future. Please God, your majesty shall make your porcelain in your own dominions!"

"Will you guarantee that? Will you undertake it?" asked the king, kindly.

"I will."

"And look ye, you are just the man to carry out what you wish. I am well satisfied with you. You have justified the confidence I placed in you when I was crown prince. You have redeemed the vow you made me then."

"I swore to your majesty that I would be faithful to the fatherland with life and property," cried Gotzkowsky, with noble ardor.

"And you have kept your word. It is not difficult in easy and prosperous times to find people to serve the state. Those are good citizens who serve her when she is in difficulty and danger.[2] You are a good citizen." And handing Gotzkowsky an open letter which lay on the writing-table, he said: "Read, it is a letter from the Marquis d'Argens. Read it aloud, I would like to hear it again."

And Gotzkowsky read with a trembling voice, and cheeks reddened with noble modesty, the following passage from a letter of the marquis, which the king pointed out to him with his finger: "Gotzkowsky is, indeed, an excellent man and a worthy citizen. I wish you had many such as he. The greatest gift which fortune can make a state is a citizen full of zeal for the welfare of his country and his prince. And in this respect I must say, to the credit of Berlin, that in these trying times I have met many of her citizens, Gotzkowsky the foremost among them, whose virtues, the old historians of Rome, had they lived at the present day, would have immortalized!"[3]

"Are you satisfied?" asked the king, as Gotzkowsky, having finished, handed him the paper. "Oh, I see you are a modest man, and blush like a young girl. But tell me, now, what brings you here? What does the city of Berlin wish?"

"Her rights, your majesty," said Gotzkowsky, seriously.

"And who is troubling her rights?"

"Your majesty."

The king frowned, and cast an angry glance on the bold jester.

Gotzkowsky continued, calmly: "Your majesty is depriving us of our good rights, in so far as you wish to prevent us from being honest people, and keeping our word sacred."

"Oh, now I understand you," said the king, laughing. "You are speaking of the Russian war-tax. Berlin shall not pay it."

"Berlin will pay it, in order that your majesty may retain her in your gracious favor; in order that the great Frederick may not have to blush for his faithless and dishonest town, which would not then deserve to be the residence of a king. How! would your majesty trust the men who refused to redeem their openly-pledged word? who look upon sworn contracts as a mouse-trap, to be escaped from as soon as the opportunity offers, and when the dangerous cat is no longer sitting at the door? Berlin will pay—that our sons may not have to blush for their fathers; that posterity may not say that Berlin had stamped herself with the brand of dishonor. We have pledged our word, and we must keep it."

"You must not, for I do not wish you to do so," cried Frederick, with anger-flashing eyes. "I will institute reprisals. The imperial court has refused the payment of the Bamberg and Wurzburg bonds."

"And your majesty considers that proceeding highly dishonest and unjust," interrupted Gotzkowsky; "and while you wish to punish the empire for its breach of faith, you punish doubly the town of Berlin by depriving her of the last thing that remained to her in her day of need and misfortune—her honorable name. You cannot be in earnest, sire? Punish, if you choose, the imperial judge, but do not make Berlin the dishonored Jack Ketch to carry out your sentence."

"But are you so anxious to get rid of your money? What is the amount that you still owe?"

"A million and a half, sire."

The king stepped back and looked at Gotzkowsky with astonishment. "And the people of Berlin insist upon paying it?"

"Yes, because their word is pledged."

The king shook his head thoughtfully. "Hark ye," said he, "you seem to me to be a dangerous agitator, who wishes to turn my peaceful citizens of Berlin into true children of Haman. Some weeks ago, after the unfortunate fight of Kunnersdorf, when I sent an express courier to Berlin and ordered the Town Council to advise the rich and well-to-do to retire from the city with their portable property, my recommendation was not followed: you yourself excited the Council to disobedience. In your self-willed obstinacy you had the impudent assurance to make your way through a country infested by the enemy; and if my colonel, Von Prittwitz, had not found you in those woods, and brought you to me in the village, your obstinate head would have adorned the lance of some Cossack or other. And what did you come for but to assure me that the well-to-do citizens of Berlin would prefer staying at home, and did not wish to run away? Yes, truly you are a queer diplomatist, and rush headlong into danger and trouble only to assure your king that his citizens will not obey him!"

The king had spoken with apparent displeasure, but around his lips there played a slight smile, and his large blue eyes were directed toward Gotzkowsky with an expression of indescribable kindness.

"In this case they do not wish to obey your majesty, because they wish to remain worthy of the name of your majesty's citizens and subjects."

The king paced up and down several times, with folded arms, and then stopped before Gotzkowsky, looking steadily in his eyes. "Now tell me, how did you manage to make the Berliners so obstinate and so lavish of their means?"

Gotzkowsky smiled. "Please your majesty, the Berliners prize their honor above their life."

The king shook his head impatiently. "You may tell that to some one else. Tell *me*, how did you bring my Berliners up to that? But the truth—mind, you tell me the truth."

"Well, then, your majesty shall know the truth," said Gotzkowsky, after a pause.

"Yes, yes, the truth," cried the king, nodding his head violently. "I wish to know how you inspired the citizens of Berlin with such bold assurance."

"The truth is, sire, that this was only the courage of cowardice, and that the prudent magistracy and merchants were perfectly delighted with your majesty's orders not to

206

pay these bonds, and that I gave myself an immense amount of trouble in vain to remind them of their pledged word and their compromised honor."

"Oh! I know it," said the king. "My good Berliners love money as well as any other of the good-for-nothing children of men. Proceed!"

"Well, when I found them deaf to the voice of honor, I let them hear the words of cowardly prudence. I painted to them the horrors awaiting them if the enemy perchance should return as conquerors, and what a fearful revenge they would take on the perjured city. I reminded them that the enemy would immediately attack all our property in Courland, Dantzic, and Livonia, and that at the Russian headquarters they had threatened me that they would publish, us in all the open commercial marts as issuers of false bonds."

"You were then in the Russian camp?"

"A fortnight ago, sire. The Council of Berlin requested me to undertake this journey to complete the transactions left unfinished by the rapid retreat of General von Tottleben."

"And did you finish them?"

"I was obliged to give General Tottleben a written agreement that I would return in four weeks to the Russian camp to carry out the transactions in the name of these merchants."

"I have been told that the Russian general would not accept the bonds for the war-tax unless you indorsed them. Is that true, too?"

"It is true."

"And what did you do?"

"I indorsed them."

The king's eye lighted up with friendship and kindness. "D'Argens is right," said he. "Cornelius Nepos and Livy would have mentioned you in their writings." And he paced up and down the room in deep thought.

A long pause ensued. Finally, Gotzkowsky was bold enough to break it. "And the tax, your majesty, may we pay it?"

The king stopped in front of him. "The tax shall be paid," said he curtly; but, as Gotzkowsky was about to break out in loud expressions of gratitude, the king waved him off with his hand. "That is," said he, "I myself will pay it, if it cannot be otherwise. Go back into the Russian camp, as you have promised. Endeavor to get some abatement of the amount, or some other profitable terms; but if you do not succeed, well, I will have to pay this million and a half for Berlin. But in return you must grant me a favor."

"What, sire? Whatever it may be," cried Gotzkowsky, ardently, "I am ready to perform any service for your majesty, even to the sacrifice of my life."

The king smiled. "Oh, no! not quite so bad as that, although the service I ask of you is more difficult to most men than dying—I mean *keeping silence*." And as he laid his hand affectionately on Gotzkowsky's shoulder, he continued: "Betray to no one what I have said to you, and only at the very last moment, if it is absolutely necessary, take the Council into your confidence."

"How, sire?" said Gotzkowsky, painfully. "You wish to deprive your Berlin citizens of the gratification of expressing to you their gratitude, their infinite affection. Berlin may not even know how kind, how gracious your majesty has been to her!"

"I don't like the jingling of words, nor the throwing of wreaths. The very people who throw laurel-wreaths would be only too glad if the laurels were hard enough to break our heads. You pay the contribution, that is to say, you advance it, and I'll return it to you.[4] That's all, and now don't say another word about it." At the same time, as if fearful that Gotzkowsky might yet venture to act contrary to his wishes, he continued more rapidly: "Now tell me a little about Berlin, and above all things about our gallery at Sans-Souci. How does it fare?"

"It is finished, sire, and the people flock to see it."

"I only, like a fugitive or a Don Quixote, am driven about," said the king to himself, "and cannot even enter my own house, and they call that royal happiness!" Turning to Gotzkowsky, he remarked aloud: "Have you seen the gallery since the enemy took up his quarters in it?"

"Yes, sire! Prince Esterhazy was this noble enemy. He protected Sans-Souci like something sacred. When he left he only took one single small picture with him, as a souvenir."

The king gave a friendly nod. "I know it," said he, "and that is the only pleasure I have had for a long time. Once more I will see my Titians and Correggios, my Rubenses and Vandycks, which you bought for me. Now tell me about Charlottenburg. But mind, give me the truth. I have noticed that no one will speak out about it, nobody will tell the truth. They are afraid of my anger. But you are a brave man, you are not even afraid of the Cossacks. You will have the courage to let your king know the facts. How is it with Charlottenburg? The Saxons have quartered there—what did they do?"

And now Gotzkowsky, often interrupted by the violent and angry exclamations of the king, told of the barbarous and cruel vandalism committed by the Saxons at Charlottenburg, their unbridled destructiveness and unsparing barbarity.

"And the Polignac collection?" asked the king, breathlessly.

"Almost entirely destroyed."

The king started up from his easy-chair, his eyes flashing with rage. He was no longer the philosopher of Sans-Souci, no longer the poet; he was now the warrior panting for battle and bloody vengeance. "Tell me, tell me! I wish to know all," said the king, laboring out each word, and taking long strides up and down.

But as Gotzkowsky gave him a more detailed account, and related the sacrilegious barbarity which did not spare even the sacred art-treasures, the king's brow became more darkened, and for a moment a burning flush of anger shot across his pale cheek. At one time he raised his arm threateningly, as if he would bring down the thunderbolts of heaven upon such wickedness and ruthlessness.

As Gotzkowsky finished, the king said, curtly and vehemently, "Good, very good!" and traversing the room with hasty steps, he threw open the door which led into the antechamber, and called out, "Saldern!"

Immediately General von Saldern appeared at the open door. The king commanded him to enter and shut the door; then, addressing him in a short, decisive tone: "Go to-morrow, quietly, with a detachment of infantry and cavalry, to Hubertsburg, take possession of the castle, and have all the valuable furniture carefully inventoried and packed up. I will have none of it. The money obtained from its ransom will be turned over to the Lazaretto, and I will not forget you."

There was a pause. General von Saldern remained at the door motionless, in stiff military attitude.

The king looked at him with astonishment. "Well! did you hear?"

"Yes, your majesty, I heard. But, may it please your majesty, this is against my honor and my oath."

The king compelled himself to be composed, for he loved General Saldern as a brave and noble officer. "You would be right," said he, "if I did not use this desperate means to a good object. But let me tell you, the head of the great lord does not feel it if you tear out the hair of his subjects. You must hit, then, where it hurts him; and that I intend to do. The Elector of Saxony shall find out how it feels when one's most cherished possession is destroyed. We will teach him to be humane, and behave himself. Go, therefore, to Hubertsburg, and do as I told you."

General von Saldern turned pale, and his countenance was expressive of deep suffering, as he answered gravely and firmly: "Your majesty may send me right off to attack the enemy and his batteries, and I will obey with my whole heart; but against my honor, my oath, and my duty, I cannot, dare not act."

The king stamped with his foot, and his eye flashed with threatening anger.

"You must obey, as is your duty; you are bound to obey no other voice than that of your king who commands you," said he with a voice of thunder.

General Saldern answered, calmly: "But, sire, I must obey the voice of my honor! Your majesty can easily transfer this commission to another."

The king turned from him with an involuntary frown, and, walking up and down hastily, he stopped near Saldern, and laid his hand gently on his shoulder. "Look ye, Saldern, obey—go to Hubertsburg."

"I cannot, sire!"

"You do not desire to enrich yourself?" said the king, as he turned away. "Do you wish your discharge? I have no use for soldiers who do not consider obedience their first duty."

"I herewith ask for my discharge, sire!"

"You have it—go!"[5]

Without saying a word, General von Saldern made a military obeisance, and left the room.

"You go too!" said the king to Gotzkowsky, who had been a silent, involuntary spectator of this scene—"go and tell my adjutant to send Quintus Icilius to me."

In a few minutes Major Quintus Icilius entered. "Go to Hubertsburg with a detachment of infantry and cavalry, and clear out the castle."

Major Quintus Icilius took good heed not to contradict the king. He had already, in the antechamber, heard of General von Saldern's fate, and he was not indisposed to execute the king's commission.

"Only a hundred thousand dollars you hand over to the Lazaretto, the rest you can keep for yourself."

"As you command, sire! Shall I proceed at once?"

210

The king cast a look of disgust on him. "Are you in such a hurry to be rich?" said he. "Go—I will appoint the time and the hour more particularly."[6]

When the king was alone again, he paced up and down the room in deep thought. At one time he stopped at the window, and his bright blue eyes were turned mournfully toward heaven. "Poor fools that we are!" said he, with a sigh. "We have only a moment to live, and we make this moment as bitter as possible to each other. We take pleasure in destroying the master-pieces of industry and art, at the same time we are erecting an accursed monument to our own devastation and our cruelty."[7]

[Footnote 1: "Lettres inedites, ou Correspondance de Frederic II.," &c., p. 120.]

[Footnote 2: The king's own words.]

[Footnote 3: "Correspondance entre Fred. et M. d'Argens," vi., p. 228.]

[Footnote 4: "Life of a Patriotic Merchant," pp. 85-254. "The king paid the contribution in fact so quietly, one hardly knew when, where, or how."—*Preuss's History of Frederick.*]

[Footnote 5: This interview is historical and literal. General von Saldern left the army, but after the peace entered it again, with high honor and distinction.—-KUSTRE, "Traits of Saldern," p. 39.]

[Footnote 6: Not till May, 1761, was the king's order carried into execution by Major Q. Icilius, in a most barbarous manner. The king was apparently satisfied; but when Q. Icilius in 1764 applied for repayment of moneys spent in executing the royal command, the king indorsed on the application—"My officers steal like crows. They get nothing."]

[Footnote 7: His own words.]

* * * * *

CHAPTER II.

The king of Prussia had left Meissen, and taken up his winter-quarters in Leipsic. The choice of this town arose from a particular need of the king. He wished to pass the winter in a university town, and, instead of the rough companions of war, to surround himself with learned men and artists, poets and musicians. He had his band brought from Berlin, and invited the professors of the Leipsic University to his table. Thus Leipsic, the rich and luxurious commercial town, found itself, for a few months, converted into a royal residence. But not willingly did she undergo this transformation; and it was against her wish that she received the Prussian king, in lieu of the troops of the allies, within her walls. Frederick knew this, and therefore exercised no mercy on this city, so rich in money and professions, whose unwelcome guest he was.

Had Leipsic welcomed the Prussian army in a ready and friendly manner, she would certainly have met with indulgence; but her defiant and sullen behavior, her warm partisanship of Austria, whose ally Saxony was, naturally only tended to increase the animosity of the king, and aggravate his ill-humor. If Leipsic insisted upon regarding the Prussians as enemies, his duty was to consider her as an enemy, and treat her as such.

Enormous contributions were laid upon the town, and in spite of the previous written promise of the king that her assessment should not, at the utmost, exceed five hundred thousand dollars, new demands were now constantly being made, and new contributions levied. In vain did the Council beg and plead for mercy and justice; in vain did the merchants protest that their means were exhausted, and that they were not able to meet any further payments. The enormous demands determined on were firmly and with iron obstinacy insisted upon; and as the refractory town did not cease to oppose them, recourse was had to threats to intimidate her. Tarred rings were hung against the houses, and it was sworn to lay the town in ashes if Leipsic did not immediately pay the million of dollars demanded. But the unfortunate inhabitants had already reached that pitch of desperation at which people are prepared for any thing, and fear nothing further because there is nothing more to lose. They declared that they could pay no more, and offered to seal their word with their death.

The tarred rings were indeed taken down from the houses, but the richest and most respectable inhabitants were seized and incarcerated. Even the authorities were not spared, and the officers of the Council were thrown into the prisons of the towns. In the most degrading manner, like a flock of sheep, they were shut up in spaces hardly able to contain them; damp straw was their bed, bread and water their only nourishment, and this was brought to them with words of cruel insult by their Prussian jailers. But to these latter the burden soon became too heavy; they were weary of their cruel service, and sought to lighten it.

212

At first they had one hundred and twenty prisoners, but, after a fortnight of useless torment, the greater number had been set free, and only seventeen retained. To be sure, these consisted of the richest and most respectable citizens of Leipsic. And these unfortunate hostages, these spoilt sons of wealth and luxury, were now forced to bear the whole weight of misfortune, the entire anger of the victorious enemy. They, whose whole life had been one of indulgence and effeminacy, had now to undergo the greatest privations, the hardest sufferings. The cold earth was their bed, a piece of bread thrown to them their nourishment; and it was a feast to them when one of the gentlewomen of Leipsic succeeded in obtaining permission to visit a brother or husband, and was able to smuggle in under her silk dress a piece of meat or a little bowl of soup for the martyrs. These cruelties would doubtless have been lessened or abolished if the king had had positive knowledge of them, or if he had believed that the king, vexed by the continually repeated complaints, out of humor at the obstinate conduct of Leipsic, and mindful of the vandal conduct of the Saxons at Charlottenburg, had issued strict orders not to trouble him with this business, and not to report to him about them until they could at the same time show that the sum demanded had been paid. And therewith sentence had been passed upon the unfortunate citizens of Leipsic. No one dared to mention to the king the torments and tortures to which the hostages of the pitiable town were subjected. No one had the courage to beg for mercy for those whose only crime was, that their riches were exhausted, their coffers empty, and that they did not possess the means to pay the inordinate sums demanded of them.

But while the population of Leipsic was undergoing this grief, this hard time of trial, an uninterrupted quiet and precious peace prevailed in the house inhabited by the King of Prussia. Music was performed, readings were held, and in the midst of these gentle diversions and this pleasant rest Frederick drew up the plans of fresh, battles and new and great undertakings. Fasch and Quanz had been brought from Berlin to play music for him, the Marquis d'Argens to philosophize for him, his dogs to amuse him. The king, who knew enough of men to despise the wavering, erring, sinful creatures, was also a sufficient connoisseur of dogs to love the faithful, obedient, submissive animals with his whole heart, and devoted a great part of his time to them. He who was deaf to the wailing and lamentations of a whole city, had his ears open to the least whine of Biche, or his favorite Psyche, and never would have forgiven him who had dared to treat one of his dogs as so many of the noble and distinguished citizens of Leipsic were being treated in his name.

* * * * *

CHAPTER III.

THE FRIEND IN NEED.

No one would have dared to speak a word for the refractory citizens and authorities of Leipsic to the king, nor act in direct contravention to his express orders. Even the Marquis d'Argens, his intimate friend and confidant, had refused to be the advocate of the unfortunate town. It seemed to be lost, without hope of redemption, and already it had been threatened with the extreme of severity. It had been announced to the chief men, the fathers and heads of families who were pining in the prisons, that they would be transported on foot to Magdeburg as recruits, with knapsacks on their backs. But at this moment the rescuer in need, of the afflicted city, made his appearance.

A tall, proud, manly form crossed the antechamber of the king. Power and energy were visible in his countenance, and his eyes sparkled with noble excitement. He was going to perform that duty from which courtiers and flatterers shrank with trembling; and what the bravest generals did not dare, he was going to undertake. John Gotzkowsky was going to tell the king the truth. John Gotzkowsky was not afraid to rouse the anger of a king, when it came to helping the unfortunate or protecting the oppressed. He had a more noble mission to perform than to sue for the smiles of a king, or the favor of the great. It was the higher mission of humanity which impelled him, and, as usual, his resolution was firm and unwavering. With bold decision he reached the door which led into the king's chamber. He had the privilege of entering unannounced, for the king expected him.

He had summoned Gotzkowsky from Berlin, to obtain information as to the progress of the Berlin industrial works, and the faithful patriot had, in obedience to the call of his king, come to Leipsic. He had seen the misery and suffering on this poor, down-trodden town, and, as he traversed the antechamber, he said to himself, with an imperceptible smile, "I brought the Russian general to clemency, and the king will not be harder than he was."

But before he threw off his cloak, he drew out of it a small package, which he examined carefully. Being satisfied with its appearance, he took it with him to the cabinet of the king. Frederick did not look at him at first. He was reclining on the floor, and around him, on silken cushions, lay his dogs, their bright eyes fixed on a dish which was placed in the midst of them. The king, with an ivory stick, was carefully dividing the portion for each dog, ordering the growling, discontented ones to be quiet, and comforting the patiently waiting ones with a light jest concerning the next piece. Suddenly he raised his eyes, and his quick glance rested on Gotzkowsky's smiling, placid face. "Ah, you laugh," said he, "and in your human conceit you find it quite beneath one's dignity to occupy one's self with dogs, when there are so many human beings. Let me tell you, you don't understand any thing about it! You don't know dogs at all, and perhaps you don't know men.—Quiet, Biche! leave that piece for Apollo. I gave it to him, and therefore it belongs to him. One would suppose you had been learning from men, and in the true spirit of

Christian and brotherly love, grudged each other a piece of bread. Quiet, Biche, and don't be vexed that I compared you to human beings. I did not mean you were quite as bad as that."

And gently stroking and caressing the offended Biche, he rose and seated himself in his velvet-covered *fauteuil*. His bright eye turned toward Gotzkowsky, and rested on the package the latter had in his hand. "What have you there?"

"A plate and a cup," said Gotzkowsky, seriously—"the first two pieces from my porcelain factory in Berlin."

The king now rose from his seat and strode hastily toward Gotzkowsky. "Give them here. I want to see what sort of potters'-ware you are going to impose upon me for porcelain." With impatient hands he tore off the paper coverings, and so eagerly was he engaged with them, that he did not perceive that Biche and Apollo were already fighting for a scrap of paper which he had thrown directly on Biche's nose, and which she consequently mistook for a delicate morsel, a prize worth a fight with Apollo. "Forsooth, it is porcelain!" cried the king, as he drew out the gold-rimmed plate and the beautifully painted cup from their wrappings, and looked at them attentively; and as his eye rested on the painting of the cup, his features assumed a soft and sad expression. "My house in Rheinsberg," muttered he softly to himself—- "a greeting from my happy days."

"In the castle Rheinsberg, I first enjoyed the favor of being presented to your majesty," said Gotzkowsky. "Castle Rheinsberg is, therefore, to me a happy recollection, and it was for that reason selected to adorn the proof pieces of my porcelain factory."

The king fastened a penetrating look upon him. "You are playing me a trick—I don't like tricks, you must know. Therefore tell me the truth. Where did you get this porcelain? It is not from Meissen. The mark is wanting, and it is whiter and stronger. Where did you get it?"

"From Berlin, sire. I promised you, when you were in Meissen, that in future you should procure your porcelain from your own dominions, and I dare not forfeit my word."

"And so you imitated the Almighty, and created a porcelain factory with the breath of your mouth?"

"Not with the breath of my mouth, but the breath of my money."

"Tell me about it, and all the particulars," said the king, still holding the cup in his hand, and looking at it attentively.

And Gotzkowsky related how, on his return from Meissen, he had accidentally made the acquaintance of a young man, who was passing through Berlin on his way to Gotha, the duke having offered to advance him the capital necessary to found a factory for the making of porcelain according to a process of his own invention. The specimens exhibited convinced Gotzkowsky that this young man was fully acquainted with the secret of porcelain-making, and he had therefore immediately determined to forestall the Duke of Gotha.

Money had in this instance, as usual, exercised its charm, and nothing more was necessary than to outbid the terms agreed on with the duke. A few thousand dollars more offered, and double purchase-money, had secured the secret of porcelain-making to Gotzkowsky, and bound the inventor down in Berlin for life.[1]

The arrangements necessary for the first attempts were made in one of the out-buildings of his house, and the articles offered to the king were the first-fruits of his factory. The king listened to him with intense interest, and when Gotzkowsky had finished, he nodded to him with a smile.

"The Marquis d'Argens is right. I wish myself I had many such citizens as you are. It would be a fine thing to be a king if all one's subjects were true men, and made it worth one's while to be to them a kind father and lord. You have fulfilled a favorite wish of mine; and let me tell you, I do not think you will call the porcelain factory yours long. I think it will soon be a royal factory."

"I founded it for your majesty."

"Good, good! you have given me a pleasure, I will give you one in return. Ask some favor for yourself. You are silent. Do you know of nothing to ask for?"

"Oh, yes, indeed," said Gotzkowsky, ardently, "I have a great favor to ask—have pity on the poor inhabitants of this town!"

The king frowned and pressed his lips angrily together. "Do you know that I have generally forbidden any one to trouble me with these Leipsic jeremiades?"

"I know it, sire."

The king looked at him with astonishment. "And yet you do it?"

"Yes, sire, I do it because I relied on the kind, noble heart of my king, and because humanity bade me not to fear your majesty's anger, when it became a question of mercy to the oppressed."

"And for this reason you wanted to bribe me with your bits of porcelain. Oh, you are a reckoner, but this time you have reckoned without your host. No pity for these obstinate Leipsigers. They must pay the eleven hundred thousand dollars, or—"

216

"Or what?" asked Gotzkowsky, as he hesitated.

The king looked angrily at him. "You are very bold," said he, "to interrupt me. The Leipsigers must pay, for I need the money for my soldiers, and they are rich; they are able to pay!"

"They are not able to pay, sire! They are as little able to pay as Berlin is if Russia insists upon her demands, and her magnanimous king does not come to her assistance. But your majesty certainly does not wish that the world and history shall say that Russia acted with more forbearance and clemency toward Berlin than Prussia did toward Leipsic? To be sure, the Russians carried off the Jewish elders into captivity because they could not pay, but then they treated these poor victims of their avarice like human beings. They did not make them sleep on rotten straw; they did not let them starve, and die of misery and filth; they did not have them scourged and tortured until they wet with their tears the bit of bread thrown to them."

"Who does that?" cried the king, with thundering voice and flashing eye.

Gotzkowsky bowed low. "Your majesty, the King of Prussia does that!"

Frederick uttered a cry of anger, and advanced with his arm raised on Gotzkowsky, who looked at him quietly and firmly. "You lie! retract!" thundered the king.

"I have, as long as I have lived, spoken the truth, sire—the truth, without fear or dread of man. Your majesty is the first man who has accused me of a lie. I have seen with my own eyes your majesty's officials treating the poor captive Leipsic merchants like dogs. What do I say—like dogs? Oh, how would the poor down-trodden men envy those dogs the delicacies contained in that dish! It may be right to compel and humble the refractory, but it is not right to tread out the human soul, and even in the conquered you should honor God's image."

The king looked at him with ludicrous surprise. "Do you wish to give me a lesson? Well, I will forgive you this time, and, as you express it, honor God's image in the owner of the Berlin porcelain factory. But hush about these hard-headed Leipsigers. They must pay. My soldiers cannot live on air, and my coffers are empty."

"The Leipsigers are very willing to contribute, but the demand must not exceed their powers."

"How do you know that?"

"The magistracy and merchant guild of Leipsic sent a deputation to me, and entreated my mediation."

"You have then already the reputation of one who knows how to use his tongue well, and goes about tattling with it."

"Sire," said Gotzkowsky, smiling, "we only follow the example of our hero-king. We all are anxious to fight, and those who have no swords must fight with the tongue. I have latterly been compelled to fight a great deal with it, and the Leipsic merchants may have heard something about that. They knew that I had some exercise with my tongue, and gained a little victory with it over the Russians in Berlin."

"How much do you think the city of Leipsic can pay?" asked the king after a pause.

"If your majesty will remit them a few hundred thousand dollars, and allow the merchants time, they are willing to bind themselves in joint bonds."

"*Parbleu*! are they willing to do that?" asked the king, derisively. "The bonds of the Leipsic merchants would be no security to me." And turning quickly on Gotzkowsky, he asked him, "Are you willing to guarantee the payment?"

"If your majesty orders it, the bonds shall be drawn out with my guaranty."

"I look to you, then, for their payment."

"At your orders, sire."

"Well, then, for your sake I will remit the Leipsigers three hundred thousand dollars; but for the rest of the million you are answerable."

"I will be answerable for it."

"I will let these gentlemen of Leipsic know that it is to your intercession and your guaranty that they are indebted for the mitigation of their contributions; and then you can, if it gives you pleasure, bargain with the rich town for some reward for your services rendered."

"That would give me no pleasure, sire!" cried Gotzkowsky, with noble indignation. "Your majesty must not think so meanly of me as to suppose that I would make a profit out of the misfortunes of others, and that I have interceded for the poor Leipsigers in order to make a trade out of them!"

"I think that you are a hard-headed, obstinate fellow, who must be allowed to have his own way," said the king, with an affable smile. "But I must bear you witness that, in your own way, you have rendered me many a good service. For that reason, you will always find me well affected toward you, and in the Sans-Souci gallery you have created a beautiful memorial to yourself."

"If your majesty would come there now, you would find the Correggio about which you wrote to the Marquis d'Argens."

218

The king's eyes sparkled. "The Correggio is mine!" said he, walking up and down slowly, with his hands behind his back. "Ah," added he, after a long pause, in a low tone, as if speaking to himself, "when will this nomadic life cease, and the world be at peace, to allow this poor, badgered king a few hours of leisure and recreation, to enjoy the contemplation of his house and his pictures? The wandering Jew, if he ever existed, did not lead such a rambling life as I do. We get at last to be like the roving play-actors, who have neither hearth nor home, and thus we pass through the world, playing our bloody tragedies, with the wailings of our subjects for chorus.[2] When will it end?"

"When your majesty has subdued all your enemies."

The king looked around with surprise—he had quite forgotten Gotzkowsky. "Ah! are you still there? and you prophesy me victory? Well, that will be as good to me as the Leipsic money. Go back home, and tell the Leipsigers to hurry with the money. And hark ye! when you get to Potsdam, greet the Correggio, and tell him I yearn for him as a lover does for his mistress Adieu!"

[Footnote 1: Porcelain-making was then a great secret in Germany, only known in Meissen; the process being conducted with closed doors, and the foreman bound by oath. Gotzkowsky paid ten thousand dollars down, a life income of a thousand dollars, and house and firewood free.—"Life of a Patriotic Merchant," p. 87.]

[Footnote 2: "Correspondance de Frederic II. avec le Comte Algarottis."]

* * * * *

CHAPTER IV.

GRATITUDE AND RECOMPENSE.

Thus did Gotzkowsky save unfortunate Leipsic from the heavy burden which weighed her down. The prisoners were released, and the merchants gave a bond, for whose punctual and prompt payment Gotzkowsky guaranteed with his signature.

He did not do this from a selfish or vain ambition to have the praise of his name sounded, nor to increase the number of his addresses of gratitude, or written asseverations of affection. He did it from love of mankind; because he desired to fulfil the vow he had made to God and himself on the highway as a shivering, starving lad: that if he should ever become rich, he would be to every unfortunate and needy one the hand which had appeared out of the dust-cloud to his relief. He did it because, as he tells us naively and simply in his Life, "I knew from my own experience how difficult it was for a community to collect such a sum, and because the idea of profiting by such misfortune was abhorrent to me."

And now there was a brilliant banquet, and no end to the words of gratitude and tears of emotion. This banquet was given by the Leipsic merchants in honor of him who had so magnanimously taken their part, saved them three hundred thousand dollars, and guaranteed their bonds. And they devoured the delicate viands and emptied the beakers to his honor, and praised him in high-sounding speeches.

When Gotzkowsky, wearied and bored by this festival, returned home, he found on his table three letters. The one which bore on its seal the arms of Prussia he opened first. It was a cabinet order from the king to his private secretary, Leinning, to pay to the merchant, John Gotzkowsky, one hundred and fifty thousand dollars. "Ah," said he, smiling, "payment on account; I bought a hundred thousand ducats' worth of paintings for the king, and he does not wish to remain always in my debt." With a slight shrug of the shoulders he opened the second letter. Suddenly he burst into a loud laugh, and his countenance assumed an expression of derisive mirth. "The Elector of Saxony, in consideration of services rendered to the town of Leipsic, appoints me his commercial privy councillor!" cried he, waving the paper in the air; "that is a good joke! The little elector, who has been my debtor for many long years, is gracious enough to throw me a bit of rank—a title! Much obliged! My name sounds well enough. It is not necessary to have a title to be a man of honor. Throw titles to numskulls, not to me—away with it!"

He then threw the paper aside with scorn, and took up the third letter. As he read it his noble countenance brightened up with proud pleasure, and his eyes sparkled. It was a document from the town of Leipsic, an address of thanks from the magistracy, the concluding words of which ran thus:

"In our extreme need we had recourse to Herr Gotzkowsky, the respected merchant and banker of Berlin, imploring the same to intercede for this town and its merchants with the king of Prussia; affording them his credit and valuable assistance, to accord to said town some reasonable respite for payment, with security. To this earnest pleading Herr Gotzkowsky yielded, and, as a true philanthropist, without any ulterior views of profit to himself, did in the most praiseworthy manner assist us, and averted this misfortune from the town. These services we are compelled to acknowledge. We therefore offer our services in return on all possible occasions, not doubting that the mercantile community of this place entertain the same sentiments, and feel themselves equally bound to all imaginable reciprocity.

[SIGNED] "The Council of Leipsic.

"Leipsic, *February* 26, 1761."

"This paper I will carry to my daughter, as a souvenir," said Gotzkowsky, folding it up carefully, and then added thoughtfully: "Who knows but what the time may come when it will be necessary to remind the merchants of Leipsic of this document? The opinions and destinies of men are very variable."

But Gotzkowsky himself was to have occasion to remind unthankful Leipsic of her professions of gratitude—not to call on her to perform reciprocal favors, but to protect himself against calumny and unfriendly suspicions. For a day came, when Leipsic forgot the affliction and grief she had suffered, and only remembered that John Gotzkowsky was her creditor, and that she owed him large sums of money. So, when at last, weary of long waiting, he pressed for payment, they accused him of self-interest, and said that he had unnecessarily mixed himself up in their affairs, and that it would have been better if he had left them to their captivity; for although they might have had much to suffer, they would have had but little to pay.

Gotzkowsky answered these accusations in a manner characteristic of his noble, proud self—he was silent about them. But hard times and oppression came again upon the rich town of Leipsic.

The Prussian king exacted fresh contributions—and now they recalled to mind the services of Gotzkowsky; again they sent him humble letters, begging him to have pity on them; and now the cunning, calculating magistracy of Leipsic saw fit to take notice of these calumnies, which they had shortly before so industriously circulated through the public newspapers, and solemnly to declare in all the journals: "We hereby certify, in compliance with truth, through these writings, that the worshipful Herr Gotzkowsky, as well in past years, as at the late Leipsic fair, out of unchanged and innate love and friendly kindness to us, this town, and its inhabitants, has given just cause for gratitude."

Gotzkowsky forgot the insults, and was again of assistance to them. A second time he persuaded the king to mitigate their contribution, and guaranteed the new bonds issued by them. A second time the magistrates and merchants thanked him in the most touching words for his noble and disinterested assistance, and a second time were they destined to forget their vows of gratitude.

* * * * *

CHAPTER V.

FOUR YEARS' LABOR.

Four years of work, of industry, of productive activity, had passed away since the stormy year of 1760. They had produced but little alteration in the life of Gotzkowsky and his daughter.

Gotzkowsky toiled and worked as he always had done; his factories were enlarged, his wealth increased and his fame as a merchant sounded through the whole world.

But all this would he have given, if he could have seen the light on the lips, the rosy glow on the cheek of his daughter, as in bygone days. But the beautiful and impassioned young girl had altered into the pale, serious, silent young woman, who had learned to throw the veil of quiet resignation over the secret of her heart, and to suppress any manifestation of pain.

Elise had grown old *internally*—old, despite her two-and-twenty years; she looked upon the life before her as a joyless, desert waste, which she had to traverse with bleeding feet and broken heart; and in the desolation of her soul, she sometimes shuddered at the death-like apathy and quiet of her feelings, broken by no sound, no note, not even the wail of woe.

She was without a wish, without a hope. Grief had spent itself on her. She wept no more—she wrestled no longer with her love, for she had conquered it. But she could not rise again to any new joys of life—she could only be resigned. She had accepted life, and she bore it as does the bird shut up in a gilded cage, robbed of freedom and fresh air, and given in return a brilliant prison. She, too, was an imprisoned bird; and her wounded heart lay in the cage of her breast, sorrowful and infinitely wretched. She prayed to God for peace, for resignation, no longer for happiness, for she did not believe happiness any more possible. She had sunk into that apathy which desires nothing more than a quiet, dreamy fading away. Her grief was deficient in the animating consolation of the thought that "it came from God." Real and sacred suffering, which does come from God, and is imposed upon us by fate, always carries with it the divine power of healing; and at the same time that it casts us down and humbles us, raises us again, steels our courage, and makes us strong and proud to suffer and to bear. Quite different is that misfortune which comes from man—which is laid upon us by the envy, hatred, and malice of mankind. This carries with it no consolation, no comfort—a misfortune full of bitterness and murmuring—a misfortune which abases us without elevating us again, which casts us down in the mire, from the soil of which not all the hot streams of our tears can purify and cleanse us. Had she lost her lover, had he been snatched away from her by death, Elise, while she gave him back to God, would have regarded this heavy and sacred affliction as her great and holy happiness; she would have accepted it as a precious promise which elevated her, and inspired her with a blissful hope.

But she had lost him by his own treachery, by worldly sin, and she had given him up, not to God, but to his own unrighteousness and disloyalty. She had therefore lost him irretrievably, and for always—not for a short space of time, but for all eternity; and she dared not even weep for him, for her misfortune was at the same time her disgrace, and even her tears filled her with humiliation and shame. For that reason she never spoke, either with her father or with Bertram, about the sad and painful past, about the errors and disappointments of her youth; and neither of them in their pure and indulgent love ever trespassed on the silence which Elise had spread over her sorrow. Toward her father she was a careful, attentive, and submissive daughter; toward Bertram a confiding and loving sister; but to both she felt as if she were only giving what was saved from the shipwreck of her affections. They both knew that Elise could no longer offer them an entire, unbroken heart. But they were both content to rest on the embers of this ruined edifice, to gather the leaves of this rose, broken by the tempest, and to remember how beautiful it was in its bloom.

Gotzkowsky only asked of his daughter that she should live, that she should become again healthy and strong for new happiness.

Bertram, in the strength and fidelity of his affections, had no other wish than that he should some day see her cheerful and content again, and once more brightened by the beams which only love and happiness can spread over a human countenance; and in his great and self-sacrificing love he said to himself: "If I only knew that her happiness lay in the remotest corner of the world, thither would I go to fetch it for her, even if she thereby were lost to me forever!"

And thus did four years pass away—externally, bright and clear, surrounded by all the brilliancy of wealth and happiness—inwardly, silent and desolate, full of privation and deep-rooted sorrow.

* * * * *

CHAPTER VI.

DAYS OF MISFORTUNE.

Gotzkowsky was alone in his room. It was an elegant, brilliantly ornamented apartment, which the greatest prince might have envied. The most select pictures by celebrated old masters hung around on the walls; the most costly Chinese vases stood on gilt tables; and between the windows, instead of mirrors, were placed the most exquisite Greek marble statues. The furniture of the room was simple. Gotzkowsky had but one passion, on which he spent yearly many thousands, and that was for art-treasures, paintings, and antiques. His house resembled a temple of art; it contained the rarest and choicest treasures; and when Gotzkowsky passed through the rooms on the arm of his daughter, and contemplated the pictures, or dwelt with her on one of the sublime statues of the gods, his eye beamed with blissful satisfaction, and his whole being breathed cheerfulness and calm. But at this moment his countenance was care-worn and anxious, and however pleasantly and cheerfully the pictures looked down upon him from the walls, his eye remained sad and clouded, and deep grief was expressed in his features.

He sat at his writing-table, and turned over the papers which lay piled up high before him. At times he looked deeply shocked and anxious, and his whole frame trembled, as with hasty hand he transcribed some notes from another sheet. Suddenly he let the pen drop, and sank his head on his breast.

"It is in vain," he muttered in a low voice—"yes, it is in vain. If I were to exert all my power, if I were to collect all my means together, they would not be sufficient to pay these enormous sums."

Again he turned over the papers, and pointing with his finger to one of them, he continued: "Yes, there it stands. I am a rich man on paper. Leipsic owes me more than a million. If she pays, and De Neufville comes, I am saved. But if not—if Leipsic once more, as she has already done three times, protests her inability to pay—if De Neufville does not come, what shall I do? How can I save myself from ruin and shame?"

Deeper and deeper did he bury himself silently in the papers. A terrible anxiety oppressed him, and sent his blood rushing to his heart and head. He arose and paced up and down the room, muttering occasionally a few words, betraying the anguish and terror which possessed him. Then standing still, he pressed his hands to his temples, as if to crowd back the pain which throbbed and ached there.

"Oh, it is terrible!" he uttered in a subdued voice; "with my eyes open I stand on the brink of a precipice. I see it, and cannot draw back. If no helping hand is stretched out to save me, I must fall in, and my good name must perish with me. And to be obliged to confess that not my own want of judgment, no rashness nor presumption on my part, but only love of mankind, love of my brethren, has brought me to this!

To each one who held out his hand to me, I gave the hand of a friend, every one in need I helped. And for that reason, for the good I have done, I stand on the verge of an abyss."

He cast his looks toward heaven, and tears shone in his eyes. "Was it, then, wrong? O my God! was it, then, culpable to trust men, and must I atone with my honor for what I did from love?"

But this compunction, this depression, did not last long. Gotzkowsky soon arose above his grief, and bearing his head aloft as if to shake off the cares which lowered around it, he said in a determined tone: "I must not lose my courage. This day requires all my presence of mind, and the decisive moment shall not find me cowed and pusillanimous."

He was about to set himself to work again, when a repeated knocking at the door interrupted him. At his reluctant bidding it opened, and Bertram appeared on the threshold. "Pardon me," he said, almost timidly; "I knew that you wished to be alone, but I could not bear it any longer. I must see you. Only think, Father Gotzkowsky, it is a fortnight since I arrived, and I have scarcely seen you in this time; therefore do not be angry with me if I disobey your orders, and come to you, although I know that you are busy."

Gotzkowsky nodded to him with a sad smile. "I thank you for it," said he. "I had ordered Peter not to admit any one. You are an exception, as you know, my son."

A pause ensued, during which Bertram examined Gotzkowsky with a searching look. The latter had seated himself again at his writing-table, and with troubled looks was examining his papers.

Bertram had been absent for nearly a year. The silent grief which day and night gnawed at his heart had undermined his health and exhausted his physical strength. The physicians had deemed a prolonged residence in Nice necessary. If Bertram yielded to their judgment and repaired to Nice, it was because he thought, "Perhaps Elise will think of me when I am no longer near her. Perchance absence may warm her heart, and she may forget the brother, some day to welcome the husband."

Returning after a year's absence, strengthened and restored to health, he found Elise as he had left her. She received him with the same quiet, calm look with which she had bid him farewell. She placed her hand as coolly and as friendly in his, and although she inquired cordially and sympathizingly after his welfare, Bertram still felt that her heart and her inmost soul had not part in her questioning.

Elise had not altered—but how little was Gotzkowsky like himself! Where was the ardent man, powerful of will, whom Bertram had embraced at his departure? where was his clear, ringing voice, his proud bearing, his energy, his burning eloquence—-

what had become of all these? What diabolical, dismal influence had succeeded in breaking this iron will, in subduing this vital power?

Bertram felt that a deep grief was corroding Gotzkowsky's life—a grief whose destructive influence was greater because he avoided the expression of it, and sought no relief nor consolation by communicating it to others. "He shall, at least, speak to me," said Bertram. "I will compel him to make me the confidant of his grief, and to lighten his heart by imparting a portion of his burden to mine." With this determination he had entered Gotzkowsky's room; he now stood opposite to him, and with gentle sympathy looked into his pale, sorrow-worn countenance.

But Gotzkowsky avoided his eye. He seemed entirely occupied with his papers, and turned them over again and again. Bertram could bear it no longer; he hastened to him, and taking his hand pressed it affectionately to his lips. "My father," said he, "forgive me; but when I look at you, I am possessed by a vague fear which I cannot explain to myself. You know that I love you as my father, and for that reason can read your thoughts. Gotzkowsky, since my return I have read much care and sorrow in your face."

"Have you?" said Gotzkowsky, painfully; "yes, yes, sorrow does not write in hieroglyphics. It is a writing which he who runs can read."

"You confess, then, that you have sorrow, and yet you hide it from me. You do not let me share your cares. Have I deserved that of you, father?"

Gotzkowsky arose and paced the room, thoughtful and excited. For the first time he felt that the sympathy of a loving heart did good. Involuntarily the crust which surrounded his heart gave way, and he became gentle and eager for sympathy. He held out his hand to Bertram and nodded to him. "You are right, my son," said he, gently, "I should not have kept my sorrows from you. It is a comfort, perhaps, to unbosom one's self. Listen, then—but no! first tell me what is said of me in the city, and, above all, what is said of me at the Bourse? Ah? you cast your eyes down—- Bertram, I must and will know all. Speak out freely. I have courage to hear the utmost." But yet his voice trembled as he spoke, and his lips twitched convulsively.

Bertram answered sadly: "What do you care about the street gossip of envious people? You know that you have enemies, because you are rich and high-minded. You have long been envied because your house is the most extensive and solid in all Europe, and because your drafts stand at par in all the markets. They are jealous of the fame of your firm, and for that very reason they whisper all sorts of things that they do not dare to say aloud. But why should you let such miserable scandal worry you?"

Bertram tried to smile, but it was a sorrowful, anxious one, which did not escape Gotzkowsky. "Ah!" said he, "these light whisperings of calumny are like the single snow-flakes which finally collect together and roll on and on, and at last become an avalanche which buries up our honor and our good name. Tell me, then, Bertram, what do they whisper?"

Bertram answered in a low, timid voice: "They pretend to know that your house has suffered immense losses; that you were not able to meet your drafts; that all your wealth is unfounded; and that—but why should I repeat all the old women's and newspaper stories?"

"Even the newspapers talk about it, then?" muttered Gotzkowsky to himself.

"Yes, the *Vossian Gazette*," continued Bertram, "has an article in which it speaks mysteriously and sympathizingly of the impending failure of one of our most eminent houses. This is said to aim at you, father."

"And the other paper, *Spener's Journal?*"

"Is sorry to join in the statement, and confirms it to-day."

Gotzkowsky broke out into a mocking laugh, his countenance brightened with indignation, and his features expressed their former energy and decision. "O world! O men!" he exclaimed, "how pitiful, how mean you are! You know, Bertram, how much good I have done these men. I have protected them as a friend in the time of their need and affliction. I saved them from punishment and shame. In return they trumpet forth my misfortunes, and that which might have been altered by the considerate silence of my friends, they cry aloud to all the world, and thereby precipitate my fall."

"It is, then, really true?" asked Bertram, turning pale. "You are in danger?"

"To-day is the last term for the payment of the five hundred thousand dollars, which I have to pay our king, for the town of Leipsic. Our largest banking-houses have bought up these claims of the king against me."

"But that is not your own debt. You only stood good for Leipsic."

"That I did; and as Leipsic cannot pay, I must."

"But Leipsic can assume a portion of the debt least."

"Perhaps so," said Gotzkowsky. "I have sent a courier to Leipsic, and look for his return every hour. But it is not that alone which troubles me," continued he, after a pause. "It would be easy to collect the five hundred thousand dollars. The new and unexpected ordinance from the mint, which renders uncurrent the light money, deprives me of another half million. When I foresaw Leipsic's insolvency, I had negotiated alone with Hamburg for half a million of light money. But the spies of the Jews of the mint discovered this, and when my money was in the course of transmission from Hamburg they managed to obtain a decree from the king forbidding immediately the circulation of this coin. In this way my five hundred thousand dollars became good for nothing."

"Horrible!" cried Bertram; "have you, then, not endeavored to save a portion of this money?"

"Yes, indeed," cried Gotzkowsky, with a bitter laugh, "I have tried. I wished to send fifty thousand dollars of my money to the army of the allies, to see if it would be current there; but Ephraim had foreseen this, too, and obtained a decree forbidding even the transit of this money through the Prussian dominions. This new and arbitrary law was only published after my money had left Hamburg, and I had grounds to hope that I would not be prevented from bringing it through the Prussian dominions, for it was concealed in the double bottom of a wagon. But avarice has sharp eyes, and the spies who were set upon all my actions succeeded in discovering this too. The wagon was stopped at the gates of Berlin, and the money was discovered where they knew it was beforehand, under this false bottom. But who do you think it was, Bertram, who denounced me in this affair? You would never guess it—the chief burgomaster, President von Kircheisen! He stood himself at the gate, watched for the wagon, and searched until he found the money."

"Kircheisen! The same, father, whom you saved from death when the Russians were here?"

"The same, my son; you shake your head incredulously. Read for yourself." He took from his writing-table a large paper provided with the official seal, and handed it to Bertram. "Read for yourself, my son. It is an order from the minister Von Finkenstein."

It was written thus: "The half of the sum is awarded by the king to President von Kircheisen, as detective and informer."

"A worthy title, 'detective and informer,'" continued Gotzkowsky. "By Heaven, I do not envy him it! But now you shall know all. It does me good to confide to you my sorrows—it lightens my poor heart. And now I have another fear. You have heard of my speculation in the Russian magazines?"

"Of the magazines which you, with De Neufville and the bankers Moses and Samuel, bought?" asked Bertram.

"Yes, that is it. But Russia would not enter into the bargain unless I made myself responsible for the whole sum."

"And you did so?" asked Bertram, trembling.

"I did. The purchase-money has been due for four months. My fellow-contractors have not paid. If Russia insists upon the payment of this debt, I am ruined."

"And why do not Samuel and Moses pay their part?"

Gotzkowsky did not answer immediately, but when he did, his features expressed scorn and contempt: "Moses and Samuel are no longer obliged to pay, because yesterday they declared themselves insolvent."

Bertram suppressed with effort a cry of anger, and covered his face with his hands. "He is lost," he muttered to himself, "lost beyond redemption, for he founds his hopes on De Neufville, and he knows nothing of his unfortunate fate."

* * * * *

CHAPTER VII.

CONFESSIONS.

Bertram raised his head again, Gotzkowsky was standing near him, looking brightly and lovingly into his sorrowful, twitching face. It was now Gotzkowsky who had to console Bertram, and, smiling quietly and gently, he told him of the hopes which still remained to him.

"De Neufville may return," he said. "He has only gone to the opening of the bank at Amsterdam, and if he succeeds in collecting the necessary sum there, and returns with it as rapidly as possible to Berlin, I am saved."

"But if he does not come?" asked Bertram with a trembling voice, fixing his sad looks penetratingly on Gotzkowsky.

"Then I am irretrievably lost," answered Gotzkowsky, in a loud, firm voice.

Bertram stepped quickly up to him, and threw himself in his arms, folding him to his breast as if to protect him against all the danger which threatened him. "You must be saved!" cried he, eagerly; "it is not possible that you should fall. You have never deserved such a misfortune."

"For that very reason I fear that I must suffer it. If I deserved this disgrace, perhaps it never would have happened to me. The world is so fashioned, that what we deserve of good or evil never happens to us."

"But you have friends; thousands are indebted to your generosity, and to your ever-ready, helping hand. There is scarcely a merchant in Berlin to whom, some time or other, you have not been of assistance in his need!"

Gotzkowsky laid his hand on his shoulder, and replied with a proud air: "My friend, it is precisely those who owe me gratitude, who are now trying to ruin me. The very fact of having obliged them, makes them my bitter enemies. Gratitude is so disagreeable a virtue, that men become implacably hostile to those who impose it on them."

"When you speak thus, my father," said Bertram, glowing with noble indignation, "you condemn me, too. You have bound me to everlasting gratitude, and yet I love you inexpressibly for it."

"You are a rare exception, my son," replied Gotzkowsky, sadly, "and I thank God, who has taught me to know you."

"You believe, then, in me?" asked Bertram, looking earnestly in his eyes.

"I believe in you," said Gotzkowsky, solemnly, offering him his hand.

"Well, then, my father," cried Bertram, quickly and gladly, "in this important moment let me make an urgent request of you. You call me your son; give me, then, the rights of a son. Allow me the happiness of offering you the little that I can call mine. My fortune is not, to be sure, sufficient to save you, but it can at least be of service to you. Father, I owe you every thing. It is yours—take it back."

"Never!" interrupted Gotzkowsky.

But Bertram continued more urgently: "At least consider of it. When you founded the porcelain factory, you made me a partner in this business, and I accepted it, although I had nothing but what belonged to you. When the king, a year ago, bought the factory from you, you paid me a fourth of the purchase-money, and gave me thirty thousand dollars. I accepted it, although I had not contributed any part of the capital."

"You are mistaken, my son. You forget that you contributed the capital of your knowledge and genius."

"One cannot live on genius," cried Bertram, impatiently; "and with all my knowledge I might have starved, if you had not taken me by the hand."

Gotzkowsky would have denied this, but Bertram continued still more pressingly: "Father, if I were, indeed, your son, could you then deny me the right of falling and being ruined with you? Can you deny your son the right of dividing with you what is his?"

"No!" cried Gotzkowsky, "from my son I could demand the sacrifice, but it is not only a question of earthly possessions, it is a question of my most sacred spiritual good, it is the honor of my name. Had I a son, I would exact of him that he should follow me unto death, so that the honor of my name might be saved."

"Well, then, let me be, indeed, your son. Give me your daughter!"

Gotzkowsky stepped back in astonishment and gazed at Bertram's noble, excited countenance. "Ah!" cried he, "I thank you, Bertram; you are a noble man! I understand you. You have found out the sorrow which gnaws most painfully at my heart; that Elise, by my failure, becomes a beggar. You wish most nobly to assist her and protect her from want."

"No, father, I desire her for her own sake—because I love her! I would wish to be your son, in order to have the right to give up all for you, and to work for you. During your whole life you have done so much for others; now grant me the privilege of doing something for you. Give me your daughter; let me be your son."

232

Gotzkowsky was silent for some minutes, then looked at Bertram sadly and sorrowfully. "You know that this has always been the wish of my heart. But what I have longed for, for so many years, that I must now refuse. I dare not drag you down in my misfortune, and even if I were weak enough to yield to your request, I cannot sacrifice the happiness of my daughter to my welfare. Do you believe, Bertram, that Elise loves you?"

"She is kind to me, and is anxious for my welfare—that is enough," said Bertram, sadly. "I have learned for many a long year to renounce all claim to her love."

"But if she loves another? I fear her heart is but too true, and has not forgotten the trifler who destroyed her happiness. Ah! when I think of this man, my heart trembles with anger and grief. In the hour of death I could forgive all my enemies, but the hatred toward this man, who has so wantonly trifled with the faith and love of my child, that hatred I will take with me into the grave—and yet, I fear, Elise has not forgotten him."

"This dead love does not give me any uneasiness," said Bertram. "Four years have passed since that unlucky day."

"And for four years have I been faithful in my hatred to him. May not Elise have been as constant in her love?"

Bertram sighed and drooped his head. "It is too true, love does not die so easily." Then after a pause he added in a determined voice: "I repeat my request—give me your daughter!"

"You know that she does not love you, and yet you still desire her hand?"

"I do. I have confidence enough in her and in myself to believe Elise will not refuse it to me, but will freely make this sacrifice, when she learns that you will only allow me, as your son, the privilege of sharing my little fortune with you. For her love to you, she will give me her hand, and invest me with the rights of a son toward you."

"Never!" cried Gotzkowsky, vehemently. "She must never be informed of that of which we have been speaking. She does not forebode the misfortune which threatens her. I have not the courage to tell her, and why should I? When the terrible event happens, she will learn it soon enough, and if it can be averted, why then I can spare her this unhappiness. For my child I wish a clear, unclouded sky; let *me* bear the clouds and storms. That has always been the object of my life, and I will remain faithful to it to the last."

"You refuse me, then?" asked Bertram, pained.

"No, my son. I accept you, and that which you have given me in this hour, the treasure of your love; that I can never lose. That remains mine, even if they deprive me of all else."

He opened his arms, and Bertram threw himself weeping on his breast. Long did they thus remain, heart to heart, in silence; but soul spoke to soul without words and without expressions of love.

When Gotzkowsky raised himself from Bertram's embrace, his countenance was calm, and almost cheerful. "I thank you, my son; you have given me new courage and strength. Now I will preserve all my composure. I will humble my pride, and apply to those who in former times professed gratitude toward me. The Council of Berlin have owed me twenty thousand ducats since the time that the Russians were here, and I had to travel twice in the service of the town to Petersburg and Warsaw. These accounts have never been asked for. I will make it my business to remind the Council of them, as in the days of their need they swore eternal gratitude to me. Come, Bertram, let us see whether these worshipful magistrates are any better than other men, and whether they have any recollection of those sacred promises which they made me in the days when they needed help, and when misfortune threatened them."

* * * * *

CHAPTER VIII.

THE RUSSIAN PRINCE.

Before the door of the first hotel in Berlin stood a travelling-carriage covered with dust. The team of six post-horses, and the two servants on the coach-box, showed that it was a personage of quality who now honored the hotel with a visit; and it was therefore very natural that the host should hurry out and open the carriage door with a most respectful bow.

A very tall, thin man descended from the carriage with slow and solemn dignity, and as he entered the house gravely and in silence, his French valet asked the host whether he had rooms elegant enough to suit the Prince Stratimojeff.

The countenance of the host expanded into a glowing smile; he snatched the candlestick hastily from the hands of the head butler, and flew up the steps himself to prepare the room of state for the prince.

The French valet examined the rooms with a critical eye, and declared that, though they were not worthy of his highness, yet he would condescend to occupy them.

The prince still remained silent, his travelling-cap drawn deep down over his face, and his whole figure concealed in the ample robe of sable fur, which reached to his feet. He motioned to the host with his hand to leave the room; then, in a few short words, he ordered his valet to see to supper, and to have it served up in an adjoining room, and as at that moment a carriage drove up to the house, he commissioned him to see whether it was his suite. The valet stated that it was his highness's private secretary, his man of business, and his chaplain.

"I will not see them to-day—they may seek their own pleasure," said the prince, authoritatively. "Tell them that our business begins to-morrow. But for you, Guillaume, I have an important commission. Go to the host and inquire for the rich banker, John Gotzkowsky; and when you have found where he lives, enter into further conversation, and get some information about the circumstances of this gentleman. I wish to learn, too, about his family; ask about his daughter—if she be still unmarried, and whether she is now in Berlin. In short, find out all you can."

The courteous and obedient valet had left the room some time, but Prince Stratimojeff still stood motionless, his eyes cast on the ground, and muttering some unintelligible words. Suddenly, with an impatient movement, he threw his furred robe from his shoulders, and cast his head-gear far into the room.

"Air! air! I suffocate!" cried he. "I feel as if this town lay on my chest like a hundred-pound weight, and that I have to conceal myself like a criminal from the eyes of men."

He threw his cloak open, and took a long and deep breath.

What was it, then, that so strangely excited Prince Stratimojeff, and shook his very bones as with an ague? It was the memory of former days; it was the painful and damning voice of Conscience which tormented him. What reason had he to inquire after Gotzkowsky the banker, and his daughter? How! Had the heart of Count Feodor von Brenda become so hardened, that when he returned to Berlin he should not long to hear of her whom he had once so shamefully betrayed?

It was indeed himself. Colonel Count Feodor von Brenda had become transformed into the Prince Stratimojeff. Four short years had passed, but what desolation had they not caused in his inner life!—four years of dissolute pleasure, of mad, enervating enjoyment; four bacchanalian years of sensual dissipation and extravagance; four years passed at the court of two Russian empresses! In these four years Elizabeth had died; and for a few days the unfortunate Peter III. had worn the imperial crown. But it had proved too heavy for him; and his great consort, Catharine, full of compassion and Russian humanity for him, had sought to lighten his load! Only, in her too great zeal, she had taken not only his crown, but his head, and changed his prison for a grave.

The Guards shouted for the new empress as they had done for the old. In the presence of their beautiful young sovereign they remembered with delight the graciousness of her predecessor, who, in the fulness of her kindness and power, had made princes of the subalterns, and great lords of the privates.

Why should not Catharine resemble Elizabeth in that respect, and show favor to the splendid soldiers of the Guards? She was merciful. She was a gracious mistress to all her subjects, but especially so to the handsome men of her empire. And the Count von Brenda was a very handsome man. He had been the favorite of Elizabeth, why should he not also be the favorite of Catharine? The former had treated him with motherly kindness, for she was old; but Catharine was young, and in her proud breast there beat an ardent heart—a heart that was so powerful and large, that it had room for more than one lover.

The young count had been for some short months the declared darling of the empress, and the whole world did homage to him, and looked upon it as a matter of course that Catharine should make him Prince Stratimojeff, and bestow on him not only orders and titles, but lands and thousands of slaves.

What a mad, intoxicating, joyous life was his! How all the world envied the handsome, rich prince, surrounded by the halo of imperial favor! But nevertheless a cloud lay always on his brow, and he plunged into the sea of pleasure like one ill of fever, who seeks something to cool the heat which is consuming him. He threw himself into the arms of dissipation, as the criminal condemned to execution, who in the intoxication of champagne revels away the last hours of life in order to banish the thought that Death stands behind him, reaching forth his hand to seize him.

236

Thus did the prince strive in the wild excitement of pleasure to kill thought and deaden his heart. But there would come quiet hours to remind him of the past, and, at times, in the middle of the night, he would start up from his couch, as if he had heard a scream, a single heart-piercing cry, which rang through his very soul.

But this scream existed only in his dreams, those dreams in which Elise's pale, sad face appeared, and made him tremble before her indignant and despairing grief. Near this light figure of his beloved appeared another pallid woman, whose sorrowful looks tortured him, and struck his soul with anguish. He thought he saw his wife, the late Countess Lodoiska von Sandomir, who, with weeping eyes, demanded of him her murdered happiness, her youth, her life.

She was dead; she had died of grief, for she had felt that the man for whom she had sacrificed every thing—her youth, her honor, and her duty—despised her, and could never forgive her for having cheated him into taking her for his wife. She died the victim of his contempt and hatred. Not suddenly, not as with a lightning-stroke, did his contempt kill, but slowly and steadily did it pierce her heart. She bore the torture for one desolate, disconsolate year, and then she died solitary and forsaken. No loving hand dried the death-sweat on her cold forehead; no pitying lips whispered words of love and hope to her; yet on her death-bed, her heart was still warm toward her husband, and even then she blessed him.

A letter written by her trembling hand in her last hours, full of humble, earnest love, of forgiving gentleness, which her husband the prince found on his writing-table, as well as another, directed to Elise Gotzkowsky, and enclosed in the first, bore witness to this fact.

Lodoiska had loved her husband sufficiently to be aware of the cause of his wild and extravagant life, to know that in the bottom of his heart he was suffering from the only true love of his life—his love for Elise; and that all the rest was only a mad and desperate effort to deaden his feelings and smother his desire.

Elise's image followed him everywhere; and his love for her, which might have been the blessing of a good man's life, had been a cruel curse to that of a guilty one. In the midst of the wild routs, the private orgies of the imperial court, her image rose before him from these waves of maddening pleasure as a guardian angel, hushing him often into silence, and stopping the wanton jest on his quivering lips.

At times during these feasts and dances, he was seized with a boundless, unspeakable dread, a torturing anxiety. He felt inexpressibly desolate, and the consciousness of his lost, his wasted existence haunted him, while it seemed as if an inner voice was whispering—"Go, flee to her! with Elise is peace and innocence. If you are to be saved, Elise will save you."

But he had not the strength to obey the warning voice of his heart; he was bound in gilded fetters, and, even if love were absent, pride and vanity prevented him from breaking these bonds. He was the favorite of the young empress, and the great of the empire bowed down before him, and felt themselves happy in his smile, and honored by the pressure of his hand. But every thing is changeable. Even the heart of the Empress Catharine was fickle.

One day the Prince Stratimojeff received a note from his imperial mistress, in which she intrusted him with a diplomatic mission to Germany, and requested him, on account of the urgency of the occasion, to start immediately.

Feodor understood the hidden meaning of this apparently gracious and loving letter; he understood that he had fallen into disgrace—not that he had committed any error or crime. It was only that Count Orloff was handsomer and more amiable than himself, or at least that he seemed so to the empress. Therefore Feodor's presence was inconvenient to her; for at that time in the commencement of her reign, Catharine had still some modesty left, and the place of favorite had not yet become an official position at court, but only a public secret. As yet, she avoided bringing the discharged favorite in contact with the newly appointed one, and therefore Feodor had to be removed before Count Alexis Orloff could enter on his duties.

Prince Feodor Stratimojeff crushed the perfumed imperial note in his hand, and muttered through his set teeth: "She has sacrificed me to an Orloff! She wishes to send me away, that she may more securely play this new farce of love. Very well; I will go, but not to return to be deceived anew by her vows of love and glances of favor. No! let this breach be eternal. Catharine shall feel that, although an empress, she is a woman whom I despise. Therefore let there be no word of farewell, not even the smallest request. She bids me go, and I go. And would it not seem as if Fate pointed out to me the way I am to go? Is it not a strange chance that Catharine should choose me for this mission to Germany?"

It was indeed a singular accident that the empress unintentionally should have sent back her discharged favorite to the only woman whom he had ever loved. He was sent as ambassador extraordinary to Berlin, to press more urgently her claims on a Prussian banker, to bring up before the Prussian department for foreign affairs the merchant John Gotzkowsky with regard to her demand for two millions of dollars; and, in case he refused to pay it, to try in a diplomatic way whether Prussia could not he induced to support this demand of the empress, and procure immediate payment.

This was the mission which Catharine had confided to Prince Stratimojeff, who, when he determined to undertake it, said to himself: "I will take vengeance on this proud woman who thinks to cast me off like a toy of which she has tired; I will show her that my heart is unmoved by her infidelity; I will present to her my young wife, whose beauty, youth, and innocence will cause her to blush for shame."

Never had he been so fascinating and lively, so brilliant and sparkling with wit, as on the evening preceding his departure. His jests were the boldest and freest; they made even the empress blush, and sent her blood hot and bounding through her veins. The court, that would have been delighted to have seen the long-envied and hated favorite now abashed and humbled before his newly-declared successor, remarked

238

with astonishment and bitter mortification that the humiliation was changed into a triumph; for the empress, charmed by his amiability and wit, seemed to turn her heart again toward him, and to entreat him with the tenderest looks to forgive her faithlessness. She had already forgotten the unfortunate embassy which was to remove Feodor from her court, when he himself came to remind her of it.

While all countenances were still beaming with delight over a precious *bon mot* which Feodor had just perpetrated, and at which the empress herself had laughed aloud, he stepped up to her and requested her blessing on his voyage to Germany, which he was going to commence that night.

Catharine felt almost inclined to withdraw her orders and request him to remain, but she was woman enough to be able to read pride and defiance in his face. She therefore contented herself with wishing him a speedy return to his duty. Publicly, in the presence of the whole court and her new favorite, she afforded Prince Stratimojeff a fresh triumph: she bade him kneel, and taking a golden chain to which her portrait was attached, she threw the links around his neck. Kissing him gently on the forehead, with a gracious smile full of promise, she said to him only, "*Au revoir!*"

* * * * *

CHAPTER IX.

OLD LOVE—NEW SORROW.

Elise was in her room. Her face expressed a quiet, silent resignation, and her large dark eyes had a dreamy but bright look. She sat in an easy-chair, reading, and whoever had seen her with her high, open forehead and calm looks, would have thought her one of those happy and fortunate beings whom Heaven had blessed with eternal rest and cheerful composure, who was unacquainted with the corroding poison of passionate grief. No trace of the storm which had raged through her life could be seen on her countenance. Her grief had eaten inwardly, and only her heart and the spirit of her youth had died; her face had remained young and handsome. The vigor of her youth had overcome the grief of her spirit, and her cheeks, although colorless and transparent in their paleness, were still free from that sallow, sickly pallor, which is the herald of approaching dissolution. She was apparently healthy and young, and only sick and cold at heart. Perhaps she only needed some sunbeams to warm up again her chilled heart, only some gleam of hope to make her soul young again, and strong and ready once more to love and to suffer. She had never forgotten, never ceased to think of the past, nor of him whom she had loved so unspeakably, whom her soul could not let go.

The memories of the past were the life of the present to her. The tree in the garden which he had admired, the flowers he had loved and which since then had four times renewed their bloom, the rustling of the fir-trees which sounded from the wall, all spoke of him, and caused her heart to beat, she knew not whether with anger or with pain. Even now, as she sat in her room, her thoughts and fancies were busy with him. She had been reading, but the book dropped from her hand. From the love-scenes which were described in it her thoughts roamed far and wide, and awakened the dreams and hopes of the past.

But Elise did not like to give herself up to these reveries, and at times had a silent horror even of her own thoughts. She did not like to confess to herself that she still hoped in the man who had betrayed her. She had, as it were, a sympathizing pity with herself; she threw a veil over her heart, to hide from herself that it still quivered with pain and love. Only at times, in the quiet and solitude of her chamber, she ventured to draw aside the veil, to look down into the depths of her soul, and, in agonizing delight, in one dream blend together the present and the past. She leaned back in her chair, her large dark eyes fixed on vacancy. Some passage in the book had reminded her of her own sad love, had struck on her heart like the hammer of a bell, and in response it had returned but one single note, the word "Feodor."

"Ah, Feodor!" she whispered to herself, but with a shudder at the name, and a blush suffused her otherwise pale cheeks for a moment. "It is the first time my lips have spoken his name, but my heart is constantly repeating it in hopeless grief, and in my dreams he still lives. I have accepted my fate; to the world I have separated from him; to myself, never! Oh, how mysterious is the heart! I hate and yet I love him." She covered her face with her hands, and sat long silent and motionless. A noise at the door aroused her. It was only Marianne, her maid, who came to announce that a strange gentleman was outside, who earnestly requested to speak to her. Elise trembled, she knew not why. A prophetic dread seized her soul, and in a voice scarcely audible she asked the name of her visitor.

"He will not give his name," answered the maid. "He says the name is of no consequence. He had a letter to deliver from the Countess Lodoiska, of St. Petersburg."

Elise uttered a cry, and sprang from her seat—she knew all. Her heart told her that he was near. It must be himself. She felt as if she must hasten to her father for protection and safety; but her feet refused to carry her. She trembled so, that she was obliged to hold on to the arm of a chair to keep herself from falling. She motioned with her hand to deny him admittance, but Marianne did not understand her; for, opening the door, she invited the stranger in, and then left him.

And now they stood in presence of each other, silent and breathless—Elise trembling with excitement and bitter feeling, wrestling with her own emotion, and deeply abashed by the meeting. Both uttered an inward prayer—but how different were their two aspirations!

"Now, God or devil!" thought Feodor, "give my words power, lend enchantment to my tongue, that I may win Elise!"

Elise prayed to herself: "Have mercy on me, O God! Take this love from me, or let me die."

In sad silence these two, so long separated, stood opposite to each other—both hesitating, he knowing that he was guilty, she ashamed of the consciousness of her love. But finally he succeeded in breaking the silence. He whispered her name, and as she, alarmed and shuddering, looked up at him, he stretched out his arms imploringly toward her. And then she felt, thought, knew nothing but him. She uttered a cry, and rushed forward to throw herself in his arms. But suddenly she stopped. Her dream was at an end, and now awaking from the first ecstasy of seeing him again, she collected herself, and stood before him in the whole pride and dignity of her offended honor. She found courage to sacrifice her own heart, and, with cold, constrained manner, bowing to him, she asked, "Colonel von Brenda, whom do you wish to see?"

The prince sighed deeply, and let his arms drop. "It is over," said he; "she no longer loves me!"

Low as these words had been spoken, Elise had seized their purport, and they touched her to the quick. "What do you wish?" she continued.

"Nothing!" said he, despondently. "I have made a mistake. I expected to find a faithful heart, a woman like an angel, ready in the hour of meeting to forget all else, and take refuge in this heart; to forgive, and, with her blessing, to wipe out the curse of my existence. This is what I sought. But God is just, and I did not deserve such happiness. I submit."

"Oh, my God!" said Elise to herself, "it is the same voice which once charmed me." She no longer found strength in herself to bid him go. She would have given her life blood to be able always to be thus near him.

"This time, young lady," said Feodor, "I come only as a messenger, the executor of the will of one who is dead." He took a letter from his bosom and handed it to Elise. "I bring you," he said solemnly, "the last will of my wife, Countess Lodoiska."

"She is no longer alive?" cried Elise, and involuntarily an almost joyful tone pervaded her voice.

This did not escape the prince. "I will win her," said he to himself. His eyes shone brighter, his countenance looked prouder, and his heart beat higher with triumphant joy. Elise had taken the letter, and still held it in her hand. "Will you not read it?" asked he, gently, and her heart trembled at the pleading tone of his voice.

"Yes, I will read it," she answered, as if awaking from a dream, and breaking the seal hastily.

The prince fixed his sharp, piercing eyes on her, and seemed to wish to read in her looks her inmost thoughts, and feeling them favorable to him, he approached still closer to her.

The letter was short and hastily written, but every word entered her soul and brought tears to her eyes. It ran thus:

"My dear Elise, when you receive this letter I shall be no more, and the heart which has suffered so much will be at rest. But when I have found repose in the grave, do you fulfil my trust. I leave you the dearest legacy that I possess. I give you back your property, the heart and love of Feodor, which never ceased to belong to you. I never have been able to win this love to myself. He gave me his hand, his heart remains yours, and that is killing me. Take it then, it is my legacy to you; and if you accept it my purified spirit will bless your reunion.

LODOISKA."

The letter dropped from her hand; completely overpowered by deep and solemn emotions, she sank in her chair, and hid her tears with her hands. Feodor felt that she was again his, that he had regained his sway over her. He rushed toward her, falling at her feet, and passionately snatching her hands from her face, he exclaimed, "Elise!

in this moment her spirit is hovering over us. She blesses this love which she has already forgiven. Oh, if you only knew what I have suffered for you, you would, at least, not be angry with me. You would pardon me for the sake of what I have undergone."

"Have I then not suffered also?" she asked, turning her face, covered with tears, toward him.

"Oh! leave me here at your feet," he continued. "Look upon me as a poor pilgrim who has wandered to the holy Sepulchre in order to cleanse his heart of its sins at the sanctuary by sincere repentance and prayers for forgiveness. You are my sanctuary, to you my heart bends; the poor pilgrim has come to you to confess and be shrived before he dies. Will you, my Madonna, hear him? May I tell you what I have endured, how much I have suffered?"

"Speak," she said, half conscious, but eagerly listening to the music of his voice. "Tell me what you have suffered, that I may forget my own sufferings when I gave you up."

"Oh!" he continued, with a shudder, "I shall never forget that fearful moment when I became aware of the deception, and discovered that it was not you, but Lodoiska, whom I held in my arms. A raving madness seized me, which threatened my own life. Lodoiska turned aside the dagger, and pronounced your name. That name recalled me to life, to the knowledge of my crime. I submitted to the punishment which I had merited, and which you had imposed upon me. I led Lodoiska to the altar, at which I had hoped to see you. I made her my wife, and my heart pronounced *your* name, while my lips bound me to *her*. It was a terrible hour, a fearful agony raged within me, and it has never left me since. It was there, when Lodoiska pressed me to her heart. It was present in the tumult of battle. Then, however, when death raged around me, when destruction thundered from the enemy's cannon, then I became cheerful, and the pang left me as I rushed amid the enemy's ranks. But even death itself retreated before me—I found on the battle-field only honor and fame, but not the object for which I fought, not death. I lived to suffer and to expiate my crime toward you, Elise. But one hope sustained me, the hope one day to fall at your feet, to clasp your knees, and to sue for forgiveness."

Completely overcome by his own passionate description, he bowed his head on her knees, and wept aloud. He had succeeded in rousing his own sympathy; he believed in his own grief. He had so feelingly played the part of a repentant sinner, an ardent lover, that for a moment probability and reality had become blended in one, and he felt himself thoroughly possessed by crushing repentance.

But Elise believed in him. His voice sounded like music in her ear, and every fibre of her heart thrilled and quivered. The past with its griefs and sorrows was gone forever, he was once more there, with no stranger to come between them, and she only felt that she loved him without bounds.

He embraced her knees, looking pleadingly up in her face. "Elise, forgive me," cried he; "say but one word, 'Pardon,' and I will go away in silence, and never again dare to approach you."

Elise had no longer power to withstand him. She opened her arms, and threw them with passionate tenderness around his neck. "Feodor, love does not forgive, it loves," she cried with unspeakable rapture, and tears of delight burst from her eyes.

Feodor uttered a cry of joy, and sprang up to draw her to his breast, to cover her face with kisses, to whisper words of delight, of tenderness, of passionate love, in her listening ear. "Oh! now all is right again—now you are again mine. These four years are as if they had not been. It was all a mournful dream—and we are now awake. Now we know that we love each other, that we belong to each other, forever. Come, Elise, it is the same hour which then called us to the altar. Come, the priest waits. For four long years have I hoped for this hour. Come, my beloved."

He threw his strong arm around her and raised her to his breast to draw her forth with him. As Elise drew herself gently back, he continued still more passionately: "I will not let you go, for you are mine. You have betrothed yourself to me for life or death. Come, the priest is waiting, and to-day shall you be my wife. This time no unfriendly hand shall impose itself between us, and Lodoiska no longer lives."

"But my father lives," said Elise, as earnestly and proudly she freed herself from Feodor's arms. "Without his consent I do not leave this threshold. It was for that the Lord punished us. My father's blessing was not upon our love, and I had sinned grievously against him. Now, it is expiated, and Fate is appeased. Let us go hand in hand to my father, and ask his blessing on our love, that love which has remained undiminished through so many years of grief."

"I submit to you. I will obey your will in every thing. But will not your father reject me? I feel that he must hate me for the tears I have caused you to shed."

"He will love you when he sees that you have taught me to smile once more," said she gently. "Come to my father."

She wished to draw him along with her. But his consciousness of guilt held him back. He wanted the daring courage to face this man whom he had been sent to ruin; and involuntarily he shrank back from his own deeds. "I dare not go before him so suddenly and unprepared," said he hesitatingly.

"Then allow me to prepare him for your presence."

"And if he denies his sanction?"

"He will not do it."

244

"He has sworn never to allow you to marry a Russian."

"Oh, that was long ago," said she, smiling, "when Russia was our enemy. Now we are at peace. The bloody streams of discord are dried up, and an angel of peace rules over all countries. Even my father will feel his influence, and make peace with you and me."

Feodor did not answer immediately. He stood thoughtful and contemplative, weighing the necessary and unavoidable, and considering what he should do. One thing only was clear. Neither Elise nor Gotzkowsky must be allowed to suspect on what extraordinary mission his empress had sent him thither. Only when Elise was irrevocably bound to him, when she was his without recall, when Gotzkowsky had given his consent to their union, then would he dare to disclose it to him. It was necessary, above all, to postpone the negotiations about the Russian demands for a day, and therefore he only gave his agents his instructions, and imposed on them silence and inactivity for a day longer. The principal thing, however, was to convince Elise and her father that their union should suffer no delay, because he was only allowed to remain a few hours. He put his arm around Elise's slender waist and pressed her to his heart. "Listen to me, my beloved; my time has been but sparingly dealt out to me. I have come on with courier horses, so as to allow me more leisure on my return with you. But to-day we must leave, for the army is on the frontier, equipped and ready for war. Only out of special favor did the empress allow me a short leave of absence, to fetch my wife. In her clemency she has done what she was able to do, and I must now obey her orders to return speedily, if I do not wish to bring her anger down upon me. That nothing might prevent or delay us, I have brought a chaplain of our Church with me, to bless our union. You see, my beloved, that every thing is ready, and all that is wanting is the wreath of myrtle in your hair."

"And the blessing of my father," she replied solemnly.

Feeder's brow darkened and an angry expression flashed across his countenance. Elise did not perceive it, for, in her noble forgetfulness of self, she had leaned her head on his breast, and all doubt and distrust were alien to her free and confiding love. The love of a woman is of divine nature; it forgives all, it suffers all; it is as strong in giving as in forgiving. Every woman when she loves is an inspired poetess; the divine frenzy has seized her, and poetic utterances of ecstasy issue from her trembling lips. This poor girl, too, had become inspired. Confidingly happy, she reposed on the breast of the man whom she had never ceased to love, whom she had blest in the midst of her bitterest tears, whom she had prayed for, earnestly entreating God to have mercy on him.

"Do you go to your father," said Feodor, after a pause. "Pray for his consent and his blessing on both of us—I hasten to prepare every thing. Tell your father that my whole life shall be spent in the endeavor to redeem every tear you have shed for me with a smile; that I will love him as a son to whom he has given the dearest treasure of life, his Elise."

He pressed her to his heart and kissed her forehead. Elise raised her face from his breast, and smiled on him with loving emotion. But he placed his hands over her eyes; he was not callous enough to be able to bear those innocent, yielding, tender looks.

"I must be gone," he said. "But this shall be our last separation, and when I return, it shall be to lead you to the altar. In an hour, dearest, you must be ready. At the end of that time, I will come to take you to St. Petersburg, and present you at the empress's court as my bride, the Princess Stratimojeff."

He looked down at her with an air of triumph, to see what impression his words would have on her. He had expected to prepare a pleasurable surprise for her with the princely title—to see her blush with proud satisfaction. But Elise felt neither elevated nor honored by the high rank. What did she care whether Feodor was a prince or a poor officer, so that he only loved her, and would never again forsake her?

She replied, with some surprise, "Princess Stratimojeff! What does that mean?"

"For three months," said he with a proud smile, "I have been Prince Stratimojeff. The empress gave me this title. The world calls me prince, but you—you will call me your Feodor?"

"Oh," said she feelingly, "my heart called you so when you did not hear me."

"Well, then, go wind the wreath of myrtle in your hair, and wait for me. In an hour I will return."

He hastened to the door, but on the threshold he turned to send a farewell greeting to her. Their eyes met and rested on each other, and suddenly a deep, indescribable feeling of grief came over him. It seemed to him as if he would never see her again; as if the threshold once crossed, Elise was lost to him forever. Once again he returned, and folded her passionately in his arms, and, completely overpowered by his painful presentiments, he bowed his head on her shoulder, and wept bitterly. He then tore himself loose. "Farewell!" he cried, but his voice sounded hoarse and rough—"farewell! in an hour I will return for you. Be prepared, do not keep me waiting in vain. Farewell!"

* * * * *

246

CHAPTER X.

THE MAGISTRACY OF BERLIN.

Gotzkowsky had conquered his proud heart; he had left his house to apply to those whom he had benefited and saved in the days of their need and distress, and who had then avowed him everlasting gratitude. He resolved now, reluctantly and with deep humiliation, rather to remind them of those days than to ask of them any favors or assistance beyond the payment of their debts to him.

First he went to the ober-burgomaster, President Kircheisen; to the man whom he had saved from death, who had clung to him, and, when he had found his speech again, had vowed with tears that he would be forever grateful to him, and would bless the arrival of the hour in which he could prove it to him by deeds.

This hour had now arrived, but Herr von Kircheisen did not bless it; on the contrary, he cursed it. He was standing at the window of his ground floor when Gotzkowsky passed by. Their eyes met. Gotzkowsky's were clear and penetrating; Kircheisen's were cast down, as he stepped back from the window. He only had time to tell the servants that he was not at home for any one, whoever it might be, when the bell rang, and Gotzkowsky inquired for Herr von Kircheisen.

"Not at home, sir."

"Not at home! but I saw him just this moment standing at the window."

"It must have been a mistake, sir. The president has just gone to the Council-chamber."

"Very well. I will go to the town-hall," said Gotzkowsky, as he left the house.

Passing by the window he looked in again. This time, however, Kircheisen was not standing before the sashes, but at the side, ensconced behind the curtain, he was spying Gotzkowsky through the window. As he saw him passing by, pale of countenance, but erect and unbent, he felt involuntarily a feeling of remorse, and his conscience warned him of his unpaid debt toward the only man who came to his rescue. But he would not listen to his conscience, and with a dark frown he threw back his head with contempt.

"He is a bankrupt—I have nothing to do with him!" So saying, he retired to his study, and in obedience to a natural instinct, he opened his strong box, and refreshed himself with a look at the thousands which he had earned from Gotzkowsky as "detective and informer." And now his conscience no longer reproached him; the sight of the shining money lulled it into a gentle slumber.

In the meanwhile Gotzkowsky continued his toilsome and humiliating journey. He met men who formerly bent humbly to the earth before him, yet who scarcely greeted him now. Others, again, as they passed him, whispered, with a malicious smile, "Bankrupt!" As he came to the corner of a street, he met the valiant editor of the *Vossian Gazette*, who was coming round from the other side. As they met, he jostled Gotzkowsky rather roughly, yet Mr. Kretschmer did not think it worth while to excuse himself, but pulling his hat over his face he walked on with a dark and scornful look. As Gotzkowsky passed the houses, he could hear the windows rattle, and he knew that it was his former good friends, who were drawing back when they saw him coming, and who, after he had passed, opened the windows again to look after him, to laugh at and mock him. It was an intellectual running of the gantlet, and Gotzkowsky's heart bled from the blows, and his feet were tired to death. What had he then done to burden himself with the cruelty and contumely of the world? Had he not been benevolent and kind, full of pity and humanity, obliging to every one? Had he not always shown himself ready to serve every one, and never requested nor desired services in return? Therein lay his fault and his crime.

He had been independent. He had never sought the favor of any man, but, trusting solely to himself, had always relied on his own strength. And now mankind wished to make him feel that he had mortified them by his self-sufficiency—for small natures never forgive one who dares to be independent of others, and finds his source of honor in himself. And this crime Gotzkowsky had been guilty of. What he was, he had made himself. He had owed nothing to protection, nothing to hypocrisy or flattery, eye-service, or cringing. Only by the strength and power of his own genius had he elevated himself above the world which he ruled.

And now that he was down, it was but natural that the world should fall upon him, tear him to pieces with its venomous fangs, to enjoy his torture, and joyfully to witness the lowering of pride and independence. Gotzkowsky arrived at the town-hall and slowly ascended the steps. How often had he gone this same road in answer to the pressing cry for help which the magistrate would utter in his distress! How often had he mounted those steps to give his advice, to lend his energy, his money, and his credit to these gentlemen of the Council!

This day the doors were not thrown open to him the beadle did not bow down to the earth before him, but proudly and with erect head stepped up to him and bade him wait in the antechamber until he had announced him to the assembled Council. He had to wait long, but finally the doors opened and he was admitted. There sat the aldermen and councillors, and the burgomaster, just as they had when, in their need and distress, they had appealed to Gotzkowsky for advice and assistance—just as they had when, in solemn session, they determined to present him with a silver laurel-wreath as an honorable testimonial.

Only the chief burgomaster was absent. Herr von Kircheisen was at home, enjoying the sight of the money he had won from Gotzkowsky. This day they did not receive him as a counsellor or friend, but more like a delinquent. No one rose to greet him— no one offered him a seat! They knew that he came to ask for something. Why, then, should they be polite to him, as he was only a petitioner like all other poor people? In the mean time Gotzkowsky did not seem to be aware of the alteration. Smiling, and with a firm, proud step he walked to a chair and sat down.

After a pause the burgomaster asked him churlishly what his business was. He drew out a parcel of papers, and laying them on the table, said, "I have brought my accounts."

A panic seized the worshipful gentlemen of the Council, and they sat petrified in their seats.

"Your worships have forgotten my claims," said Gotzkowsky quickly. "However, that I can easily understand, as the accounts are somewhat old. It is now four years since I have had the honor of having the Council of Berlin as my debtor; since I thrice performed the perilous journey to Koenigsberg and Warsaw in order to negotiate the war contribution in the name of the town. At that time, too, I was obliged, in the service of the Council, to take with me many valuable presents. I may enumerate among them the diamond-set staff for General von Fermore, and the snuff-box, with the portrait of the empress, surrounded by brilliants, which I delivered to the General Field-Marshal Count Butterlin, in the name of the magistracy and town of Berlin. But, gentlemen, you will find the accounts of all these things here."

The gentlemen of the Council did not answer him; they seized upon the papers hastily, and turned them over, and looked into them with stern and sullen eyes. Not a word was said, and nothing was heard but the rustling of the papers, and the low muttering of one of the senators adding the numbers, and verifying the calculation. Gotzkowsky rose, and walked to the window. Raising his looks to heaven, his countenance expressed all the pain and bitterness to which his soul almost succumbed. Ah! he could have torn the papers out of the hand of this miserable, calculating, reckoning senator, and with pride and contempt have thrown them in his face. But he thought of his daughter, and the honor of his name. He had to wait it out, and bend his head in submission.

At last the burgomaster laid the papers aside, and turned scowlingly toward Gotzkowsky. The latter stepped up to the table with a smile, making a vow to himself that he would remain quiet and patient.

"Have you read them, gentlemen?" he asked.

"We have read them," answered the burgomaster roughly, "but the Council cannot admit that it owes you any thing."

"No?" cried Gotzkowsky; and then, allowing himself to be overcome by a feeling of bitterness—"I believe you. Those in authority seldom take cognizance of what they owe, only what is owing to them."

"Oh, yes, indeed," said the first councillor with solemn dignity, "we know very well that we owe you thanks for the great services you have rendered the town."

Gotzkowsky broke out into a loud, ironical laugh. "Do you remember that? I am glad that you have not forgotten it."

"It is true," continued the councillor, in a tone of conciliation, "at the request of the magistracy you took charge of the affairs of the town. You travelled to St. Petersburg to see the empress; twice did you go to Warsaw to see General Fermore, and twice to Saxony to visit the king. You see the Council knows how much it is indebted to you."

"And we are cheerfully willing to be grateful to you," interrupted the burgomaster, "and to serve you when and in what manner we can, but these debts we cannot acknowledge."

Gotzkowsky looked at him in dismay, and a deep glow suffused his cheek. "You refuse to pay them?" he asked, faintly.

"It pains us deeply that we cannot recognize these claims. You must abate somewhat from them if we are to pay them," answered the burgomaster rudely.

"Do you dare to propose this to me?" cried Gotzkowsky, his eyes flashing, his countenance burning with anger and indignation. "Is this the way you insult the man to whom four years ago on this very spot you swore eternal gratitude? In those days I sacrificed to you my repose, the sleep of my nights; for, when the town was threatened with danger and alarm, there was no Council, no authority in existence, for you were base cowards, and abjectly begged for my good offices. With tears did you entreat me to save you. I left my house, my family, my business, to serve you. At the risk of my life, in the depth of winter, I undertook these journeys. You did not consider that Russian bayonets threatened me, that I risked health and life. You thought only of yourselves. I have not put down in the account the sleepless nights, the trouble and anxiety, the privation and hardships which I suffered. I do not ask any money or recompense for my services. I only ask that I may be paid back what I actually expended; and you have the assurance to refuse it?"

"No, we do not," said the burgomaster, quite unmoved by Gotzkowsky's noble excitement. "We do not refuse payment; we only desire a reduction of the amounts."

"You wish to cheapen and bargain with me," said Gotzkowsky with a hoarse laugh. "You take me for a chapman, who measures out his life and services by the yard; and you wish to pay me for mine by the same measure. Go, most sapient gentlemen; I carry on a wholesale trade, and do not cut off yards. That I leave to shopkeepers, to souls like yours."

The burgomaster rose up proud and threateningly from his seat. "Do you dare to insult the Council?"

"No, the Council of Berlin insult themselves by their own deeds. They dare to chaffer with me!"

"And they have a right to do so," cried the burgomaster, quite beside himself with rage. "Who asked you to play the great lord in our name, and distribute royal presents—diamonds and gold snuff-boxes? You could have done it much more cheaply. The Russian is not so high-priced. But it was your pleasure to be magnificent at our expense, and to strut about as a bountiful gentleman."

"Silence!" cried Gotzkowsky, in such a commanding tone that the burgomaster was struck dumb, and sank back in his chair. Gotzkowsky said no more. He took the accounts from the table, and, casting a look of anger and contempt on the worthy gentlemen, tore the papers in pieces, and threw the scraps at their feet. "I am paid!" he said, proudly, and turned to leave the room.

One of the town councillors hastened after him, and held him back. "You are too hasty: we may yet agree."

"No!" said Gotzkowsky, striving to free himself. "I do not chaffer and bargain for my right."

The other held him tight. "But the Council are not averse to paying you, if you—"

"If I will only traffic with you, is it not so?" interrupted Gotzkowsky. "Let me go; we have done with each other."

"You will regret having repulsed the Council," said the burgomaster, threateningly.

"I never regret an action when my honor is satisfied," said Gotzkowsky, with proud contempt; and then, without honoring the worthy gentlemen with another look, he left the hall, and returned into the street.

* * * * *

CHAPTER XI.

THE JEWS OF THE MINT.

Herr Itzig was a very pious and devout Jew. He kept the Sabbath strictly after the custom of his ancestors. He was charitable to the poor; and no Jew beggar ever left his door without a gift.

He sat in his room, performing his morning devotions, and so deeply was he immersed therein, that he did not hear a repeated knocking at the door until a low, gentle voice whispered, "Good-morning, Herr Itzig!"

Itzig first finished his prayer; for all the world he would not have broken off before the end of it: "Be gracious and merciful to us, Jéhovah, and incline us to be compassionate and helpful to all who approach us with supplication, even as we desire that thou shouldst be to us." And now the pious Jew closed his prayer-book, and turned slowly around.

That pale, bent man, who greeted him with a sorrowful smile—could it possibly be—could it be John Gotzkowsky, the celebrated banker, the honored and bright hero of the Exchange, the money-king before whom all Europe bowed down?

An expression of malicious joy stole over Itzig's face; but he suppressed it immediately, for the last words of his prayer still floated around his lips, and somewhat purified them. "Ah!" said he, in a friendly tone, as he stepped toward Gotzkowsky, stretching out both his hands to him, "the great and powerful John Gotzkowsky does me the honor to visit me. What joy for my humble house!"

Gotzkowsky did not allow himself to be misled by this seeming politeness. He observed him with sharp and penetrating eyes, and then proudly said: "Listen, Itzig; let us be candid with each other. You know the reports which are current about me in the city and on the Bourse."

"I know them, but do not believe them," cried Itzig, with an altered, earnest mien. "Yes, I know these reports, and I know too what they are worth. They are a speculation of Ephraim, that your notes may be depreciated, that he may buy them in at a low rate. I know that Gotzkowsky is a rich man; and a rich man has judgment, and whoever has judgment is prudent—does not venture much, nor stand security for other people."

"I have perhaps less of this judgment than you think," said Gotzkowsky. "It may be that I have stood security."

"Then you will certainly know how to pay?" said Itzig, with a forced laugh.

"But how if I cannot pay?" said Gotzkowsky, sadly.

Itzig stepped back, and gazed at him horrified.

"If I cannot pay," continued Gotzkowsky, impressively; "if I am unable to pay half a million for Leipsic, another half million for the Russian claims, after having lost the same amount yesterday by the new treasury ordinance—what would you say to that, Itzig?"

Itzig listened to him with increasing terror, and gradually his features assumed an expression of hatred and savage rage. When Gotzkowsky had finished, he raised his clasped hands to heaven, as if imploring the wrath of God on the head of the sinner. "My God! sir, are you, then, going to fail?"

Gotzkowsky seized his hand, and looked into his quivering face with an expression of intense anxiety. "Listen to me, Itzig. I may yet be saved; every thing depends upon my obtaining a delay, that my credit may not be shaken. You are rich—"

"No, I am poor," interrupted Itzig, vehemently. "I am perfectly poor; I have nothing but what I earn."

"But you can earn a great deal," said Gotzkowsky, with a faint smile. "I wish to effect a loan from you. Take my word of honor as security."

"Your word of honor!" cried Itzig, thrusting back his hand. "What can I do with your word of honor? I cannot advance any money on it."

"Consider! the honor of my name is concerned—and this, till now, I have kept unsullied before God and man!" cried Gotzkowsky, imploringly.

"And if my own honor was concerned," exclaimed Itzig, "I would rather part with it than my money. Money makes me a man. I am a Jew. I have nothing but money—-it is my life, my honor! I cannot part with any of it."

But Gotzkowsky did not allow himself to be repulsed. It seemed to him that his future, his honor, his whole life hung upon this moment. He felt like a gambler who has staked his last hope upon one throw of the dice. If this fails, all hope is gone; no future, no life is left, nothing but the grave awaits him. With impetuous violence he seized the hand of the rich Itzig. "Oh!" said he, "remember the time when you swore eternal gratitude to me."

"I never would have sworn it," cried Itzig—"no, by the Eternal, I never would have done it, if I had thought you would ever have needed it!"

"The honor of my name is at stake!" cried Gotzkowsky, in a tone of heart-rending agony. "Do you not understand that this is to me my life? Remember your vow! Let your heart for once feel sympathy—act as a man toward his fellow-man. Advance me money upon my word of honor. No, not on that alone—on my house, on all that belongs to me. Lend me the sum I need. Oh! I will repay it in a princely manner. Help me over only these shoals, and my gratitude to you will be without bounds. You have a heart—take pity on me!"

Itzig looked with a malicious smile into his pale, agitated face. "So the rich, the great Christian banker, in the hour of his trouble, thinks that the poor derided Jew has a heart; I admit that I have a heart—but what has that to do with money? When business begins, there the heart stops. No, I have no heart to lend you money!"

Gotzkowsky did not answer immediately. He stood for an instant motionless, as if paralyzed in his inmost being. His soul was crushed, and he scarcely felt his grief. He only felt and knew that he was a lost man, and that the proud edifice of his fortune was crumbling under him, and would bury him in its ruins. He folded his hands and raised his disconsolate looks on high; he murmured: You see my suffering, O God! I have done my utmost! I have humbled myself to begging—to pitiful complaining. My God! my God! will no helping hand stretch itself once more to me out of the cloud?"

"You should have prayed before to God," said Itzig, with cruel mockery. "You should have begged Him for prudence and foresight."

Gotzkowsky did not heed him. He fought and struggled with his immense suffering, and, being a noble and a brave man, he at length conquered it. For a moment he had been cowed and downcast, but now he recovered all the power of his energetic nature. He raised again his bowed head, and his look was once more determined and defiant. "Well, then, I have tried every thing; now I accept my fate. Listen, then, Herr Itzig, I am going to suspend payment; my house must fail!"

Itzig shuddered with a sudden terror. "My God!" cried he, "only yesterday I bought a draft of yours. You will not pay it?"

"I will not do it, because I cannot; and I would not do it, if I could. I have humbled myself before you in the dust, and you have stretched out no hand to raise me. Farewell, and may that now happen which you would not prevent when you could! You punish yourself. Farewell!"

Itzig held him convulsively back, and cried, in a voice drowned by rage, "You will pay my draft?"

"I will not," said Gotzkowsky. "You have judged; take now your reward." He threw Itzig's hands from him, and hastened from the spot.

254

Behind him sounded the wailing and raging of Itzig, who implored Heaven and hell to punish the criminal who had cheated him of his money.

* * * * *

CHAPTER XII.

THE LEIPSIC MERCHANT.

Exhausted and weary, Gotzkowsky returned to his house, and retired to his room, to give himself up to the sad and terrible thoughts which tortured him. He could not conceal from himself that the sword above his head was only suspended by two thin threads. If De Neufville did not return from Amsterdam, and if the courier did not bring a relief from Leipsic, then was he lost without redemption, and the deadly sword must fall. For the first time did he think of death; for the first time did the thought of it flash like lightning through his brain, and make him almost cheerful and happy.

He could die; it was not necessary that he should bear the pain and humiliation of life. He could take refuge in the quiet, silent grave under the turf, which would soon be decked with flowers over his agonized breast. He had worked much; his feet were sore, and his heart weary, from his walk through life. Why should he not lay himself down in the grave to rest, to dream, or to sink in the arms of eternal, dreamless sleep?

But this enticing thought he cast forcibly from him. He had not yet lost all hope. His anticipations rose as the door opened, and the servant handed him a large sealed letter, which the courier from Leipsic had just brought. With hasty hand he seized the letter, and motioned to Peter to retire. But as soon as he was alone, and was about to break the seal, he drew back and hesitated. This letter might, indeed, contain his salvation; but it might also contain his death-sentence. He weighed it in his hand thoughtfully, and muttered to himself: "It is as light as a feather, and yet its contents may be heavy enough to hurl me down the abyss. But this is foolish," he exclaimed aloud, drawing himself up proudly. "At least I will know my fate, and see clearly into the future."

With a firm hand he broke the seal. But as he read, horror and dismay were depicted in his countenance, and his whole frame shook. Violently he flung the paper on the ground. "This, then, this is my reward—reproaches, accusations, instead of thanks; scorn and malice, instead of compassion. Reproaches, because I assisted them; accusations, that I had offered to help them; only because without me it would have been impossible for the King of Prussia to raise so much money. Without my mediation, they say, they would not have paid, but at the utmost would have had to endure a somewhat longer imprisonment, which would have been more tolerable than the loss of such immense sums."

He paced impatiently up and down, and as he came to the letter he spurned it with his foot, like a poisonous adder, too loathsome to touch. "I have deserved this punishment," cried he, laughing aloud from inward pain.

256

"Who bade me love mankind? who bade me help them, instead of like a highwayman falling upon and plundering them, when they were defenceless? Fool that I was to give to life any other interpretation, any other end!" He threw himself in a chair, and was soon buried in thought. Once more he reviewed his whole past, and as he made up the accounts of his life, he had to confess that the total of his hours of happiness was but small, while that of his years of misery and toil was heavy enough to bear him down. But there was still one hope, and as long as he could expect De Neufville's arrival all was not lost, and he must still wait in patience, still struggle with the worm that gnawed at his heart. With such painful thoughts as these was he busied when the door opened, and Elise entered with a glowing countenance.

She was so happy, that in her selfishness she did not perceived his troubled and care-worn looks. "Oh" said she, kissing his hand, "I am so happy at last to find you alone at home. Several times have I sought you here."

"With letters for me?" asked he, hurriedly, for he had not observed Elise's excited countenance. Both were so occupied with their own thoughts and feelings, that they took note of nothing else. "Have not letters arrived?" asked he once more.

"No letters have arrived," said she, smiling joyously, "but happiness has come."

"De Neufville is here, then!" cried Gotzkowsky, anxiously, hurrying toward the door.

"What has De Neufville to do with it?" asked Elise, with surprise holding him back.

Gotzkowsky stared for a moment, terrified at her bright face, and then a sad smile stole across his own. "Poor fool that I am!" he muttered; "I complain of the egotism of men, while I am selfish enough to think only of myself." He drew Elise toward him, and looking at her with infinite tenderness, said, "Well, my child, speak: what happiness has arrived?"

"Look at me," said she, playfully; "can you read nothing in my looks?"

Sadly he looked down deep into her large bright eyes. "Oh, your eyes shine as bright as two stars of hope, the last that are left me!"

Elise threw both her arms around his neck, and kissed him, then drew him with gentle force toward the ottoman, and, as she forced him down on the cushions, she took her own seat, smiling, on the stool at his feet. "How often, my father, have you sat here and cared for me! Ah! I know well how much sorrow I have caused you in these last four sad years, I could not command my heart to forget. You knew this, and yet you have been considerate and gentle as a mother, and kind as the best of fathers. You were never angry with me on account of my grief; you knew of it, and yet you allowed me to weep." She took his hand in hers, and for a moment covered her hot, burning face with it, then looked cheerfully up in his face. "See," she said,

"I do not shed any more tears, or, if I do, they are tears of joy. My father, I come to ask your blessing. Feodor is again here; he has come to ask me of you for his wife. Oh, forgive him, and grant your blessing to a love which till now has been the anguish of my life, but which hereafter will be its chief happiness!"

Blushing and with maiden modesty she nestled in her father's breast. Gotzkowsky felt himself paralyzed with terror. He pressed his child's head warmly to his breast, saying to himself, "And this, too, my God! you try me sorely. This is the greatest sacrifice you have demanded of me yet; but my pride is gone. This offering, too, will I make."

"Well, my father, you do not answer?" asked Elise, still leaning on his breast. "All is right, is it not? and you will give us your fatherly blessing, and forgive Feodor the errors of former years, and receive him as a son?"

Gotzkowsky, with his eyes still raised to heaven, moved his lips in silent prayer. At last, after a long, painful pause, he said solemnly: "Well, let it be so; I give my consent."

Elise uttered a cry of joy, and, amidst tears of unalloyed delight, kissed him, as smiling, and often interrupted by her own deep emotion, she narrated her meeting with Feodor, Lodoiska's death, and the letter she had written to her. "Oh, how delightful this hour would be," continued she, after finishing her narrative, "if I could only remain with you! Love bids me go, and yet it keeps me here! I have promised Feodor to go with him, but I did it in my haste, seeing only him and listening only to his prayers. Now I see you, my father, and it seems to me as if I could not leave you to-day."

"To-day!" cried Gotzkowsky, and a ray of joy shone from his face. He arose, and, with folded arms, paced the room. His soul was full of gratitude to God, to whom he had prayed in his despair. Was this not a sign that God was with him, even if men forsook him?—that God had pity on him, even if all others were pitiless. This day his child wished to leave him, to enter on a brilliant destiny. He had, therefore, no longer any need to be anxious about her fate; and, as she was going to leave at once, he would be spared the torture of having her as a witness to his disgrace and degradation. He took her to his breast, and kissed her with heartfelt fervor. "Farewell, my child, my only happiness; you wish to leave me. I will be alone, but I will have time to think of and pray for you." He then cast her from him almost roughly, for he felt as if his grief would unman him. "Go," he cried, "your bridegroom is waiting for you; go, then, and order your bridal ornaments."

Elise smiled. "Yes, I will adorn myself; but you, father, will place the wreath of myrtle on my head, will you not? That is the sacred and last office of love with which a mother sends a daughter from her arms. I have no mother. You are both father and mother to me. Will you not crown me with the myrtle-wreath?"

258

"Yes," said he, with a sigh, "I will place the myrtle on your brow, and God grant it may not turn to a crown of thorns! Go now, my child, adorn thyself, and leave me alone to pray for you."

He greeted her smilingly, and accompanied her to the door. But when she had left the room he felt indescribably lonesome, and, pressing his hands against his breast to suppress the cry which choked him, he muttered in a low tone, "I have lost her—she is mine no longer. Every thing forsakes me. The unfortunate is ever alone!"

Once more a knocking, repeated at his door, awakened him from his reverie. Peter his servant entered, and announced Herr Ephraim.

A ray of joyful astonishment flashed across him, and, as he stepped hastily toward the rich Jew of the mint, he said to himself: "Is it possible that this man comes to have pity on me in my distress? Will he be more magnanimous than Itzig? Will he assist me?"

* * * * *

CHAPTER XIII.

EPHRAIM THE TEMPTER.

"You seek me?" asked Gotzkowsky, as Ephraim entered and saluted him in silence.

Gotzkowsky's sharp glance had detected in his insolent hearing and contracted features that it was not pity or sympathy which had brought the Jew to him, but only a desire to gloat over the sufferings of his victim. "He shall not enjoy his triumph. He shall find me collected and determined, and shall not suspect my grief." Thus thinking, he forced his features into a cheerful expression, and handing a chair to the still silent Ephraim, said laughingly: "Indeed, I must be in a dangerous plight, if the birds of prey are already settling around me. Do you already scent my death, Herr Ephraim? By Heaven! that would be a dainty morsel for you!"

"You are angry with me," said Ephraim, shaking his head slowly; "but you shall know how much injustice you do me. I bring you an important and fearful piece of news."

"It must be fearful, indeed," interrupted Gotzkowsky, "as you do yourself the pleasure of bringing it to me in person."

Ephraim shrugged his shoulders and abruptly replied, "De Neufville has failed!"

A cry of horror escaped Gotzkowsky's lips; he staggered, and was obliged to support himself by a chair to keep himself from falling. This was the last, decisive blow, and it had wounded him mortally. "De Neufville has failed!" he muttered low to himself.

"Yes, he is bankrupt!" said Ephraim with scarcely suppressed malice. "The proud Christian merchant, whose greatest pleasure it was to look down with contempt upon the Jew Ephraim, he is bankrupt. The Jew stands firm, but the Christian merchant is broken." And as he spoke, he broke into a scornful laugh, which brought back to Gotzkowsky his composure and self-possession.

"You triumph!" he said, "and on your brow is marked your rejoicing over our fall. Yes! you have conquered, for De Neufville's failure is your deed. It was you who persecuted him so long, and by cunning suspicions and calumny undermined his credit until it was destroyed, and the whole edifice of his honorable industry fell together."

"It *is* my work," cried Ephraim exultingly, "for he stood in my way, and I have pushed him out of it—what more? Life is but a combat; whoever is the strongest—that is, has the most money—is conqueror."

260

"De Neufville has fallen—that is a hard blow," muttered Gotzkowsky; and as his wandering eye met Ephraim's, he added with an expression of complete prostration: "Enjoy my suffering; you have succeeded—I am hurt unto death!"

"Listen to me, Gotzkowsky," said Ephraim, approaching nearer to him; "I mean well by you."

"Oh, yes!" said Gotzkowsky, bitterly; "after you have hastened my downfall, you condescend to love me. Yes, indeed! I believe in your friendship; for none but a friend would have had the heart to bring such a Job's message."

Ephraim shook his head. "Listen to me," said he; "I will be quite candid with you. Formerly I hated you, it is true, for you were more powerful and richer than I was; you were renowned for being honest and punctual, and that hurt me. If a large bargain was to be made, they were not satisfied unless Gotzkowsky was concerned in it, and if your name stood at the bottom of a contract, every one was pleased. Your name was as good as gold, and that vexed me."

"And for that reason you wished to overthrow me, and worked unceasingly for my downfall; because you knew that I expected this remittance of light money from Hamburg!"

"I procured the decision that the light money should be declared uncurrent, that is true. I succeeded. From this hour I am more powerful and richer than you. You shall see that I only hated your house, not yourself; I have come to help you. You must indeed fail; that I am aware of, and that if you were to put forth all your power, you could not stand this blow, You must and will fail, and that this very day."

Gotzkowsky muttered some unintelligible words, and covered his face with his hands. "Yes," he cried, piteously, "I and all my hopes have suffered shipwreck."

Ephraim laid his hand suddenly upon his shoulder. "Seek, then, to save some plank from the wreck, on which you may swim. You can no longer save your creditors; save yourself."

Gotzkowsky removed his hands slowly from his face, and looked at him with astonishment and wonder.

Ephraim met his look with a smiling and mysterious expression, and bending down to Gotzkowsky's ear, whispered: "I think you will not be such a fool as to give up all you have to your creditors, and to go out of your house a poor man. Intrust me with your important papers, and all that you possess of money and valuables, and I will preserve them for you. You do not answer. Come, be reasonable; do not allow the world the pleasure of pitying you; it does not deserve it. Believe me, mankind is bad; and he is a fool who strives to be better than his fellows." He stopped, and directed an inquiring look toward Gotzkowsky.

The latter regarded him proudly and with contempt. "This, then, is your friendship for me? You wish to make me a cheat!"

"Every man cheats his neighbor," cried Ephraim, shrugging his shoulders; "why should you alone be honest?"

"Because I do not wish to be ashamed of myself. It is the fault of others that I fall to-day. It shall not be said that Gotzkowsky is guilty of any crime of his own."

"It will be said, nevertheless," interrupted Ephraim; "for whoever is unfortunate, is in the wrong, in the eyes of men. And if he can help himself at the expense of others, and does not do it, do you think men will admire him for it? No! believe me, they will only laugh at him. I have often been sorry for you, Gotzkowsky; for, with all your good sense, your whole life through has been a miscalculation—"

"Or rather say," said Gotzkowsky, sadly, "I have not calculated enough, and from all the experiences of my life I have not drawn the sum total."

"You miscalculated," said Ephraim, "for you calculated on gratitude. That is a bad investment which does not bear interest. Mankind cannot be grateful, and when any one tries to be so he must sink, for others are not so. Whoever wishes to succeed in this world, must think only of himself, and keep his own interest in sight."

"You wise men of the world are right!" cried Gotzkowsky, with a hoarse laugh.

Unhindered by Gotzkowsky's vehement and scornful bearing, Ephraim continued: "If I had thought as you did, I would not have been able to operate against you, nor could I have brought the mint ordinance to bear on you. Then, to be sure, I would have been grateful, but it would not have been business-like. Therefore I thought first of my own welfare, and after that I came here to serve you, and show you my gratitude."

"I do not desire any gratitude. Let me go my way—you go yours."

Ephraim looked at him almost pityingly. "Be reasonable, Gotzkowsky; take good advice. The world does not thank you for being honorable. Mankind has not deserved the pleasure of laughing at you. And they will laugh!"

"Leave me, I tell you!" cried Gotzkowsky; "you shall not deprive me of my last possession, my conscience!"

"Conscience!" sneered Ephraim. "You will starve on that capital."

262

Gotzkowsky sighed deeply and dropped his head on his breast. At this moment there were heard from without loud hurrahs and jubilant sounds, mingled with the tones of martial music.

King Frederick II. was returning this day to Berlin, after a long absence, and the happy and delighted Berliners had prepared for him a pompous and brilliant entry. They had built triumphal arches, and the guilds had gone forth to accompany him into the city, now adorned for festivity. The procession had to pass by Gotzkowsky's house, and already were heard the sounds of the approaching music, while the shouts and cries of the people became louder and shriller.

Ephraim stepped to the window, opened it, and pointing down into the street, he said, with a mocking laugh: "Just look, Gotzkowsky! There is the true test of your beautiful, high-toned principles. How often has Berlin not called you her benefactor, and yet she is overjoyed on the very day you are going to ruin! The whole town of Berlin knows that Gotzkowsky fails to-day, and yet they pass by your house with merry music, and no one thinks of you."

"He is right," murmured Gotzkowsky, as the huzzas sounded under his window. "He is right! I was a fool to love mankind."

Ephraim pointed down into the street again. "See," said he, "there comes Count Salm, whom you saved from death when the Russians were here. He does not look up here. Ah, there goes the banker, Splittyerber, whose factories in Neustadt Eberswald you saved at the same time. He, too, does not look up. Oh! yes, he does, and laughs. Look there! There goes the king with his staff. You have caused his majesty much pleasure. You accomplished his favorite wish—you founded the porcelain factory. You travelled at your own expense into Italy, and bought pictures for him. You preserved his capital from pillage by the Austrians and Russians. The Dutch ambassador, who at that time interfered in favor of Berlin with the Austrians, him has the king in his gratitude created a count. What has he done for you? What Verelse did was but a trifle in comparison with your services, yet he, forsooth, is made a count. What has the king done for you? See, the king and his staff has passed by, and not one of them has looked up here. Yesterday they would have done so, for yesterday you were rich; but to-day they have forgotten you already: for to-day you are poor, and the memory of the people is very short for the poor. Ah! look down again, Gotzkowsky—so many gentlemen, so many high-born people are passing! Not one looks up!"

Against his will Gotzkowsky had been drawn to the window, and, enticed by Ephraim's words, he had looked down anxiously and mournfully at the brilliant procession which was passing by. How much would he not have given if only one of the many who had formerly called themselves his friends had looked up at him, had greeted him cordially? But Ephraim was right. No one did so. No one thought of him who, with a broken heart, was leaning beside the window, asking of mankind no longer assistance or help, but a little love and sympathy. But, as he looked down into the street again, his countenance suddenly brightened up. He laid his hand hastily on Ephraim's shoulder, and pointed to the procession.

"You are right," said he; "the respectable people do not look up here, but here comes the end of the procession, the common people, the poor and lowly, the workmen. Look at them! See how they are gazing at me. Ah, they see me, they greet me, they wave their hats! There, one of them is putting his hand to his face. He is a day-laborer who formerly worked in my factory. This man is weeping, and because he knows that I have been unfortunate. See! here come others—poor people in ragged clothes—women with nurslings in their arms—tottering old men—they all bend dewy eyes on me. Do you see? they smile at me. Even the children stretch up their arms. Ah, they love me, although I am no longer rich."

And turning with a beaming face and eyes moistened with tears toward Ephraim, he exclaimed: "You tell me that I have miscalculated. No! you are mistaken. I calculated on the kernel of humanity, not on the degenerate shell. And this noble kernel of humanity resides in the people, the workmen, and the poor. I trusted in these, and they have not betrayed my confidence."

Ephraim shrugged his shoulders. "The people are weathercocks; they will stone to-morrow the same men whom they bless to-day. Only wait until public opinion has condemned you, and the people, too, will forsake you. Protect yourself, then, against men. When you were rich, every one partook of your liberality; now that you are poor, no one will be willing to share your misfortune. Therefore save yourself, I tell you. Collect whatever papers and valuables you may have. Give them to me. By the God of my fathers I will preserve them faithfully and honestly for you!"

Gotzkowsky repulsed him with scorn, and indignant anger flashed from his countenance. "Back from me, tempter!" cried he, proudly. "It is true you possess the wisdom of the world, but one thing is wanting in your wisdom—the spirit of honor. I know that this does not trouble you much, but to me it is every thing. You are right: I will be a beggar, and men will point at me with their finger, and laugh me to scorn. But I will pass them by proudly, nor will I bend my head before them, for my dignity and honor as a man are unconnected with gold or property. These are my own, and when I die, on my tomb will be written—'He died in poverty, but he was an honorable man.'"

"Fool that you are!" exclaimed Ephraim, laughing in contempt. "You are speculating on your epitaph, while the fortune of your life slips away from you. Take my advice: there is yet time to secure your future."

"Never, if it is to be accomplished by frauds!"

"Think of your daughter."

264

A painful quivering flitted across Gotzkowsky's face. "Who gives you a right to remind me of her?" asked he angrily. "Do not soil her name by pronouncing it. I have nothing in common with you."

"Yes, you have, though," said Ephraim with a wicked smile. "You have done me a good deed, and I am thankful. That is something in common."

Gotzkowsky did not answer him. He crossed the room hastily, and stepped to his writing-table, out of a secret drawer of which he drew a dark-red case. He opened it and snatched out the diamond ring that was contained in it.

"I do not wish your gratitude," said he, turning to Ephraim, anger flashing from his countenance—"and if you could offer me all the treasures of the world, I would throw them to the earth, as I do this ring!" And he cast down the costly jewel at Ephraim's feet.

The latter raised it coolly from the ground and examined it carefully. He then broke out into a loud, scornful laugh. "This is the ring which the Jews presented to you when you procured our exemption from the war-tax. You give it to me?"

"I give it to you, and with it a curse on the tempter of my honor!"

"You repulse me, then? You will have none of my gratitude?"

"Yes; if your hand could save me from the abyss, I would reject it!"

"Let it be so, then," said Ephraim; and his face assumed an expression of hatred and malice—for now it could be perceived that the rich Ephraim was again overcome by Gotzkowsky, although the latter was a poor and shattered man. His sympathy and his help had only met with a proud refusal from him whom he had not succeeded in humbling and dragging down to the dust.

"Let it be so, then!" he repeated, gnashing his teeth. "You will not have it otherwise. I take the ring," and looking at Gotzkowsky maliciously, he continued: "With this ring I will buy you a place in the churchyard, that the dishonored bankrupt may, at least, find an honorable grave, and not be shovelled in like De Neufville the suicide!"

"What do you say—De Neufville is dead?" cried Gotzkowsky, hurrying after him as he neared the door, and seizing him violently by the arm. "Say it once more—De Neufville is dead?"

Ephraim enjoyed for a moment, in silence, Gotzkowsky's terrible grief. He then freed himself from his grasp and opened the door. But turning round once more, and looking in Gotzkowsky's face with a devilish grin, he slowly added, "De Neufville killed himself because he could not survive disgrace." And then, with a loud laugh, he slammed the door behind him.

Gotzkowsky stared after him, and his soul was full of inexpressible grief. He had lost in De Neufville not only a friend whom he loved, and on whose fidelity he could count, but his own future and his last hope were buried in his grave. But his own tormenting thoughts left him no leisure to mourn over his deceased friend. It was the kind of death that De Neufville had chosen which occupied his mind.

"He came to his death by his own hand; he did not wish to survive his disgrace. He has done right—for when disgrace begins, life ends—and shall I live," asked he aloud, as almost angrily he threw his head back, "an existence without honor, an existence of ignominy and misery? I repeat it, De Neufville has done right. Well, then, I dare not do wrong; my friend has shown me the way. Shall I follow him? Let me consider it."

He cast a wild, searching look around the room, as if he feared some eye might be looking at him, and read desperate thoughts in the quivering of his face. "Yes! I will consider it," whispered he, uneasily. "But not here—there in my cabinet, where every thing is so silent and solitary, no one will disturb me. I will think of it, I say." And with a dismal smile he hurried into his study, and closed the door behind him.

* * * * *

CHAPTER XIV.

ELISE.

The bridal costume was completed, and with a bright face, smiling and weeping for sheer happiness, Elise stood looking at herself in a large Venetian mirror. Not from vanity, nor to enjoy the contemplation of her beauty, but to convince herself that all this was not a dream, only truth, delightful truth. The maiden, with blushing cheeks, stood and looked in the glass, in her white dress, till she smiled back again; so like a bride, that she shouted aloud for joy, kissed her hand to herself, in the fulness of her mirth, as she greeted and smiled again to her image in the mirror. "I salute you, happy bride!" said she, in the exuberance of her joy. "I see in your eyes that you are happy, and so may God bless you! Go forth into the world and teach it by your example, that for a woman there is no happiness but love, no bliss but that of resting in the arms of her lover. But am I not too simply clad?" cried she, interrupting herself suddenly, and examining herself critically in the glass. "Yes, indeed, that simple, silly child is not worthy of such a handsome and splendid cavalier: a white silk dress and nothing else! How thoughtless and foolish has happiness made me! My Heaven! I forgot that he comes from the land of diamonds, and that he is a prince. Oh! I will adorn myself for my prince." And she took from her desk the costly set of diamonds, the legacy of her mother, and fastened the glittering brilliants in her ears, on her arms, and the necklace set with diamonds and emeralds around her snow-white neck.

"Now that looks splendid," said she, as she surveyed herself again. "Now perhaps I may please him. But the last ornament is still wanting—my myrtle-wreath—but that my father shall put on." Looking at the wreath, she continued, in a more serious and sad tone: "Crown of love and of death! it is woven in the maiden's hair when she dies as a maiden, whether it be to arise again as a wife or as a purified spirit." And raising her tearful eyes to heaven, she exclaimed: "I thank Thee, O God, for granting me all this happiness. My whole life, my whole future, shall evince but gratitude toward Thee, who art the God of love."

Soon, however, it became too close and solitary in this silent chamber. She wished to go to her father, to throw herself on his breast, to pour out to him all her happiness, her affection, her joy, in words of thankfulness, of tender child-like love. How the white satin dress rustled and shone! how the diamonds sparkled and glittered, as, meteor-like, they flitted down the dark corridor! With a bright, happy smile, holding the wreath in her hand, she stepped into her father's room. But the apartment was empty. She crossed it in haste to seek him in his study. The doors were locked and no one answered her loud calls. She supposed he had gone out, and would doubtless soon return. She sat down to await him, and soon sank into deep thought and reverie. What sweet and precious dreams played around her, and greeted her with happy bodings of the future!

The door opened, and she started up to meet her father. But it was not her father—it was Bertram. And how altered—how pale and troubled he looked! He hardly noticed her, and his eye gleamed on her without seeing her. What was it that had so changed him? Perhaps he already knew that she was to be married to-day, and that her lover, so long mourned, had returned to her. She asked confusedly and anxiously for her father.

"My God! is he not here, then?" asked Bertram in reply. "I must speak to him, for I have things of the greatest importance to tell him."

Elise looked at him with inquiring astonishment. She had never seen him so intensely excited in his whole being, and unwillingly she asked the cause of his trouble and anxiety.

Bertram denied feeling any anxiety, and yet his eye wandered around searchingly and uneasily, and his whole frame was restless and anxious. This only made Elise the more eager to find out the cause of his trouble. She became more pressing, and Bertram again assured her that nothing had happened.

Elise shook her head distrustfully. "And yet I do not deceive myself! Misfortune stands written on your brow." Then, turning pale with terror, she asked, "Do you bring my father bad news?"

Bertram did not answer, but cast his eyes on the ground to escape her searching gaze. There awoke in her breast all the anxiety and care of a loving daughter, and she trembled violently as she implored him to inform her of the danger that threatened her father. He could withstand her no longer. "She must learn it some time; it is better she should hear it from me," muttered he to himself. He took her hand, led her to the sofa, and, sitting down by her side, imparted to her slowly and carefully, always endeavoring to spare her feelings, the terrible troubles and misfortunes of her father. But Elise was little acquainted with the material cares of life. She, who had never known any extreme distress, any real want, could not understand how happiness and honor could depend on money. When Bertram had finished, she drew a long breath, as if relieved from some oppressive anxiety. "How you have frightened me!" said she, smiling. "Is that all the trouble—we are to be poor? Well, my father does not care much about money."

"But he does about his honor," said Bertram.

"Oh, the honor of my father cannot stand in any danger," cried Elise, with noble pride.

Bertram shook his head. "But it is in danger, and though *we* are convinced of his innocence, the world will not believe it. It will forget all his noble deeds, all his high-mindedness and liberality, it will obliterate all his past, and only remember that this day, for the first time in his life, he has it not in his power to fulfil his word. It will condemn him as if he were a common cheat, and brand him with the disgraceful name of bankrupt." With increasing dismay Elise had watched his countenance as he spoke. Now, for the first time, the whole extent of the misfortune which was about to befall her father seemed to enter her mind, and she felt trembling and crushed. She could feel or think of nothing now but the evil which was rushing in upon her parent, and with clasped hands and tears in her eyes she asked Bertram if there was no more hope; if there was no one who could avert this evil from her father.

Bertram shook his head sadly. "His credit is gone—no one comes to his assistance."

"No one?" asked Elise, putting her hand with an indescribable expression on his shoulder. "And you, my brother?"

"Ah, I have tried every thing," said he; and even in this moment her very touch darted through him like a flash of delight. "I have implored him with tears in my eyes to accept the little I possess, to allow me the sacred right of a son. But he refused me. He will not, he says, allow a stranger to sacrifice himself for his sake. He calls me a stranger! I know that my fortune cannot save him, but it may delay his fall, or at least cancel a portion of his debt, and he refuses me. He says that if I were his son, he would consent to what he now denies me. Elise," he continued, putting aside, in the pressure of the moment, all consideration and all hesitation, "I have asked him for your hand, my sister, that I may in reality become his son. I know that you do not love, but you might esteem me; for the love I bear your father, you might, as a sacrifice to your duty as a daughter, accept my hand and become my bride."

He ceased, and looked anxiously and timidly at the young girl, who sat blushing and trembling by his side. She felt that she owed him an answer; and as she raised her eyes to him, and looked into his noble, faithful face, which had never changed, never altered—as she thought that Bertram had always loved her with the same fidelity, the same self-sacrifice—with a love which desired nothing, wished for nothing but her happiness and contentment, she was deeply moved; and, for the first time, she felt real and painful remorse. Freely and gracefully she offered him her hand.

"Bertram," she said, "of all the men whom I know, you are the most noble! As my soul honors you, so would my heart love you, if it were mine."

Bertram bent over her hand and kissed it; but as he looked at her, his eye accidentally caught sight of the sparkling jewels which adorned her arms and neck, and aware for the first time of her unusually brilliant toilet, he asked in surprise the occasion for it.

"Oh, do not look at it," cried Elise; "tell me about my father. What did he answer you when you asked him for my hand?"

"That he would never accept such a sacrifice from his daughter, even to save himself from death."

"And is his fall unavoidable?" asked Elise thoughtfully.

"I almost fear it is. This morning already reports to that effect were current in the town, and your father himself told me that if Russia insisted on payment, he was lost irretrievably. Judge, then, of my horror, when I have just received from a friend in St. Petersburg the certain intelligence that the empress has already sent a special envoy to settle this business with the most stringent measures. This half a million must be of great importance to the empress, when, for the purpose of collecting it, she sends her well-known favorite, Prince Stratimojeff!"

Elise started from her seat in horror, and stared at Bertram. "Whom did she send?"

"Her favorite, Stratimojeff," repeated Bertram, calmly.

Elise shuddered; her eyes flashed fire, and her cheeks burned. "Who has given you the right to insult the Prince Stratimojeff, that you call him the favorite of the adulterous empress?"

Bertram looked at her in astonishment. "What is Prince Stratimojeff to you?" said he. "The whole world knows that he is the favorite of Catharine. Read, then, what my correspondent writes me on the subject." He drew forth a letter, and let Elise read those passages which alluded especially to the mission of the imperial favorite.

Elise uttered a scream, and fell back fainting on the sofa; every thing swam before her; her blood rushed to her heart; and she muttered faintly, "I am dying—oh, I am dying!" But this momentary swoon soon passed over, and Elise awoke to full consciousness and a perception of her situation. She understood every thing—she knew every thing. With a feeling of bitter contempt she surveyed all the circumstances—her entire, pitiable, sorrowful misfortune. "Therefore, then," said she to herself, almost laughing in scorn, "therefore this hasty wedding, this written consent of the empress—I was to be the cloak of this criminal intercourse. Coming from her arms, he was anxious to present me to the world. 'Look! you calumniate me! this is my wife, and the empress is as pure as an angel!'" She sprang up, and paced the room with hasty steps and rapid breathing. Her whole being was in a state of excitement and agitation. She shuddered at the depth of pitiable meanness she had discovered in this man, who not only wished to cheat and delude her, but was about, as if in mockery of all human feeling, to make herself the scapegoat of her imperial rival.

She did not notice that Bertram was looking at her in all astonishment, and in vain seeking a clew to her conduct. "This is too much!" cried she, half soliloquizing. "Love cannot stand this! Love! away with the word—I would despise myself if I could find a spark of this love in my heart!" She pressed her hands to her breast, as if she wished thereby to extinguish the flames which were consuming her "Oh!" she cried, "it burns fearfully, but it is not love! Hate, too, has its fires. I hate him! I know it now—I hate him, and I will have vengeance on the traitor! I will show him that I scorn him!" Like an infuriated tigress she darted at the myrtle-wreath which lay on the table. "The bond of love is broken, and I will destroy it as I do this

270

wreath!" she exclaimed, wildly; but suddenly a gentle hand was laid upon her extended arm, and Bertram's soft and sympathizing voice sounded in her ear.

What he said, what words he used—he who now understood all, and perceived the fulness of her grief—with what sincere, heart-born words he sought to comfort her, she neither knew nor understood. But she heard his voice; she knew that a sympathizing friend stood at her side, ready to offer a helping hand to save her from misery, and faithfully to draw her to his breast. She would have been lost, she would have gone crazy, if Bertram had not stood at her side. She felt it—she knew it. Whenever she had been threatened with calamity, he was always near, to watch and shield, to afford her peace and comfort.

"Bertram! Bertram!" she cried, trembling in every limb, "protect me. Do not shut me out from your heart! have pity on me!" She leaned her head on his breast and wept aloud. Now, in her sorrow, she felt it to be a blessing that he was present, and for the first time she had a clear consciousness that God had sent him to her to be a helping friend, a guardian angel.

The illusions and errors of her whole life fell from before her eyes like a veil, and she saw in a clear light both herself and Bertram. And now, as she leaned her head upon his breast, her thoughts became prayers, and her tears thank-offerings. "I have entertained an angel unawares," said she, remembering, unintentionally, the language of Holy Writ. When Bertram asked the meaning of her words, she answered, "They mean that an erring heart has found the right road home."

She wiped away her tears with her long locks. She would no longer weep, nor shed a single tear for the false, intriguing traitor, the degenerate scion of a degenerate race. He was not worthy of a sigh of revenge, not even of a reproach. A mystery had slept in her breast, and she thought to have found the true solution in the word "Feodor!" but she was mistaken, and God had allowed this long-mourned, long-desired man to return to her, that she might be allowed to read anew the riddle of her heart more correctly, to find out its deceitful nature, its stubborn pride, and to conquer them. Thus thinking, she raised her head from Bertram's breast, and looked at him "You asked my father for my hand. Do you still love me?"

Bertram smiled. This question seemed so strange and singular! "Do I love you?" asked he. "Can he ever cease to love who has once loved?"

"Do you still love me?" she repeated.

"Faithfully and honorably," said he, with feeling.

"Faithfully and honorably!" cried Elise, deeply moved. "Oh those are words as strong as rocks, and like the shipwrecked sailor, I will cling to them to save myself from sinking. Oh, Bertram, how good you are! You love my father, and desire to be his son, only for the sake of helping him."

"And if need be, to work for him, to give up my life for him!"

With her bright eyes she looked deeply into his, and held out her hand to him. "Give me your hand, Bertram," said she, softly. "You were a better son to my father than I have been a daughter. I will learn from you. Will you be my teacher?"

Bertram gazed at her astonished and inquiringly. She replied to this look with a sweet smile, and like lightning it shot through his heart, and a happy anticipation pervaded his entire soul. "My God! my God! is it possible?" murmured he, "is the day of suffering, indeed, past? Will—"

He felt Elise suddenly shudder, and pressing his hand significantly, she whispered, "Silence, Bertram, look there!"

Bertram followed the direction of her eyes, and saw Gotzkowsky, who had opened the door of his study, and was entering the room, his features pale and distorted, and his gaze fixed. "He does not see us," whispered Elise. "He is talking to himself. Do not disturb him."

In silence she pointed to the curtains just behind them, concealing a recess, in the middle of which stood a costly vase. "Let us conceal ourselves," said she, and, unnoticed by Gotzkowsky, they glided behind the curtains.

* * * * *

CHAPTER XV.

THE RESCUE.

Gotzkowsky had closed with life and earthly affairs. He had signed the document declaring him a bankrupt, and he had delivered over all his property to his creditors. The die had been cast. He had been powerful and great through money, but his power and greatness had now gone from him, for he was poor. The same men who yesterday had bowed down to the ground before him, had to-day passed him by in pride and scorn; and those who had vowed him eternal gratitude, had turned him from their door like a beggar. Why should he continue to bear the burdens of a life which had no longer any allurements, and whose most precious jewel, his honor, he had lost?

De Neufville had done right, and only a coward would still cling to life after all that was worth living for had disappeared. They should not point scornfully at him as he went along the streets. He would not be condemned to hear whispered after him, "Look! there goes Gotzkowsky the bankrupt." No, this fearful word should never wound his ears or pierce his heart.

Once more only would he pass through those streets, which had so often seen him in his glory—once more, not poor, nor as the laughing-stock of children, but so that those who now derided him should bow down before him, and honor him as the mourning emblem of departed honor: only his body should pass by these men who had broken his heart. He had determined to quit this miserable existence, to leave a world which had proved itself to him only a gulf of wickedness and malice, and his freed spirit would wing its way to regions of light and knowledge.

With such thoughts he entered the room which was to be the scene of his last hours. But he would not go down to the grave without bearing witness to the wickedness and malice of the world. His death should be a monument of its disgrace and ingratitude.

For this purpose he had sought this room, for in it was the costly *etagere* on which stood the silver pitcher presented to him by the Council of Leipsic as a token of their gratitude, and from it he would drink his fatal draught. He took it and emptied into it a small white powder, that looked so innocent and light, and yet was strong enough to drag him down with leaden weight into the grave. He then took the water-goblet and poured water on it. The draught was ready; all that was necessary was for him to put it to his lips to imbibe eternal rest, eternal oblivion.

Elise saw it all—understood it all. She folded her hands and prayed; her teeth chattered together, and all that she could feel and know was, that she must save him, or follow him to the grave. "When he raises the pitcher to his lips, I will rush out," she whispered to Bertram, softly, and opened the curtains a little in order to watch him.

Gotzkowsky had returned to the *etagere*. He took the silver-oaken wreath, the civic crown presented to him by the city of Berlin, and looked at it with a bitter, scornful smile. "I earned this," he said, half aloud—"I will take it with me to the grave. They shall find my corpse crowned with this wreath, and when they turn away in shame, the broken bankrupt, John Gotzkowsky, will enjoy his last triumph over a degenerate world." And as if in a dream, in the feverish delirium of grief, he placed the wreath on his brow, then for a moment stood with his head bent in deep thought.

It was a strange picture to see his proud, tall figure, his pale, nervous face, crowned with the silver wreath, and opposite to him, looking through the curtains, his daughter, whose glowing eyes were eagerly watching her father.

And now Gotzkowsky seized the silver pitcher, raised it on high—it had already touched his lips—but suddenly he staggered back. A dearly-loved voice had called his name. Ah, it was the voice of his daughter, whom he had forgotten in the bitterness of his grief. He had believed his heart dead to all feeling, but love still lived in him, and love called him back to life. Like an electric shock it flew through his whole frame.

He put the pitcher down, and covering his face with his hands, cried, "Oh, unnatural father! I forgot my child!"

Behind him stood Elise, praying to God eagerly and fervently. She wished to appear quite composed, quite unsuspicious, that her father might not have even an inkling of her knowledge of his dark design. Her voice dare not tremble, her eye must remain clear and calm, and a smile play about her lips, which yet quivered with the anxious prayers she had just offered to God. "My father!" she said, in a low but quiet voice—"my father, I come to beg your blessing. And here is the myrtle wreath with which you were to adorn me."

Gotzkowsky still kept his face covered, but his whole frame trembled. "I thank Thee, O my God! I thank Thee! the voice of my child has saved me." And turning round suddenly, he stretched out both arms toward her, exclaiming aloud: "Elise, my child, come to my heart, and comfort your father."

Elise uttered a cry of joy, rushed into his arms, and nestled close to his heart. She whispered in his ear words of fervent love, of warmest affection. They fell on Gotzkowsky's heart like soothing balm; they forced tears of mingled joy and repentance from his eyes.

A long while did they remain locked in each other's arms. Their lips were silent, but their hearts spoke, and they understood each other without words. Then Elise raised herself from her father's embrace, and, again offering him the myrtle-wreath, said with a smile, "And now, my father, bless your daughter."

274

"I will," said Gotzkowsky, drying his eyes. "Yes, from my whole soul will I bless you. But where is the bridegroom?"

Elise looked at him inquiringly. "Will you bid him, also, welcome?"

"That I will with all my heart!"

Elise approached the curtain, drew it back, and taking Bertram's hand, led him to her father, saying, with indescribable grace: "My father, bless your children."

"This is your bridegroom?" asked Gotzkowsky, and for the first time a sunbeam seemed to flash across his face.

Bertram with a cry of delight drew Elise to his heart. She clung to him, and said warmly: "I will rest on your breast, Bertram. I will be as true and as faithful as yourself. You shall reconcile me to mankind. You will make us both happy again. My father and I put our hope in you, and we both know it will not be in vain. Is it not so, my father?" She extended her hand to Gotzkowsky.

He took it, but was too much affected to speak. He pressed it to his eyes and his breast, and then looked with a smile into the countenance of his daughter.

Elise continued: "Look, father, life is still worth something. It gives you a son, who is happy to share your unhappiness with you. It gives you a daughter, who looks upon every tear of yours as a jewel in your crown; who would be proud to go as a beggar with her father from place to place, and say to all the world, 'Gotzkowsky is a beggar because he was rich in love toward his fellow-men; he has become poor because he was a noble man, who had faith in mankind.'" And as she drew her father into her own and Bertram's embrace, she asked him, smiling through her tears, "My father, do you still wish to leave your children?"

"No, I will live—live for you!" cried Gotzkowsky, as, almost overcome with emotion and pleasure, he threw his arms around their necks, and kissed them both warmly and lovingly. "A new life is to begin for us," said he, cheerfully. "We will seek refuge in a quiet cottage, and take with us none of the show and luxury for which men work and sell their souls—none of the tawdriness of life. Will you not be content, Elise, to be poor, and purchase the honor of your father with the loss of this vain splendor?"

Elise leaned her head on his shoulder. "I was poor," she said, "when the world called me rich. Now I am rich when it will call me poor. Give up every thing that we possess, father, that no one may say Gotzkowsky owes him any thing, and has not kept his word." With ready haste she loosened the necklace from her throat, the bracelets from her arms, and the drops from her ears. "Take these, too," said she, smiling. "Add them to the rest. We will keep nothing but honor, and the consciousness of our probity."

275

"Now I am your son, father," cried Bertram, with beaming eyes. "Now I have a right to serve you. You dare no longer refuse to accept all that is mine for your own. We will save the honor of our house, and pay all our creditors."

"That we will do," exclaimed Gotzkowsky; "I accept your offering, my son." And joining Elise and Bertram's hands together, he cast grateful looks to heaven, saying: "From this day forward we are poor, and yet far richer than many thousands of rich people; for we are of sound health, and have strong arms to work. We have good consciences, and that proud contentment which God gives to those only who trust in His help."

* * * * *

CHAPTER XVI.

RETRIBUTION.

The appointed hour had arrived, and in the full splendor of his rich uniform, decorated with orders, and glittering with diamonds bestowed upon him by the favor of two empresses, Prince Feodor von Stratimojeff entered Gotzkowsky's house. With the proud step of victory he ascended the stairs that led to the apartments of his bride. The goal was at last reached. The beautiful, lovely, and wealthy maiden was finally to become his wife. He could present her at the court of St. Petersburg, and with her beauty, her virtue, and his happiness revenge himself on the fickle empress. These were his thoughts as he opened the door and entered Elise's room. There she stood in her white bridal attire, as delicate, as slender, and as graceful as a lily to the sight. There stood also her father, and the friend of her youth, Bertram. The witnesses to the ceremony were present, and nothing more was necessary but to lead her to the altar. Elise had requested of her father that she herself should see the prince, and give him his dismissal. She had also requested that Bertram should be present. She wished to show him that her heart had, at once and forever, been healed of its foolish and unholy love, and that she could face the prince without trembling or hesitation. This was an offering which she wished to bring to the honor of her future husband and her own pride; and she would have despised herself if a motion of her eyebrow or a sigh from her breast had betrayed the sadness which, against her will, she felt in her heart. She looked, therefore, with a cold and calm eye on the prince as he entered, and for the first time he seemed no longer the handsome man, the being endowed with numberless fascinations, of former days. She read only in his flaccid features the sad history of the past. The charm was broken which had held her eyes captive. Her vision was clear again, and she shuddered before this wild, demoniacal beauty which she had once adored as God's image in man. As she looked at him, she felt as if she could hate him, because she had loved him; because she had spent her first youth, her first love, her first happiness, on him; because he had defrauded her of the peace and innocence of her heart; and because she no longer had even the right of weeping for her lost love, but was forced to turn away from it with blushes of shame.

Feodor approached with an air of happy triumph and satisfaction, and, bowing low to her father, said, with a most exquisite smile, "I have come to seek my bride—to request Elise's hand of her father."

With eyes beaming with pleasure he offered Elise his hand, but hers remained calm and cold, and her voice did not tremble or falter as she said: "I am a bride, but not yours, Prince Stratimojeff;" and extending her hand to Bertram, she continued: "This is my husband! To-day, for the third time, he has saved me—saved me from you!"

Prince Feodor felt annihilated, and staggered back as if struck by an electric shock. "Elise! is this the way you reward my love?" asked he sadly, after a pause. "Is this the troth you plighted me?"

She stepped up close to him, and said softly: "I kept my heart faithful to my Feodor, but he ceded it to Prince Stratimojeff. Elise is too proud to be the wife of a man who owes his title of prince to the fact of being the favorite of an empress."

She turned and was about to leave the room, but Feodor held her back. No reserve, no concealment were any longer possible to him. He only felt that he was infinitely wretched, and that he had lost the hope of his life. "Elise," he said, in that soft, sad tone, which had formerly charmed her heart, "I came to you to save me; you have thrust me back into an abyss. Like a drowning man I stretched out my hand to you, that in your arms I might live a new life. But Fate is just. It hunts me back pitilessly from this refuge, and I must and will sink. Well, then, though the waves of life close over me, my last utterance will be your name."

Elise found herself capable of the cruel courage of listening to his pathetic words with a smile: "You will yet have time to think over your death," said she, with proud composure; and, turning to her father, she continued, "My business with this gentleman is finished. Now, father, begin yours." She gave her hand to Bertram, and, without honoring the prince with another look, she left the room with her betrothed.

"And now," said Gotzkowsky coldly, "now, sir, let us proceed to our affairs. Will you have the kindness to follow me to my counting-room? You have come to Berlin to rob me of my daughter and my property! You have been unsuccessful in the one; try now the other."

"That I will, that I shall!" cried the prince, gnashing his teeth, and anger flashing from his eyes. "Elise has been pitiless, I will be so too."

"And I would hurl your pity from me as an insult," said Gotzkowsky, "if you offered it."

"We are then enemies, for life and death—"

"Oh, no! We are two tradesmen who bargain and haggle with each other about the profits. There is nothing more between us." He opened the door and called in his secretary and his cashier. "This gentleman," said Gotzkowsky, with cutting coldness, "is the agent of Russia, sent here to negotiate with me, and in case I cannot pay, to adopt the most severe measures toward me. You, gentlemen, will transact this business with him. You have the necessary instructions." He then turned to the prince, who stood breathless and trembling from inward excitement, burning with anger and pain, and leaning against the wall to keep himself from falling. "Prince," said he, "you will be paid. Take these thirty thousand dollars; they are the fortune of my son-in-law. He has given it cheerfully to release us from you. Here, further, are my daughter's diamonds. Take them to your empress as a fit memorial of your German deeds, and my pictures will cover the balance of my indebtedness to you."[1]

278

"It is too much, it is too much!" cried Prince Feodor; and as if hunted by the furies, he rushed out, his fists clinched, ready to crush any one who should try to stop him.

[Footnote 1: Gotzkowsky paid his debt to Russia with thirty thousand dollars cash; a set of diamonds; and pictures which were taken by Russia at a valuation of eighty thousand dollars, and formed the first basis of the imperial gallery at St. Petersburg. Among these were some of the finest paintings of Titian, some of the best pieces of Rubens, and one of Rembrandt's most highly executed works—the portrait of his old mother.]

* * * * *

CHAPTER XVII.

TARDY GRATITUDE.

John Gotzkowsky, the rich merchant of Berlin, had determined to struggle no longer with Fate; no longer to undergo the daily martyrdom of an endangered honor, of a threatened name. Like the brave Sickenhagen, he said to himself, "Better a terrible end than an endless terror," and he preferred casting himself down the abyss at once, to be slowly hurled from cliff to cliff. He had given notice to the authorities of his failure, and of his intention of making over all his property to his creditors. He was now waiting to hand over the assets to the assignees, and leave the house which was no longer his. Not secretly, however, but openly, in the broad daylight, he would cross the threshold to pass through the streets of that town which was so much indebted to him, and which had formerly hailed him as her savior and preserver. It was inevitable—he must fall, but his fall should at the same time be his revenge. For the last time he would open the state apartments of his house; for the last time receive his guests. But these guests would be the legal authorities, who were to be his heirs while he was yet alive, and who were to consign his name to oblivion before death had inscribed it on any tomb-stone.

The announcement of his fall had spread rapidly through the town, and seemed at last to have broken through the hardened crust which collects around men's hearts. The promptings of conscience seemed for a moment to overcome the voice of egotism. The magistrates were ashamed of their ingratitude; and even the Jews of the mint, Ephraim and Itzig, had perceived that it would have been better to have avoided notoriety, and to have raised up the humbled Gotzkowsky, than to have trodden him in the dust entirely.

Instead of the officials whom he had expected, however, a committee of the Council, accompanied by Ephraim and Itzig, entered his house and asked to speak with him. He received them in his apartments of state, with his children at his side. His figure was erect, his head proudly raised, and he regarded them, not as an unfortunate, downcast man, but as a superior would regard his inferiors; and they lowered their eyes before his penetrating glances, ashamed and conscious of wrong.

"The Council have sent us," said one of the aldermen.

"I have no further business with the Council," said Gotzkowsky, contemptuously.

"Gotzkowsky, do not be angry with us any longer," said the aldermen, almost imploringly. "The magistracy, in acknowledgment of your great services to the city, are ready and willing to pay the sum you demand." Gotzkowsky shook his head proudly. "I am no longer ready to accept it. The term has expired; you can no longer buy me off; you remain my debtors."

"But you will listen to us," cried Itzig. "We come in the name of the Jews."

"We are empowered to assist you," added Ephraim. "We have been instructed by the Jews to give you, on the security of your signature and the prepayment of the interest, as much money and credit as will prevent your house from failing."

Gotzkowsky's large bright eyes rested for a moment searchingly and speculatively on Ephraim's countenance; and the light, mocking smile which stood on the lips of the Jew confirmed his determination, and strengthened him in his resolution. "My house has failed," said he, quietly and proudly, and, reading the anxiety and terror depicted on their countenances, he continued almost exultingly: "yes! my house has failed. The document in which I announced it and declared myself a bankrupt, has already been sent to the magistracy and the merchant's guild."

"You dare not fail!" cried Itzig, in a rage.

"You dare not put this insult upon the Council and the town," exclaimed the aldermen, with dignity. "We cannot allow posterity to say of us, 'The town of Berlin left the noblest of her citizens to perish in want and misery.'"

"It will be well for me if posterity should say so, for then my name and my honor will be saved."

"But the magistracy will be delighted to be able to show its gratitude toward you."

"And the Jews will be delighted, too," cried Itzig. "The Jews are ready to help you."

Gotzkowsky cast an angry look at him. "That is to say, you have calculated that it will not profit you if I do fail. You have large drafts on me, and if I fail, you only get a portion of your debt; whereas, if I stand, you get the whole. You would be magnanimous from self-interest, but I do not accept your magnanimity—you shall lose. Let that be your punishment, and my revenge. You have wounded my heart unto death, therefore I will strike you on the only spot in which you are sensitive to pain: I attack your greed of money. You come too late; I am bankrupt! My drafts are no longer current, but my honor will not die with my firm."

They were all silent, and gazed down to the earth frowningly. Only one looked toward Gotzkowsky with a clear, bright eye. This was Ephraim, who, mindful of his conversation with Gotzkowsky, said to himself, triumphantly, "He has taken one lesson from me—he has learned to despise mankind."

But Itzig was only the more furious. "You wish our ruin," said he, angrily. "You will be ungrateful. The Jews, who made you a present of a handsome ring, have not deserved that of you. What will the world say?"

"The world will learn the cause of my ruin, and condemn you," said Gotzkowsky. "Go, take all that I have; I will reserve nothing; I despise riches and estate. I wish to be poor; for in poverty is peace. I turn my back upon this house, and I take nothing with me but this laurel-wreath and you, my children."

Smilingly he gave his hands to Bertram and Elise. "Come, my children! let us wander out in the happiness of poverty. We shake the dust from our feet, and are light and free, for though we are poor, we are rich in love. Yes, we are poor; but poverty means freedom. We are no longer dependent upon prejudices, conventionalities, and forms. We have nothing more to conceal or hide. We need not be ashamed of our poverty, for we dare to show it to all the world; and when we go through the streets as ragged beggars, these rich people will cast down their eyes in shame, for our poverty will accuse them, and our rags testify against them. Come, my children, let us begin our life of poverty. But when death comes to take me away, crown my cold brow with this laurel-wreath, given me by the city of Berlin, and write on my coffin: 'This is the world's reward!'"[1]

And firm and erect, leaning on his children, Gotzkowsky crossed the room. No one dared to detain him. Shame and remorse, anger and terror, kept them all spell-bound. "Let us go, let us go; I have a horror of this house, and this splendor sickens me."

"Yes! let us go," said Elise, throwing her arms around her father's neck. They went out into the street. How refreshing did the cool air seem to them, and how soft and sweet did the calm blue sky look down upon them! Gotzkowsky gazed up at it. He did not perceive the multitude of people which stood before his own door, or rather he did not wish to see them, because he took them for a portion of the idle, curious populace, which follows misfortune everywhere, and finds a spectacle for the amusement of its *ennui* in the suffering of others.

But for this once, Gotzkowsky was mistaken; it was indeed only poor people who were standing in the street, but their countenances bore the marks of sympathy, and their looks were sad. They had heard of his misfortunes, and had hastened hither, not from curiosity, but from interest in him. They were only factory-hands, to whom Gotzkowsky had been benefactor, friend, and adviser; they were the poor whom he had supported and comforted, who now stood before his house, to bid him a last farewell. To be sure, they could render him no assistance—they had no money, no treasures—but they brought their love with their tears.

At the head of the workmen stood Balthazar, with his young wife, and although his eyes were dimmed with tears, he still recognized his master who had done him so much kindness; and although his breast was stifled with grief, yet he controlled himself, and cried out, "Long live Gotzkowsky, our father!"

"Hurrah for Gotzkowsky! Long may he live!" cried the crowd, not jubilantly, but in a sad tone, half smothered by tears.

Gotzkowsky's countenance beamed with joy, and with a grateful smile he stretched out his hand to Balthazar. "I thank you, my friend," he said; "you have often shouted in compliment to me, but never has it given me so much pleasure as to-day."

"Never has it been done more cordially and sincerely," said Balthazar, pressing Gotzkowsky's hand to his lips. "You have always been a father and a friend to us, and we have often been sorry that you were so rich and powerful that we could not show you how dear you were to us. Now that you are no longer rich, we can prove that we love you, for we can work for you. We have come to an agreement among ourselves. Each of us will give one working-day in the week, and the proceeds shall go to you, and as there are one hundred and seventy of us workmen, you shall at least not starve, Father Gotzkowsky."

Gotzkowsky looked at him with eyes glistening with pleasure. "I thank you, my friends," said he, deeply moved; "and if I do not accept your offer you must not think that I do not appreciate its greatness or its beauty. Who can say that I am poor when you love me, my children?"

At that moment, a carriage stopped at the door. Bertram had brought it to convey them to their new and modest residence.

"Are you going, then, to leave us forever?" said Balthazar mournfully.

"No, my children, I remain among you, in the midst of you. I am only going to exchange this large house for a smaller one."

"Come," cried Balthazar, "come, my friends, we will escort our father, Gotzkowsky, to his new house. The town of Berlin shall see that only rich people are ungrateful, and that the poor never forget their benefactor and their friend. Come, let us take out the horses. We will draw Father Gotzkowsky through the streets."

The crowd answered with a thundering hurrah; and with busy haste they proceeded to the work. The horses were unharnessed, and twelve of the most powerful workmen crowded around the pole. In vain did Gotzkowsky beg them to refrain, not to make him an object of general curiosity. But the people paid no heed to his request—it was a necessity to their hearts to give him a public proof of their love. Almost by force they raised him into the carriage, and compelled Bertram and Elise, who had mixed with the crowd for the purpose of escaping attention, to take their seats beside him. And now the procession advanced. Women and workmen went on before, rejoicing and jumping about merrily at the side of the carriage; and when they met other workmen, these latter stopped and waved their hats, and greeted Gotzkowsky, calling him the great factory-lord, the father of his workmen, the benefactor of Berlin. Especially when the procession came to the low houses and the poor cottages, the small dusty windows were thrown open, and sun-browned faces looked out, and toil-hardened hands greeted and waved.

The forsaken, the ruined Gotzkowsky celebrated this day a splendid triumph. The jubilant voice that thus did him homage was that of the people—and the voice of the people is the voice of God!

[Footnote 1: With these words Gotzkowsky closes his autobiography.]

* * * * *

CHAPTER XVIII.

THE AUCTION.

All was now over—the curtain had fallen: Gotzkowsky had run his brilliant career, and retired into oblivion. His fall was for some days the topic of conversation of the good Berliners; but it was soon superseded by some other novelty, and without either sympathy or ill-feeling they passed by the deserted house with the closed windows which had once been Gotzkowsky's residence. The king had purchased it, in order to carry on, at the expense of the royal government, the porcelain factory which Gotzkowsky had founded.

Months had passed by. How many changes had taken place in this short space of time! How many tears had been shed there, how many hopes destroyed!

Elise had become Bertram's wife; and she lived with him in the small, quiet residence which they had selected in the most remote quarter of the town. The three had entered the low, narrow rooms, which were to be their home, with the firm determination not to let themselves be annoyed by such slight material privation as they might have to endure, but to pass them over with cheerful equanimity and proud indifference, consoling themselves with the conviction that no one could rob them of their great and pure love. And besides this, their honor and their reputation were untouched, for every one was acquainted with Gotzkowsky's fate, every one knew that he had not fallen through his own fault, but through the force of circumstances, and the baseness of mankind.

He might have cause of complaint against the world, it had none against him. With his creditors he had been honest. All that he possessed he had given up to them, and they were all satisfied. With proud step and unbent head could he pass through the streets, for no one dared to follow him with insulting words. Nor had he need to be ashamed of his poverty, for it was in itself a proof not only of his unmerited misfortune, but of his integrity. All this he said and repeated to himself daily, and yet it pained him to go through the streets, feeling solitary and downcast. His eyes even filled with tears, as one day passing by his house he saw the gates open, and equipages, as in former days, at his door, while genteel and rich people, with cold, apathetic countenances, were entering his house as they had done of yore. Formerly they came to Gotzkowsky's splendid dinners, now they had come to the auction. The *fauteuils* and velvet-covered sofas, the carpets and gold-embroidered curtains, the chandeliers of bronze and rock crystal, the paintings and statuary, the silver table-ware, and the costly porcelain service, all these were now exposed for sale.

There is something sad and mournful about an auction. It speaks always of the ruin and breaking up of a man's life and the happiness of his family, of the wreck of a shattered existence, and the sad remains of what was once, perhaps, a brilliant destiny. On the day of an auction there ceases to be a home, the sacred secrets of family life vanish; home is no longer the abode of peace, and the long-cherished *penates* hide their heads in grief.

Then the gates are opened, and the curious multitude rushes in, and with callous eye spies into each corner and every room; tries the sofas on which, perhaps, yesterday some poor widow sat weeping for her lost husband; throws itself down on the bed which once had been the sacred temple of their love; and coldly and unfeelingly examines the furniture of parlor and boudoir, which yet retains the appearance of comfort and of genial repose, though soon to be scattered to the winds, to proclaim aloud its sad and secret story in the gaudy show-room of some second-hand dealer. All the beauty and splendor of Gotzkowsky's former days were now to be displayed at auction. For this reason there stood so many carriages before his door; for this reason did so many noble and wealthy persons come to his house, and, mixed with brokers and speculators, crowd into those halls, which they had formerly trod with friendly smiles and in costly dresses.

No one took any heed of the figure of a man crouching, leaning against the staircase, with his hat pressed down over his brow, and the collar of his cloak drawn up high over his face. No one perceived how he shuddered when the auctioneer handled the beautiful articles and called on the public to bid. It was to him a terrible grief to assist at these obsequies of his past life, and yet he could not tear himself away. He felt fascinated, as it were, by some supernatural power, and forced to remain in the house and attend this horrible ceremony. In the tediousness of his lonesome, inactive, idle misery, it was a species of diversion to him, something to arouse him from his dull rumination, to be present at this disintegration and demolition of his own house.

As Jeremiah once sat among the ruins of Jerusalem, so sat Gotzkowsky with concealed face at the threshold of his house, listening with savage joy to the strokes of the auctioneer's hammer—albeit each blow struck him to the heart, and made its wounds smart still more keenly. At times, when a well-known voice fell on his ear, he would raise his head a little, and look at the bidders, and examine their cold, unsympathizing faces. How many were there among them whom he had once called his friends, and to whom he had done good! And now, like vultures, they flocked to the carcass of his past; they bought his treasures, while their eyes glistened with malicious joy. They were delighted to be able to boast that they possessed a souvenir of the rich Gotzkowsky.

When Gotzkowsky saw this, he felt ashamed that he had once smiled lovingly on these men, had confided in them, and believed in their assurances of friendship. He rose to leave, feeling himself refreshed and strengthened, for his depression and grief had left him. Never had he walked the streets more proudly than on the day when he returned from the auction to his dark, lowly dwelling. Never had he looked upon mankind with greater pity or more bitter scorn. And yet it pained him to reenter this dismal, quiet house, and to force himself back into the *ennui* and indolence of his inactive life. It was such a sensitive, burning pain, so, in the fulness of his strength and manhood to be condemned to do nothing more than drag on a weary existence— to sleep, to eat, and to dream of the past! And yet he would repeat to himself, he was strong and active to work and create; and nevertheless, he was condemned to idleness, to live by the favor and toil of others, even if these others were his children.

286

But they worked for him with so much pleasure and so much love! Bertram had accepted the situation of book-keeper in a large factory, and his salary was sufficient to support the three. To be sure, they had to manage carefully, and provide scantily enough. But Elise was active and notable; though as the spoilt child of wealth, she had, indeed, been able to learn nothing of those minor offices of life which are called by women "housekeeping." Still the instinct of her sex had enabled her soon to acquire this knowledge, and in a short time she became mistress of it. It was, indeed, a pleasant sight to see Elise, with the same quiet cheerfulness, acting at one moment the part of cook in the kitchen, at another setting her little chamber to rights with busy hands, and making amends in cleanliness and neatness for what was wanting in elegance and beauty. True, she was altered, but never since she had been. Bertram's wife had her brow been darkened or her eye dimmed. Her face was always bright and clear: for her husband, when he returned home, she had always a smile of welcome, a cordial greeting—never a word of complaint or of mourning over the privations she was obliged to undergo, or the wealth she had lost. Elise felt rich—for she loved her husband; not with that ardent, consuming passion which she had once felt, and which had been the cause of so much disappointment and so many tears; but with that gentle, affectionate flame which never dies out, but is constantly supplied and nourished by esteem and appreciation.

Bertram was no longer her brother; he was her beloved, her friend, her counsellor, and comforter, above all. With him she was always certain to be understood and appreciated, to find comfort and help. As on a rock, she could now rely on the noble heart of one who was at the same time so firm, and yet so soft in loving, that he had never doubted her, never turned away from her. Her whole heart was given up to him in gratitude and affection, and with her whole life did she wish to reward him for his noble love, for the self-sacrificing gratitude with which he had given up his entire fortune to her father, and saved the name and honor of his house from disgrace and shame. She desired neither splendor nor jewels. Surrounded by the halo of her love, and of her quiet, peaceful happiness, this poor, little dwelling seemed to her as a temple of peace and of holy rest; and, locked in Bertram's embrace, her wishes never reached beyond its narrow sphere.

But Gotzkowsky was not as yet able to attain this resignation. This repose was to him an annihilating torment, and the inactive vegetation a living death. With each day the torture increased, the soreness of his heart became more corroding and painful. At times he felt as if he must scream out aloud in the agony of his despair. He would strike his chest with his clinched fists, and cry to God in the overflow of his sufferings. He who his whole life long had been active, was now condemned to idleness; he who through his whole life had worked for others, was now obliged to lay his hands in his lap, and allow others to labor for him. How had he deserved this? What crime had he committed, that after he had toiled and worked honestly, he should go down, whilst others who had enriched themselves by fraud and lying, by cunning and malice, should drive through the streets in splendid carriages, surrounded by elegance and wealth, while he was obliged to creep along, bowed down with sorrow? He had gone down, while Ephraim had risen higher and higher. He had become poor because he was honest; but Ephraim had grown rich on usury. His firm had failed, while Ephraim continued to coin money. What did the Jew care that his name was branded by the people, that they spoke with cutting sarcasm of the pewter-money to which he had so skilfully imparted the appearance of silver coin, and that he was derided by all? Gotzkowsky's name, too, had been scoffed at, and he had been a benefactor of the people, while Ephraim had been their blood-sucking leech.

At last, Gotzkowsky came to a firm determination that he would have revenge—yes, revenge on this ungrateful generation which had betrayed and forsaken him—-revenge on the men who had shown themselves so small and pitiful. He wanted to remind those who were flourishing in pride and splendor, of their meanness and ingratitude. He would accuse no one, but his whole life was an indictment, not against individual men, but whole communities and cities, against the king himself. They had all been ungrateful toward him. They were all his debtors, and in presence of the whole world he would cast their ingratitude, their meanness, their malice, and knavery in their face, and humble them by recalling the past. He wrote for that purpose *The History of his Life*, not in anger and scorn; he did not dip his pen in gall, he made no ill-natured reflections, no contemptuous remarks. He did nothing more than quietly and simply, clearly and truthfully, describe his life and his deeds, and whenever it was necessary, confirm his assertions by quotations from the official documents relating thereto.[1]

The very simplicity and truthfulness of this *"Biography of a Patriotic Merchant"* procured for it an enormous success, and made the long-forgotten, much-calumniated Gotzkowsky for a while the topic of conversation, not only in Berlin, but throughout all Germany. Every one wanted to read the book. All wished to have the malicious pleasure of seeing how much people of rank, communities, cities, and princes, were indebted to this man, and how pitilessly they had let him sink.

The natural consequence was that the book, though written simply and with reserve, gave great offence. Gotzkowsky had accused no one, but the facts accused. His present poverty and need condemned the proud, high-born people, and showed to the world their cold-heartedness and miserable conduct. He had not exposed *individuals* to the judgment of the world; no—his book accused the whole magistracy of Berlin of deeds of ingratitude; and it even included the king, for whom he had bought a hundred thousand *ducats'* worth of pictures, and who had only paid him back a hundred and fifty thousand *dollars*.

If his book had contained the smallest untruth, if there had been the least false statement in it, they would have stigmatized him as a calumniator and scandalizer of majesty. But Gotzkowsky had only told the truth. They could not, therefore, punish him as a false witness or slanderer. Consequently they had to content themselves with suppressing "The Life of a Patriotic Merchant."

The booksellers in Berlin were therefore ordered to give up all the copies, and even Gotzkowsky received an order to return those in his possession. He did so; he gave up the book to the authorities, who persecuted him because they had cause to blush before him; but his memory he could not surrender. His memory remained faithful

288

to him, and was his support and consolation, whenever he felt ready to despair; this made him proud in his misfortune, and free in the bonds of poverty. And now they were really poor; and penury, with all its horrors, its humiliations and sufferings, crept in upon them.

Gotzkowsky's book had awakened all those who envied and hated him, and they vowed his ruin. It showed how much the merchants of Berlin were indebted to him, and how little of this indebtedness they had cancelled. It was therefore an accusation against the wealthy merchants of Berlin, against which they could not defend themselves, but for which they could wreak revenge. Not on him, for he had nothing they could take from him—no wealth, no name, no credit, and, in their mercantile eyes, no honor. But they revenged themselves on his family—on his son-in-law. The rich factory-lord, whose book-keeper Bertram had been, deprived him of his situation; and in consequence of a preconcerted arrangement, he could find no situation elsewhere. How could he now support his family? He was willing to work his fingers to the bone for his wife, for his father, for his child; who looked up so lovingly to him with its large, clear, innocent eyes, and dreamt not of the anxiety of its father, nor of the sighs which told of the anguish of its young mother. But nowhere could he procure employment—nowhere was there a situation for the son-in-law of Gotzkowsky, who had accused the merchants, the magistrates, yea, even the king! And now they were indeed poor, for they had no work; but, condemned to inactivity, to comfortless brooding, they shudderingly asked themselves what was to become of them—how this life of privation was to end.

But while Bertram and Elise remained sad and dispirited, Gotzkowsky suddenly brightened up. For a long time he had walked up and down in silent thought. Now, of a sudden, his countenance assumed the cheerful expression of former days, and energetic self-reliance was expressed in his features. Elise looked on with astonishment. He drew out from his chest the last remains of by-gone days, the silver oak-wreath set with diamonds, presented him by the town of Berlin, and the golden goblet given by the town of Leipsic. He looked at them for a long time attentively, and then went out, leaving Elise alone, to weep and pray to God to send them help, and to console Bertram when he came home from his fruitless search after a situation.

It was some hours before Gotzkowsky returned, but his countenance still retained its cheerfulness, and his features exhibited the energy and activity of past days. He stretched out his hands to both of his children, and drew them affectionately toward him and embraced them. "Are we then really poor, possessing one another? I say that we are still rich, for our hearts are yet warm, and our honor is not yet lost. But we have not yet learned to bear the indigence of our outer life, We have covered our poverty with the gloss of respectability; we have been ashamed to appear in the streets in coarse clothes; we have not yet learned to distinguish the necessary from the superfluous; we have endeavored to be poor, and yet happy, in a city. That has been our mistake. The happiness of poverty does not reside within the cold walls of a town. It is not sown among the paving-stones of a street. It is only in Nature, who is rich enough to nourish and give to all those who trustingly cast themselves on her bosom—only in Nature, and the privacy of country life, that we can find rest and peace. Come, my children, let us leave this town; let us have the courage to become children of Nature and free citizens of poverty. Let us cast the show and glitter of a city life behind us, and wander forth, not over the sea nor into the desert, but to a cottage in a wood. I have stripped off the last vestige of the past, and the silver wreath and the golden goblet have been of some use, for they have furnished us the means to found a new existence. Bertram, have you the courage to commence life anew and become a peasant?"

Bertram smiled. "I have both the courage and the strength, for I am hearty and able to work."

"And you, Elise, are you not too proud to bring up your child as a peasant?"

Elise kissed her child, and handed him to her father. "Let us bring him up to be a good and healthy man—a man like you and his father, and he will overcome the world and poverty, and be happy."

"Oh! I well knew that I could count upon you; and now I know how we all can be helped. We are rich enough to buy, in some corner of the world, a little piece of land that we can cultivate, and on which we can build a cottage. The product of my valuables is sufficient for that purpose; and what we can realize from these articles of furniture will be sufficient to defray our travelling expenses. Get ready, then, children; to-morrow we leave for Silesia. In the mountains there we will look out some quiet, secluded valley, where the newly-made peasants can build them a cottage. There we will forget the past, and cast all its sufferings behind us; or if we do speak of them, it will be as of the tales of our childhood. Come, my children, let us return to Nature, God, and contentment. Do you remember, Elise, how I once related to you that as a lad I once lay hungry and wretched on the high-road? The hand which was then stretched out to me did not proceed out of the cloud, but from heaven. It was not the consolation of an alms that it gave me, but the comforting assurance of love which raised me up and strengthened me, directing my looks to God, and teaching me to love Him in all His works. God dwells and speaks in Nature. Let us seek Him there, and serve Him in the sweat of our brow and in the coarse peasant's frock."

* * * * *

And they went, and did as Gotzkowsky said. They moved to Silesia, and bought themselves there, among the mountains, a piece of land and a cottage, in which they led a quiet, retired, happy life. The world forgot them. Gotzkowsky's name passed into oblivion. But history preserved it, and still holds him up as an example, not only of the most noble patriotism, but also of the ingratitude of men. His book, too, is left us, and bears witness for him. But as we read it, we become sad, and are ready to cry out, as he does, *"This is the world's reward!"*

290

THE END.

Made in the USA
Middletown, DE
23 September 2016